A

History of

Hope and

Caergwrle

Rhona Phoenix & Alison Matthews

bridge
books

A History of Hope and Caergwrle
first published in Wales in 2006
by
Bridge Books
61 Park Avenue
Wrexham
LL12 7AW

ISBN 978-1-84494-034-9

A CIP entry for this book is available from the British Library

Printed and bound by
Cromwell Press Ltd
Trowbridge

Contents

Foreword

The authors of *A History of Penyffordd and Penymynydd* have done it again! This time Alison Matthews and Rhona Phoenix have directed their attention to the villages of Hope and Caergwrle and have made an impressive contribution to the published knowledge of our heritage. This work provides the wider context for other accounts, including the already published *Hope & Caergwrle Heritage Trail*. It helps us to see the place of the two villages in the history of Wales and Britain. I would commend it to anyone who, having gained an outline of British history, wants to see the impact of national events within the locality.

A detailed history of Hope and Caergwrle has been long overdue and this one has been produced with a considerable amount of painstaking research. There are those who have attempted something similar before, but they all failed to see the project to fruition. With local histories having been written on so many villages in recent years, the absence of one on these two villages has been a glaring omission. I am sure members of the local community will unite with me in expressing thanks to Alison and Rhona for producing this important work on the local heritage, which will also be of considerable interest to visitors and those with fond memories of past visits to the area.

David Healey
Chairman
Hope and Caergwrle Heritage and Conservation Society

Acknowledgements

We wish to thank everyone for their kindness and support in our venture. Our special thanks to Mrs Pat Murrells (Blackwell), as a 'native' of Caergwrle, for her help in pointing us in the right direction! Also to Mr Roy Madeley and the daughter of the late Mr Roy Mathers (Wendy) for their many post cards and pictures. We would also like to thank ALL the staff in the Flintshire Record Office, Hawarden, especially Archivists Mrs Claire Harrington, Miss Elizabeth Pettitt and Mr Paul Mason, also Miss Joy Thomas Local Studies Centre Wrexham.

Many thanks to Mr David Healey for his proof reading, which was invaluable. Finally we wish to thank our publisher Mr Alister Williams not only for his encouragement and guidance but also for his professionalism.

Mr Mike Arden

Mr Bannister, Plas y Bwl

Boys' Brigade/ Mr Harry Gould/ Mr Norman Jones

Mr Ronnie Bradshaw, Caergwrle

Mrs J. Clark, Broxton

Mr & Mrs Carstesan, Bryn Iorcyn

Mrs Doris Clarke, Caergwrle

Mr & Mrs Philip & Irene Clegg

Mrs Norah Clubb, Caergwrle

Mrs Alison Davies, Cartographer

Mrs Felicity Davies, Archaeologist

Mr Chris Davies, Mold

Mr Ifan Davies, Headteacher, Ysgol Estyn

Mr & Mrs T. Eccleston, Penyffordd

Mrs Beryl Edwards, Caergwrle

Mr Paul Edwards, Castell Alun

Mrs Kathleen Evans

Miss Norma Evans, Nercwys

Mr J. Evans, Hope

Mr Russell Fidler

Mr Albert Fielding

Mrs L. Fielding, Hope

Mr Sydney Fielding, Whitchurch

Mrs Sheila Ford, Penyffordd

Mrs Gabriel, Hope Hall

Mr & Mrs Warren & Vera Gittins

Mrs Kathleen Graham, Penyffordd

Mr H. E. Griffiths, Mold

Mr Ken Lloyd Gruffydd /Revd. Eirlys Gruffydd

Dr G. Harrap, PhD

Mr Charles Harston

Miss Leanne Hayes

Mr David Healey

Mr & Mrs Henshaw, Sarn House

Mrs Margaret Hillman, Hope

Mr Howell Hughes, Penyffordd

Mrs Mavis Hughes, Hope

Mr Cyril Jackson, Hope

Mrs Beryl Jones, Wrexham

Mr D. Jones, Llanfynydd

Mr & Mrs Les & Pat Jones, Cymau

Mr Rod Jones, Gwersyllt

Mr Les Kendrick

Mrs G. Leaney

Mrs J. Ledgard

Mr Peter Lee.

Mrs Wendy Lloyd, Hope

Mr & Mrs Ann & David Lovatt

Mr Roy Madeley, Hope

Mr John Manley, Archaeologist

Mrs Jane Marriott, Hope

Dr David Mason, Archaeologist

Members of Hope Community Council

Mr Harold Mount

Mr David Mountfort, Headteacher, Ysgol Castell Alun

Mr & Mrs Geoffrey and Patricia Murrells

Mrs Gwyneth Nesbitt, Penyffordd

Mr Philip Owen, Cymau

Mr Alan Parsonage

Mr Ray Parsonage

Mr David Phoenix

Mr Mike Phoenix

Mr & Mrs Alun & Liz Poynton

Mrs Helen Price

Mr & Mrs Jeff Pugh

Mr Colin Purton

Mrs Rosemary Quant (née Whittingham)

Mr Gordon Roberts, Archivist, Salvation Army

Mr Mike Roberts

Mr & Mrs T. E. & H. Roberts, Hope

Mrs J. Ross Jones

Mr Alun Rushden, Clerk to Hope Community Council

Mr George Scattergood.

Mrs Sherlock, Rhyddyn Hall

Mr Cliff Shone, Hope

Mr Roger Shone, Chester

Revd. Martin Snellgrove, Rector

Mr & Mrs Ian & Liz Sumpter

Mrs Sutcliffe, Penyffordd

Mr I. Swain, Headteacher, Abermorddu

Mrs Kath Swale, Hope

Miss Joy Thomas, Local Studies Librarian, Wrexham

Mr J. Trematick

Mr John Whittingham, Baschurch.

Mrs Hazel Webb, Penyffordd

Mr & Mrs Alan & Sue Webb, Buckley

Mr & Mrs Geraint & Gwyneth Williams

Mrs Williams, Rhyddyn Hill

Mrs Margaret Williams, Caergwrle

Mrs Cheryl Wilson

Mr & Mrs George & Olga Woodhall, Penyffordd

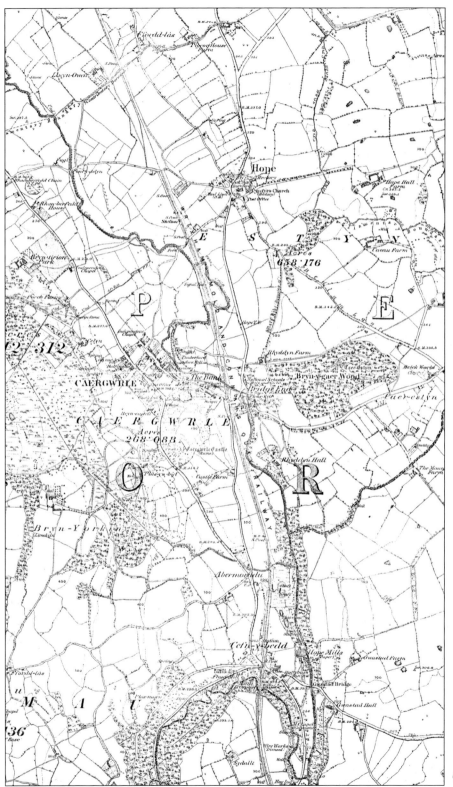

Hope and Caergwrle, 1871.

Introduction

Researching the story of Hope and Caergwrle has proved to be an exciting project. We were delighted with the response we received when asking about various aspects of the history of these two villages. We are indebted to everyone for his or her kindness and hospitality, and so we have acknowledged the many people who have helped us to gather this history.

There are and have been many local historians, Mr D. G. Evans, Mr Elfed Roberts, Mr John Trematick, Mr Charles Harston, Mr David Healey, who have already written important work about this area. There was also 'Captain Wilson's manuscript diary' which we were unable to trace — this apparently had some wonderful stories.

We have tried to approach the history from a different angle, endeavouring to find out how people lived so many years ago, and what influenced them, using both primary and secondary sources plus lots of photographs.

It was difficult to plan how to set out the history of this fascinating area and so we have divided it into different aspects of development and growth, working through the ages.

This area provides wonderful material for study, partly because it is adjacent to Cheshire and also the lordships of Hawarden and Ewloe, which differ greatly from the lordship of Hope. In the lordship of Hawarden Welsh place names are few however in the lordship of Hope there are varying proportions of Welsh and English.

Hope — it is important to remember that 'Hope' was the all encompassing name given to the villages of Hope, Caergwrle and even Penyffordd. The village of Hope lies in the township of Estyn and gives its name to the parish. It is mentioned in the Domesday Book of 1086, becoming at one time Queen's Hope in 1398, and Hope Regina 1430. 'Hop' means 'a plot of enclosed land especially in marshes or waste'. *Yr Hob* must be taken as an adaptation of Hop, and reflects the strength of the Welsh language in the area.

Stryt Isaf — 'lower street' the Netherstrete. This is an ancient road. It is also known as Stryt Isa and Stryt Issa.

Sarn Lane — 'causeway'

Caer Estyn — *Estyn* means eastern village, *caer* meaning fort. This fort is on the hill to the east of the River Alyn at Wat's Dyke. Caer Estyn and Caergwrle are almost twins, one on each side of the River Alyn and Wat's Dyke.

Rhos Estyn — *rhos* is 'moor or heathland' in the north corner of Estyn.

Rhyddyn Hall — 'ryding or clearing'.
Celyn — 'holly'.
Gwalia — *gwaliau* 'town walls'.
Rhanberfedd — *rhan* 'a part', *perfedd* 'the middle'.
Bryn Tirion — *tirion* 'gentle' *bryn* 'hill. '

Caergwrle — this village is engulfed in legend. One popular explanation is that Gwrle was a giant whose castle was the remains of his fort and that he was buried in the tumulus in Cefn-y-Bedd. The earliest reference in 1278 spelled it as 'Kaierguill', and there have been various spellings ever since. Earlier forms show that gwrle was formed from two English words. The old English word 'cron' or 'corn' meaning bird or crane. The 'ley' part of Caergwrle means wood, or clearing in a wood. Putting the two meanings together it means a 'wood or clearing in the wood beside the River Alyn where the cranes were often seen'. *Caer* as we have mentioned means fort.

There are two rivers, the River Alyn and the River Cegidog. As the River Alyn has had some changes to its name over the centuries, we have decided to use the spelling we are most familiar with *circa* 1700. In 1337 it was the Alun; 1373, Elyn; and in 1539, Alen. This river meanders through the villages, and in the distant past was believed to have been used to transport goods. Rising north of Llangollen it flows through or near to Llandegla, Llanarmon-yn-Iâl, Llanferres, Cilcain, Rhydymwyn, Mold, Caergwrle, Gresford and then into the River Dee.

The River Cegidog was noted for the hemlock (*cegid*) a poisonous plant which was used in medicine. This river rises in Blanau to the east of Rhydtalog and flows through Ffrith, Cefn-y-Bedd and into the River Alyn at Sydallt.

For a fuller explanation of names and their various spellings please refer to, as we did, *The Place Names of East Flintshire* by Hywel Wyn Owen.

The 1875 O. S. map shows the area we have researched. There are many other interesting areas we would have liked to investigate, such as Shordley however we felt this could wait for another time as there was enough to do collecting the history of Hope and Caergwrle!

We hope you enjoy reading this book. We realise that some of the events included have already been recorded and written about, however as these are an integral part of the villages' history they cannot be ignored. We acknowledge that there are other aspects of the local history which will need further investigation in time.

Rhona Phoenix and Alison Matthews

1. Early History

Physical Features

Hope and Caergwrle are part of an area which is borderland, between the lowlands of the Cheshire Plain and the uplands of the Clwydian range and beyond. The River Alyn meanders through a flat valley where there are thick glacial deposits of sand and gravel. To the west of the river is Hope Mountain, an outlier of the upland area, which rises steeply to its summit at 330m. The eastern slopes of Hope Mountain are of Cefn-y-fedw sandstone, a millstone grit formed under marine delta conditions. Two smaller outliers, Bryn-y-gaer and Castle Hill, are also of the same stone. The western slopes of Hope Mountain towards Uwchymynydd Ucha are underlain by carboniferous limestone. This rock is rich in invertebrate fossils having been formed in shallow water. Coal measures are accessed in the valleys and are made up of rotted vegetation deposited in primeval swamps and marshes.

Hope village is situated above the flood plain of the River Alyn and has developed around the church on the south and west facing slopes of the valley. Wat's Dyke follows the line of a low ridge just north of the village.

As the Alyn flows southward the valley narrows and the river is squeezed between two small hills, Castle Hill and Bryn y gaer. The builders of Caer Estyn hill fort and Caergwrle Castle took full advantage of these strong defensive positions. The village of Caergwrle has developed around the castle, on the lower eastern facing slopes of Hope Mountain.

A tributary river, the Cegidog, joins the Alyn at Sydallt, south of Cefn y bedd, and the Alyn itself flows into the River Dee south-east of Rossett.

Prehistoric Flintshire

Flintshire has a long history of human settlement beginning with the Palaeolithic culture of the Stone Age, 250,000—8,000BC, when people hunted mammoth and horse, and engraved pictures on rocks.

A standing stone which has been incorporated into a stone wall at Horeb, Hope Mountain.

11

The Caergwrle Bowl. [National Museum of Wales]

The further back we go, however, the less accurate is our knowledge of these times and the way people lived, and for this we depend on the findings of archaeologists. Megaliths (standing stones) belonged to the Neolithic and Bronze Ages, possibly between 3500BC and 1500 BC, and had a number of functions, not least being the focal point of a community. There are two standing stones at Horeb on Hope Mountain.

The Bronze Age

About 2,000 BC a new people came to Britain from what is now France. Objects which have been left behind by these people enable us to have some understanding of their way of life.

The Caergwrle Bowl is a unique artefact which was found in 1823 to the south-west of Rhyddyn Hall, buried by the River Alyn, which was a significant place, near water, the river being a tributary of the River Dee. The river was likely to have been the focus for religious or ritual life for the Bronze Age people living along its banks. It is possible that the Sarn in Hope, which means 'causeway across the river' could have been one such site. This is the description of the Caergwrle Bowl, by Stephen Aldhouse-Green:

> a votive model of an ancient skin boat. None of the raw materials are native to this area. The gold might be from west Wales or Ireland; the tin probably comes from Cornwall, the shale from Dorset. The boat model is in itself a work of high craftsmanship and no precisely similar objects are known elsewhere in the world.

For many years it was believed to have been made of oak. However, after some time it was realised that this was a shale material derived from Kimmeridgian oil shale in Dorset.

> It is decorated with gold leaf applied both on and just below the rim. Engraved or stamped on the gold are discs, which have been interpreted as sundiscs or shields hung on the gunwales of the boat, there also appear to be depicted oars and waves, the lower view the ribs. At either end are pairs of 'eyes', which would suggest the 'warding off' of evil, as can be seen on boats in Mediterranean ports.

The age of the bowl is believed to be typical of the Bronze Age 'Penard period' 1200–1000 BC, a time when a warrior élite emerged in Wales. They used large sheet metal vessels for ceremonial feasting.

Eighty years ago the fragments of this find were put together by the British Museum. Recently, however, an x-ray has been taken in order to discover the original pieces, with a view to correcting it and finding its true original shape. It is now in the National Museum of Wales, Cardiff.

Other finds

A bronze socketed axe was discovered by Mr Llewelyn Bowman at Hope Hall. The implement is 95mm long x 50mm broad at the extremity of the cutting edge — the mouth of the socket measures 30mm x 25mm with marks on one side of the broken tong. This is now in St Asaph's Cathedral Museum.

Excavations at Sarn Lane, Hope (1993) revealed a lithic (stone) blade, 25mm long by 7mm wide, and also beyond the eastern edge of the modern settlement, a spindle whorl, or net sinker.

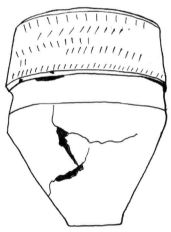

The Caergwrle Urn.
Ellis Davies, The Prehistoric and Roman Remains of Flintshire.

Another exciting find was in the tumulus in a field called Bryn yr Orsedd which belonged to Hafod Farm, in 1822. There is an account of the discovery of a sepulchral urn written by H. W. Eyton of Leeswood in which he describes how the urn was found in a bank of sand and gravel near the road from Caergwrle to Mold. The urn contained several portions of human bones that had not been consumed by fire, part of a jaw and tooth, as well as a piece of rib. The urn after examination is believed to be of the Middle Bronze Age, but unfortunately its location is not known.

Changes from one period to another, such as Bronze Age and Iron Age, in reality were far less clear cut but gradual, which is why dates may vary.

Iron age 750 BC–47 AD Hill Fort/ Caer Estyn

The Bronze Age people had been in Britain for about 1,000 years when new invaders crossed the Channel. These newcomers were the Celts a people who had learned to smelt and cast iron, and were, therefore, able to defend themselves with far better weapons. Iron is a hard and strong metal, so their knives and axes were much sharper. Also, the iron shod plough, drawn by a pair of oxen, made it possible for these people to cultivate the soil more

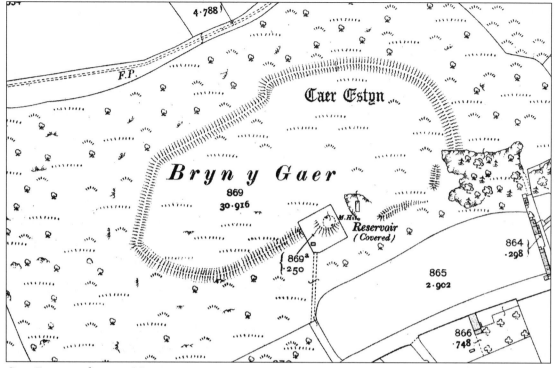

Caer Estyn on the 1912 OS map.

efficiently. There were many hill forts around Flintshire, Caer Estyn being one of the smaller structures.

This hill fort occupies the top of a long hill called Bryn y Gaer, overlooking the hill on which Caergwrle Castle stands; the River Alyn flows in the valley between these two hills. It is described in the Royal Commission of Ancient Monuments of Wales and Monmouth (1912) thus:

The area enclosed is irregular oval ... on the north east exists a triple line of bank with intervening ditches, the breadth of the defences is 77 feet. The entrance is in the centre of the north face.

Water was available from three or four springs within the camp.

Over the years, extensive quarrying has taken place. When a small group of local historians decided to do a limited excavation in 1957, part of the fort was already

Beehive quern found in the Rectory garden.

destroyed. From their excavation they surmised that the wall and rampart was probably five feet in height with a base of four feet. The excavation team did, however, find a flint blade and three possible hammer stones.

In Hope, the upper stone of a Bee Hive Quern was discovered in the Rectory garden and this is also believed to be from the Iron Age period.

The story of the Celts brings an end to the prehistoric era, their language surviving in the Welsh and Gaelic tongues. The Celtic tribe, the Deceangli lived in Flintshire at the beginning of the Christian era, and occupied the forts when the Romans appeared.

The Romans 48-399AD

The Roman conquest of southern Britain was completed when Wales was finally subdued. This invasion brought about many changes. The fort at Deva (Chester) was built in 70–74AD, a strategic place for access and control of north Wales and the north-west of England. By the second century, this walled town had become an important trading centre for our borderlands.

The local tribe, the Deceangli, after strong opposition, appeared to have learned to integrate with the Romans, settling into a peaceful and comfortable life, accepting Roman authority and culture. At this time, in this area, there would have been a number of settlements, a mixture of single farmsteads, fenced or ditched enclosures and small hamlets.

According to the historian Tacitus, the Romans were anxious to conquer Wales for its valuable lead mines and minerals. One such lead mine at the Ffrith was reached by the Roman route from Chester and part of this road is visible in some areas but ill-defined in others. According to one local historian, it leaves Chester from the Southgate and bridge through to the Lache and on to Dodleston. The road is hard to trace as there is a gap of four miles across low-lying ground from Dodleston to Caergwrle where the hilly country begins abruptly. It then continues from Abermorddu, south of Caergwrle, onto the winding road to the Ffrith. An alternative theory is that this route, using the native trackways, would have passed Bryn Iorcyn, on to Cymau, then, crossing the River Cegidog, to Ffrith. This road probably crossed the River Alyn at some point between Caergwrle and Cefn-y-bedd; other possibilities are the Sarn (pitching on road) Hope, or perhaps the ford at Bridge End, Caergwrle.

There have been discoveries of Roman coins or other metallic objects, some in Shordley, which because of their size could easily have been carried to that place. A Roman coin was found by Thomas Rogers in 1930 in the garden of Eastfield Hope. This was apparently given to Mr J. F. Sharpe of Hawarden County School, who mislaid it. His description was that it was a silver coin, a denarius from the time of Constantine. It bore on the reverse side the figure of Victory. Another coin found at Caergwrle Castle, a sestercius from the time of

Antoninus Pius, dated AD 150, is now in the Grosvenor Museum, Chester.

Accounts of discoveries *circa* 1585 have led to the suggestion that there was a Roman occupation in the Hope/Caergwrle area, however there does not appear to be any conclusive evidence, such as buildings or any other structures — as yet — to support this claim.

There is the possibility of a settlement around the crossing of the river, which is not yet known, but again there is no evidence at this time to support the theory.

Confusion about a Roman settlement seems to have arisen because the ruins of Roman buildings which were discovered at Ffrith in the sixteenth century were described as being found 'in the parish of Hope' or near Caergwrle.

This idea of a Roman settlement came from Campden's words:

> At Hope was there a Roman Stoupe or hole (recte hote--hot) howse digged up 5 elnes (ells) long, four broad, one and halfe deep ... On the tyles was written Legio XX, which sometime laye at Chester six miles off.

This description led Pennant and subsequent writers, who largely depended on him, to connect the discovery with Caergwrle, which is less than a mile south of Hope village. This debate will no doubt continue, and as excavations continue at the castle possibilities of new discoveries are ever-present.

Around 400 AD the Romans began to withdraw from Deva, resulting in more changes as trade and authority began to disappear. Raids from the Picts and Scots from the north, and Anglo Saxons from the east drove the desperate population of north Wales further west into the mountains and forests leaving a sparsely populated area with much confusion as law and order disintegrated.

Emergence of Wales 400—1070AD

In the early years of the fifth century there were many changes due to great social unrest. Trade and commerce ceased as we moved into the Dark Ages. In about 550AD the Saxon advance resumed. A hundred years later, most of what would become England was under their control. On reaching the Welsh mountains, however, the expansion became a spent force.

The Battle of Chester in 613 AD resulted in Chester being taken by the Angles after a great battle between the troops of Aethelfrith, ruler of the Anglian kingdom of Northumbria and those of Selyf, prince of Powys. Thus Chester became an alien stronghold and the Northumbrian armies loomed ominously on the Welsh horizon.

The Welsh tried desperately to stop Aethelfrith's advance into their territory. Historians regarded this battle as significant because from this time on Wales as a nation had to defend itself almost continuously against various kings from the region which we now call England, a bitter struggle to keep land, language, livestock and traditions alive.

The lands between the rivers Dee and the Clwyd from now on were to become battlegrounds, fought over by the armies of the English kingdoms of Mercia and Northumbria on one side, and the Welsh kingdoms of Gwynedd and Powys on the other. The rise of the kingdom of Mercia posed a real threat in the seventh century.

The Dyke Systems

Wat's Dyke is an important boundary and feature of the archaeological landscape of the Welsh Marches. The Dyke follows a strategic contour, having gaps to control crossing and trade. The sketch shows Wat's Dyke in relation to the villages of Hope and Caergwrle. It is believed that Wat's Dyke marked the formal boundary and defensive line dividing Anglo-Saxon Mercia and the Celtic west. The western limit of the region extends for over 62km from Maesbury in the south to Basingwork in the north.

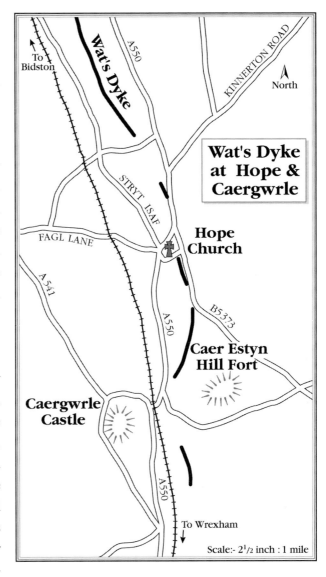

There are currently differing views by historians, about the date of its construction. As this is an ongoing discussion, we can only give you an idea of these different theories.

Is it a seventh century defensive line to keep out the Welsh, an eighth century boundary marker built by a Mercian King, or the work of a post Roman local King or powerful warlord during the last gasps of the Romans before they 'abandoned' Britain?

Sir Cyril Fox (1934) considered that the details of design construction and overall strategy were part of the 'Mercian school of dyke builders', as was Offa's Dyke, therefore placing the date around the mid to late eighth century. If this was indeed the date, then it

Wat's Dyke at Hope, 2006. The ditch and bank clearly visible.

would seem that at this time the north-eastern part of the present county of Flintshire was permanently Anglian or Saxon.

During the years 716—757AD Mercia was ruled by Aethelbald, king of the whole of Anglo-Saxon Britain according to the historian Bede, the principal English monarch of his day.

A recent new dating, based on radio carbon dating of remains from an archaeological investigation of a site near Oswestry, suggests that the deep ditched boundary rampart was constructed 300 years earlier than previously accepted. Other historians, however, argue that this carbon dating can only suggest a probable date before the dyke was built, as it is based on a sample collected from a hearth on the ground under the dyke.

In the parish of Hope, Wat's Dyke sometimes appears to have been confused with Offa's Dyke, which runs further to the west. Historians suggest that this confusion was because of the wording in the 1378 Charter which was granted to Hope, the "Offediche" of the Charter is really Wat's Dyke.

Offa's Dyke was built by Offa, King of Mercia, who in 780AD ordered the building of a dyke from sea to sea. Offa's Dyke essentially defined the territory of Wales, and is generally acknowledged to have been built during his documented campaigns against the Welsh, 757—96AD. It is unlikely that it was built in a single year and is believed to have been in existence by the early 790s.

There is still much speculation about the purpose of Wat's Dyke. A report by Sir Cyril Fox in 1934 described it as a frontier, a boundary rampart, but not a line of defence. He believed it not to be continuous, but built only where natural features such as rivers, forests and marshes would not serve the same purpose. However, later work on the dyke led to the theory that pre-historic earthworks along the dyke have been re-occupied and re-used suggesting a defensive dyke. This defence was considered to have been built by peoples of the east against those of the west, not against a large army, but against small groups of raiders whose attacks made agriculture very difficult along the Mercian border. It is also believed to have afforded some protection for Chester.

This linear earthwork consisted of a bank and ditch and was a form of construction known as far back as when people first became settled farmers, with a need to enclose and defend their land. It is argued that this is the first boundary which Mercians were able to establish between themselves and Welsh, the deep ditch was always on the west, the Welsh, side, clearly indicating that the threat came from that direction.

Lastly who was Wat? One suggestion was that the name came from a figure of folklore in the area of Schleswig-Holstein, from which the royal house of Mercia originated. Another historian argues that it could be the name of a local dignitary, or was even taken from the folk hero Wada, the Wada Haelsingum ruler of Haelsingas. We may never know for certain.

By the year 816 AD Mercian power was in decline as the Saxon kingdom of Wessex became more powerful. It was not until 973 AD, when eight British rulers, amongst them the prince of Gwynedd and the king of Mercia, submitted to Edgar, ruler of Wessex, recognising his authority to become king of England. It seems that, whatever the dating may reveal, Wat's Dyke marked the formal boundary to north-west Mercia, and its importance as the western limit of the region lasted until the Norman Conquest.

There was, however, a successful Welsh uprising in this area, led by Gruffydd ap Llywelyn who was king of all Wales 1055–63, when he was murdered by Welsh traitors. He was successful in reclaiming from English settlers lands to the east of Offa's Dyke. His conquest of areas of north-east Wales which were formerly part of the earl of Chester's domain, meant that they would remain Welsh and become part of the later counties of Flintshire and Denbighshire.

Wales was once more broken up into various kingdoms. This latest campaign had increased the prestige of Harold, the earl of Wessex, and marked him out for kingship on the death of Edward the Confessor. On his accession in 1066, however, he was called upon to defend his claim against William the Norman.

The Impact of the Normans

The Normans invasion of England in 1066, perhaps the best known date in English history, is considered to be a crucial turning point in the nation's story. Four years later in 1070, Edwin, the Saxon nobleman of Chester, surrendered to King William. At this time Wales was largely independent, made up of a loose federation of small princedoms.

The Domesday survey provides us with the most comprehensive and detailed document of the eleventh century. It was written in 1086, and provides a picture of Flintshire 900 years ago. Here is the description of Hope manor:

Hope — the same Gilbert holds Hope. Eadwin held (it); he was a freeman. There is one hide that pays geld. There is land (enough) for one plough; it is there with 2 villeins and (there are) 2 acres of wood (land). It is worth 7s; it was waste and he found it so.

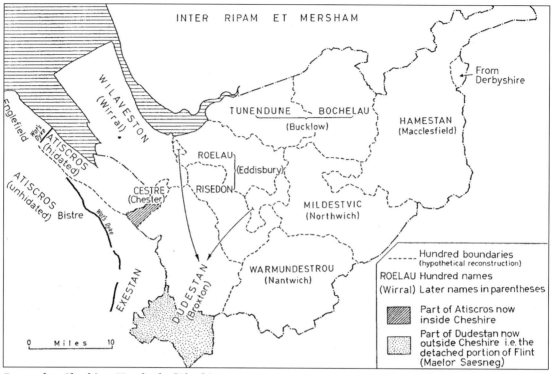

Domesday Cheshire: Hundreds. [Cheshire Community Council Publications Trust]

NB — Gilbert de Venables of Kinderton was one of the chief Cheshire barons.

A hide was a unit of land measurement reckoned at 60–120 acres, adequate for one family and its dependants.

A villein was a labourer.

The land was divided into hundreds, which were districts within a shire, whose assembly of notables and village representatives met once a month. These units of land extended from the Dee valley to Wat's Dyke and included the hundred of Exestan. The Domesday Book shows that by 1086 the affairs of the earldom and the borderlands of north Wales were closely linked together. Their close proximity meant there were often scenes of intermittent warfare. The earldom of Chester was considered to be a bulwark against Welsh invasion, its position in relation to Wales a distinct military advantage, lying in the northern part of the Marches, an ill-defined zone that separated England and Wales.

The hundred of Exestan, which included Hope, comprised of twenty-one hides, twenty-one plough lands, eight plough teams and a population of forty-five people. The population density in this poorly developed territory varied from five to less per square mile. Much of the lowland or borderland was moor, marsh or forest, a description of which was written by the chronicler for William the Conqueror:

He made large forests for deer and enacted laws therewith, so that whoever killed a hart or a hind should be blinded. As he forbade the killing of deers so also the boars. As he loved the tall Stags as though he were their father. He also appointed concerning the Hares that they should go free. The rich complained and the poor murmured but he was so sturdy that he recked nought of them.

The people of Flintshire were soon to become familiar with the sight of mail clad knights and the sound of their Norman-French tongue. Entering their bloodiest era, the borderlands became a battleground for conflicts between the indigenous Welsh and the Normans.

One of William's followers, a Flemish nobleman Gherbod, became the earl of Chester, but was soon replaced by William's nephew, Hugh, in 1071, the first of a long line, who ruled continuously until 1237, when the earldom passed to the Crown. Hugh was considered to be the first earl of Chester. He was a borderer from Avranches in Normandy, and was well versed in border warfare and defence. It was his job to help restore the wastelands. He was an able soldier but a cruel ruler, feared and hated by the Welsh. Described as a coarse, worldly man, he became better known as Hugh the Gross (the Fat) and later Hugh Lupus (the Wolf). He is described by Orderic Vitalis, an English monk and historian:

This man with the help of many cruel barons, shed much Welsh blood. He was not so much lavish as prodigal. His retinue was more like an army than a household ... Each day he devastated his own land and preferred falconers and huntsmen to cultivators of the same and ministers of heaven.

The Earl of Chester was allowed freedom to rule his kingdom. He had his own army, which enabled him to enlarge his territory by seizing land from the Welsh. With the aid of a young Norman, named Robert, he quickly brought the lowlands between Chester and Basingwerk under Norman control.

The Normans were skilful in the art of war, more so than either the Welsh or Saxons, for their ability to build castles served them well as places to retreat to when under attack, unlike their enemy, who had to fight their battles in the open countryside and flee to the mountains to avoid being cut to pieces.

A Norman knight. [D. Phoenix]

Another advantage was the armoured knight who fought on horse back. Norman knights on their great battle horses, galloping in line with couched lances to charge a company of footmen, must have been a terrifying sight. Knights were the élite troops of medieval European warfare. At a time when peasants travelled on foot and merchants on the back of mules, owning a horse made the knight a person of higher social standing. He was accompanied by his squire and attendants who carried his shields and took care of the animals. Knights had expensive equipment: a sword and lance, a helmet and a coat of mail, the latter consisting of a long shirt made of fine, steel hoops, skilfully looped together. A typical Norman raid would use the art of surprise, attacking and slaughtering the men whilst abducting the women. The manors, including Hope, were wasted by enemy action and as a result were virtually abandoned.

The people who lived in the Hope area at that time were described as: villeins or labourers who carried manure, hedged and ditched and did other 'humble work'; bodors, who lived in small cabins made of mud and wattle and held a small section of land on the condition they supplied eggs, poultry and other articles of food for the table of the Lord; serfs, who were of a lower rank than villeins, and reduced to a state of bondage, peasants permanently attached to the feudal manor who were inherited by each new lord, having few legal rights.

There were huge forests, which expanded steadily at this time, reaching their widest extent during the reign of Henry II in the late twelfth century. These forests were not reserved just for hunting but contained pastureland and villages. The two forests in our area were the Forests of Rusty (possibly derived from the Welsh name *Yr Estyn*) and Loidcoid/Lloitcoit.

The basic economy during this period depended upon agriculture and it was a difficult time for peasants. Famine was commonplace; crops could easily be ruined by too much or too little rain. Spring crops of barley and oats were introduced at this time, however tilling the land was exhausting work for these poor malnourished people.

The Normans of Chester had penetrated into a great deal of north Wales and although the area colonised was limited, their lordships were established over numerous *cantrefs* and *commotes* that had previously formed portions of the kingdoms of Gwynedd and Powys.

2. Late Medieval & Early Modern History

The Welsh Princes

During a period of renewed conflict in the reign of William II (1087-1100), the political situation in the north was reversed, so that after 1094 much of the land which had previously been lost to the Normans, was gradually recovered by the Welsh princes of northern Wales.

The twelfth and thirteenth centuries were a period of royal campaigns and Welsh offensives. The Welsh were unable to completely eject the Norman invaders from their lands. Throughout this period the position and power of the crown by and large drove the affairs with the Welsh.

Owain Gwynedd, who died in 1171, had been recognised as a powerful leader holding land from Anglesey to the river Dee. At this time Welsh rule was well established, the areas of Hope and Caergwrle were in the possession of the Prince of Powys.

Dafydd ap Gruffudd

During the early part of the thirteenth century, Llywelyn ap Iorwerth (known as Llywelyn *Fawr*, the 'Great') a skilled and respected statesman, united all Wales, bringing peace to the borderlands through his friendship with the earl of Chester. After his death in 1240, he was succeeded by his son Dafydd who, unable to maintain the unity established by his father, lost control of parts of Flintshire. He died suddenly in 1246 and his three nephews, Owain, Llywelyn and Dafydd (the sons of his brother Gruffydd), fought amongst themselves to become ruler of Gwynedd. By 1254 Llywelyn had taken control. It is believed that the bone of contention between the brothers was the partition of lands.

The Welsh complained bitterly about the harsh treatment they received from officials of the Marcher lords in general and Prince Edward of England (who later became Edward I) in particular. Llywelyn, with the help of his brother Dafydd, successfully attacked the English forces and drove them out of north Wales, gaining control of the whole region by 1262. On 29 September 1267 the Treaty of Montgomery was signed between Gwynedd and England, recognising Llywelyn as the Prince of Wales. This was a period of momentous importance in the shaping of the nation's political destiny.

For the next ten years there was an uneasy peace; Llywelyn still refused to pay homage to the English king, whilst Dafydd's loyalty lay with Edward I, along with other Welsh

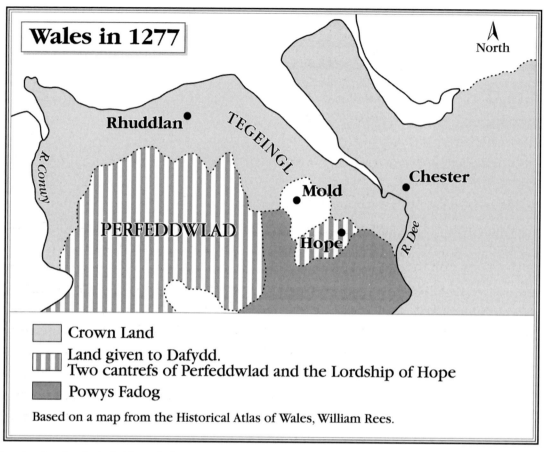

Wales in 1277

North

Rhuddlan

TEGEINGL

R. Conwy

Mold

Chester

PERFEDDWLAD

Hope

R. Dee

Crown Land

Land given to Dafydd.
Two cantrefs of Perfeddwlad and the Lordship of Hope

Powys Fadog

Based on a map from the Historical Atlas of Wales, William Rees.

border lords. It is believed that in 1274 Dafydd plotted with the lord of southern Powys, Gruffydd ap Gwenwynwyn, to assassinate Llywelyn in the hope of being proclaimed Prince of Wales. The plot failed when Llywelyn was informed of the conspiracy and Dafydd and Gruffydd fled across the border, seeking the protection of Edward I. They were well received and spent the next few years plundering and burning Llywelyn's lands. In 1277, King Edward invaded north Wales, forcing Llywelyn to agree terms which confined his rule to Gwynedd, west of the river Conwy. Dafydd was granted the lordship of Hope by the King and was given a grant of 100 marks for works carried out at *Castrum Kaierguill* (Caergwrle Castle), where he lived for five years. The peace did not last, however, as Dafydd felt his services had not been adequately rewarded: the King had promised him a larger share of north Wales, but had introduced other royal officials, such as Reginald de Grey the Justice of Chester, to govern the conquered lands. There appears to be no doubt that this was the turning point in Dafydd's relationship with the Crown. He disliked the manner in which Grey treated him, particularly as he had been loyal to Edward. Grey's regime was aggressive and severe, resulting in an end to the peaceful times. Eventually, this uneasy period would result in the outbreak of war.

On the night of 21/22 March, Dafydd, with possibly many men from Hope, attacked Hawarden Castle, killing the English garrison and capturing the lord, Roger de Clifford. Within days, rebellion flared throughout the north, west and east of Wales, the King's men were being killed and driven out. Llywelyn had little choice but to take the lead in the rebellion and he and his brother were at last fighting on the same side, their personal hostility on hold. Edward I, however, had the power to crush this rebellion by striking from several directions at once, with commanders being appointed for each part of Wales. Reginald de Grey, Justice of Chester was put at the head of forces to strike north Wales. The troops recruited by the King consisted of cavalry and infantry and some English and Welsh lords, old adversaries of Llywelyn, would fight for Edward.

The infantry included crossbowmen, armed with weapons made of Spanish yew and whalebone. There were 1500 of these men who were Gascons, trained to use this formidable weapon. There were only 250 Englishmen. The other infantrymen were archers, many of whom were inexperienced at using the longbow, a powerful weapon in the right hands. This army must have struck fear into the hearts of the ordinary Welsh peasants.

Reginald de Grey's woodsmen cut down the forests on either side of the invasion route in order to lessen the risk of surprise attacks. The Welsh had laid waste to the lowlands and taken their families to the mountains. Edward I tried to encourage the Welsh to remain in their homes by offering them peace, liberty and their lands if they served him faithfully. Many, who were tired of war, decided to do this. The King, however, would never again favour Dafydd; he had changed sides once too often.

> We welcomed him when an exile, endowed him out of our own lands, and favoured him under the cloak of our wing, placing him amongst the greatest of our palace.

The war which began at the end of March 1282, following the fall of Hawarden, was a defining moment in Welsh history. Reginald de Grey pushed his troops up the valley of the Dee towards Hope where the castle had been severely damaged by Dafydd. By mid summer, the numbers of troops assembled was immense with hundreds of cavalry and crossbowmen, and thousands of foot soldiers, with the main thrust starting in Chester. Edward made his way from Flint to Rhuddlan which he made a base for his attack on Llywelyn and Dafydd's stronghold of Snowdonia. When Edward arrived in early July there were 45 Cheshire cavalry at Hope and a large body of archers. Grey maintained this small force in the area to guarantee the security of the castles at Hope, Hawarden and Ewloe.

Llywelyn was killed in December 1282, in a skirmish with English knights near Builth. At first they did not realise who he was. The official report of his death was sent to Edward:

Know sire, that the forces that you placed under my command fought with Llywelyn ap Grufydd in the land of Builth on Friday after the feast of St Nicholas, and that Llywelyn ap Grufydd is dead, his army are broken, and all the flower of his men killed, as the bearer of this letter will tell you.

Llywelyn's head was cut off and sent to the king, then to London for display at the Tower. Dafydd was captured on 28 June and taken to Shrewsbury where he became the first man to be barbarously hanged, drawn and quartered. His head was also sent to London to be put on the White Tower, while his quartered remains were sent to Bristol, York, Northampton and Winchester. The two brothers had burned the king's towns and killed many of his subjects and Edward wreaked a terrible revenge.

The Principality of Wales after 1282

With the deaths of Llywelyn and Dafydd, Welsh independence came to an end and Edward I took control of the territories of the princes of Gwynedd. He organized the building of a series of castles in north Wales, Chester being the base for this massive undertaking, conscripting labour from all areas of England.

During the two years from 1282 to 1284, it is believed Edward I spent a great deal of time in north Wales arranging the future government of the country, and for the next two centuries, 1283–1484, the lordship of Hope was held by one or other of the royal family or their direct representative. It seems that there is a distinct possibility that the King actually visited Caergwrle Castle in July 1282.

In the records kept in the National Archives, known as 'Chancery Miscellanea', there is a detailed roll of expenditure at this castle. This source of information gives us a wonderful insight into who worked on the building and also how it was defended as the work was being carried out.

Wages of knights and squires	£246 8s.
Pay of carpenters and stone masons	£154 1s. 7½d.
Cost of necessaries etc July 13	£9 3s. 11½d.
Payments to officials, workmen, messengers, etc; cost of carriages etc from 13 July	£85 5s. 2½d.
Pay of (a) archers (£851 1s. 4d.) and (b) Diggers (£48 5s. 5d.)	£899 6s. 9d.
Wages of crossbowmen	£71 18s. 11d.
Total expenditure	£1,466 4s. 5½d.

Artist's impression of the completed Caergwrle Castle. 'For most of its short life the castle was a building site. The courtyard would have been crowded with piles of stones, timber, supplies, animals, craftsmen and labourers and of course soldiers.' [Extract from the Caergwrle Castle leaflet, published by Flintshire Countryside Services].

*Views of Caergwrle
Castle, 2006.*

The rebuilding of the castle was supervised by Hugh de Pulford. During the first month 430 wood-men were engaged to provide timber from the surrounding forest. There were 340 carpenters and 31 masons working under Heyn de Thoroy, master mason. In addition, there were 382 labourers and by July 600 diggers. It is thought that the diggers were used to extend the moat to a barbican mound making a gateway with a wooden footbridge. The internal building was most likely

Part of the North Tower of Caergwrle Castle.

constructed of timber and included a chapel. There was a chamber for pay clerks, also one over the gate, and yet another of the purpose of which is unknown. The work was probably under the control of Master James of St George, the King's architect in north Wales.

The castle was a hive of activity; all the equipment had to be transported by men and horses to the castle site at the top of a steep hill. These materials included water, timber, sacks of charcoal, lime, rope, iron, nails and tools such as picks and shovels, most of which were brought from Chester.

Two days before Edward's departure, the mason, Henry of Turvey, was paid 12*d*. for the demolition of the old keep. There can be little doubt that on this site were the remains of a great circular tower, the stones from which were reused to build again. It is not known why the tower was demolished, it may have been built years before Dafydd's time or possibly Dafydd had built it but damaged it during the rebellion. The well, a vital source of water, had been blocked by the Welsh with stone, and a miner was paid 3*d*. per day to unblock it. Once this was achieved, two barrels of water were sent to King and Queen at Rhuddlan Castle as proof. It has been reported to the authors that, during the miners strike of 1926, a miner named Roberts went down the well to unblock it once more and discovered a

Remains of the east curtain wall, Caergwrle Castle, 2006.

Base of a pillar at Caergwrle Castle.

door. He opened it and a blast of stale air hit him in the face. He shut it quickly.

The whole site needed to be protected, and, as shown in the expense account, the greatest expenditure was on these men who were based around the castle. The head of a Welshman was worth 12*d.*, equivalent to a workman's weekly wage. In fact, twenty-seven Welshmen lost their heads, presumably being captured on the wrong side of Offa's Dyke which lay two miles to the west of the castle.

It would appear that the renovations were not completed by the end of the season and the castle walls were covered to protect them from the winter weather. There is no evidence, however, of work recommencing the following spring as, by the middle of March 1283, work had begun on Edward's magnificent castle at Aberconwy.

On 24 February 1283 Edward gave the castle at Hope to his consort, Eleanor of Castille, along with 'all the land of Hope, which David son of Griffin, the King's enemy and rebel formerly held. Queen Eleanor was granted a Charter on 25 June 1283 allowing her to have a weekly market on Tuesdays and an annual four day fair on the feast of St Peter. At this time the area was known as Queen's Hope.

This was the beginning of a century of exploitation of the Welsh in the borderlands. Land was allocated to those willing to become burgesses, and evidence of their allocation can still be seen on the map which will appear later. Residence was restricted to English settlers, the indigenous Welsh being expelled to make way for the immigrants. Later, a few favoured Welshmen were allowed to live in the borough.

On 27 August 1283 there was a fire at the castle — whilst the King and Queen were in residence — and there is speculation about the cause. Was it an accident or arson?

The Middle Ages 1300–1536

The Statute of Wales (or Statute of Rhuddlan), signed in 1284, created the first Welsh counties, five of them in the north and west Wales, the sixth in north-east Wales, namely Flintshire.

A Welsh uchelwr *(lord) of c.1282. [Michael Roberts, Samhain Welsh Medieval Society]*

Excavations of Caergwrle Castle 1988 by Clwyd Archaeological Service, headed by John Manley, MA, archaeologist.

Caergwrle Castle has a short but impressive history which was influenced by two very different men, Edward I of England and Dafydd ap Gruffudd of Wales. In July 1988 excavations began at the castle.

The structure of the castle has suffered badly from the robbing of the stone and quarrying activities, and so large sections have been lost. An examination of all the quarries on Castle Hill suggests that the most likely source of the sandstone for building the castle was a large quarry on the north-west side of the castle.

The excavation revealed a barbican mount (watch tower) on the north side of the castle which is believed to be a vital clue to the original gateway. Also discovered are the remains of a massive circular tower at least 48 feet in diameter. This tower commanded extensive views north, south and east, a great strategic point.

Other important finds included a large well, which was blocked by Dafydd before the castle was occupied by Edward I and also an impressive stone bread oven which seems to have originally been square in shape, with two flues at the front of the oven guided hot air up the dome. Stone footings found by the east wall could indicate the presence of a long timber built hall.

During the dig a large amount of medieval pottery was discovered which dated 1278–1283. These included both fine wares and coarser cooking vessels. It seems that wild boar was on the menu!

Metal objects such as broken horseshoes, two padlock keys, barbed iron arrow head about 3.5 cm long, iron nails and slag fragments suggested the presence of a castle smith's hearth in the open courtyard.

Other finds were the bronze end or chape of the scabbard. The scabbard would have been of leather, also a bronze knuckle attachment for a leather belt.

Coins which were discovered included two Edward I silver pennies, an Edward I farthing, pennies of Edward III and Edward IV, and an eighteenth century Wicklow halfpenny token.

To the east of the castle a low grassy bank encircles the summit of the hill. A section of this was excavated revealing stone walls infilled with loose, sandy silt and stones.

It is thought that it could have had a defensive capacity and pollen tests show that it was constructed through an area of mature oak woodland. This find points to an earlier native occupation or re occupation during the late Roman period or in the much less documented Dark Ages.

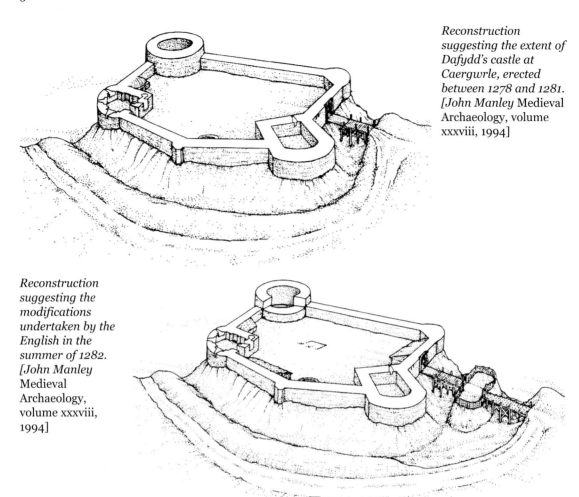

Reconstruction suggesting the extent of Dafydd's castle at Caergwrle, erected between 1278 and 1281. [John Manley Medieval Archaeology, volume xxxviii, 1994]

Reconstruction suggesting the modifications undertaken by the English in the summer of 1282. [John Manley Medieval Archaeology, volume xxxviii, 1994]

We have provided ...that there shall be a Sheriff of Flint under whom shall be the Cantred of Englefeud, the land of Mailor Sexenyth, and the Land of Hope, and ... [he] shall be obedient unto our Justice of Chester, and shall answer for the Issues of the same Commote at our Exchequer of Chester. There shall be coroners in the same counties ... and bailiffs of the commotes who shall faithfully do their offices ... according to what shall be given them in charge by the Justices and Sheriffs. [from Bowen, *The Statute of Wales*]

In 1301 the counties were granted to Edward's eldest son who was to become the first English Prince of Wales. As the county of Flintshire was attached to the earldom of Chester, the prince also had the title Earl of Chester (as does the present Prince of Wales). The chief officers of the earldom were: the Justice, who was in charge of the administration of its castles, armed forces and courts of law; the Chamberlain, who was head of the exchequer at Chester. All the money's collected were paid to the Chamberlain who then paid the wages of chief officials and maintenance costs.

Mrs Felicity Davies of the Wirral and North Wales Field Archaeology Group conducted an excavation in the autumn of 2003.

Attention was drawn to the site on the north east slope of Caergwrle Castle Hill by local historian Mr Charles Harston. Mr Harston was concerned that tree damage was destroying several features that he was convinced were important. Therefore, following consultation with the local council, Cadw and the Royal Commission for Historic Monuments in Wales, work began on the site.

After an initial survey had been conducted, it was realised that potentially, the site could be very large. It was decided therefore; that excavation be confined to an area that comprised of what appeared to be 2 large circular structures and 2 adjacent platforms.

However, as work progressed it became apparent that these were not circular structures, but seemed to be a passageway leading to a well, and a D shaped structure, one side of which comprised large stones revetted against the high wall of the passageway.

After dismantling part of the revetted wall, and excavation of one of the platforms, it is now apparent that there are at least 2 lines of large stones that enclose the well. These lines of stones have been covered over with quarry waste.

There is a paucity of finds, but from their nature and context, it is possible to reconstruct in part, at least, the history and context of the site itself.

Typographically, the large stones are Neolithic/ Bronze Age. It is possible that during either the Iron Age, or Medieval period, the large stones were covered over with quarry waste to provide a base for castle defences. It is probable that the original entrance to the Castle Hill runs along one side of the site. From the quarry waste were recovered 2 hammer stones, and fragments of animal bone, which have a 90% probability of coming from the Dexter type cattle.

Also included in the finds is a fragment of 1st century dusted mica ware from Gaul — Lyon, probably brought over by the Romans during the Claudian invasion. There is also a small piece of 11th century pottery, and some glass probably the same date.

Fragments of 17th century pottery and glass, also small pieces of lead indicate that Civil War

activity may have been present; this activity is borne out by the known history of the area. There is also a large amount of Victorian/ Edwardian pottery and glass, evidence of the many visitors to Caergwrle at this time.

It is hoped that the site will eventually come under the protection of CADW.

After the death of Queen Eleanor, Edward granted the 'farm' of Hope and its castle to Lord John de Warenne, earl of Surrey and Sussex, on 7 Feb 1301, for life, and an annual payment of £40 was given to the treasury at Chester. It is believed, however, that he must have been in possession earlier, for his bailiff in Hope was ordered to raise men for Edward in 1298 [Close Rolls, 1298]. It must be noted that only Welsh tenants were called on for military service, not the English settlers. This knight had fought in many wars with Edward, and in 1299 was involved in the battle of Falkirk. Here William Wallace faced the English king, who had at his disposal 25,700 troops, half of whom were Welsh mercenaries. It is believed that the success of this battle was achieved mainly by the use of the Welsh longbow.

Unfortunately, John de Warenne was not popular as he treated the tenants badly. The men of Hopedale and Kinnerton presented a petition to the king, claiming their ancient rights were being denied. and were not allowed to use the forests or to make use of their products, such as cutting down trees and clearing land to grow crops. Warenne died in 1304 and Hope lapsed back to the crown. On 29 June 1308, it was granted for life to John de Crumbwelle with the:

> castle, manor, knights fees, advowsons (the right to present a clergyman to a benefice, a nomination subject to the approval of a diocesan bishop), mills, woods, escheats, liberties and other appurtences. So that he may forthwith repair at his own expense the castle which is now in ruins. [Calendar of Patent Rolls, 1308]

In Hopedale the English lived mainly in 'Hope ad Castrum', which means Hope at, or below, the castle, and nearby Eston. English settlers were persuaded to come to the county by generous grants of land, made to them by the king. Such land was rented at 4d. an acre, and was known as 'English land', as no Welshman could have any part of it if an Englishman wanted it.

Ministers accounts

The Minister's Accounts from 1301–60s are an invaluable source of information, giving us an insight into the payments and expenses, also the work done in Hope at this time.

These were difficult times as, during in 1316–18, the whole of Europe suffered famine, men were away fighting and could not attend to food production. Also between 1315 and 1320 the weather became wetter and colder which again had a profound effect on agriculture, causing harvest failures as well as livestock diseases such as cattle plague.

In 1349–50, the borough of Hope had two bailiffs, Reynold Balle and John de Troghford. There was also a receiver named Richard de Eston. The rent of the borough was paid annually at the Feast of St Michael — '101s. 6d. for the burgages and of 'divers lands' in the hands of the burgesses of Hope — 7s. from the pasture of 'le Castelhull' — 30s. from the farm of the toll to the said vill and of the fairs during the same period'.

The expenses paid show the activities of this time. For example, the costs of the new mill; a carpenter had been appointed to construct one new mill for 60s. The hiring of 113 carts to carry timber from the wood cost 30s. 2d. Iron nails were bought for 3s. 6d., and for enclosing the pond or dam behind the mill, brushwood was used and many workmen were hired also to collect stone. The total cost came to £6 8s. 5½d. Bars were made for the prison in Hope for 12d.

Apparently the castle was not repaired, although requested by the King, and John de Crumbwelle had to explain why. He explained that, as he was fighting overseas, he had left his bailiffs to rebuild the castle. This work, however, had been hindered by raids of Welshmen who also encroached on the King's wastes and carried off corn and money from the King's mills. The bailiffs had not been able to protect the English inhabitants.

The Fighting Welsh

In 1330, Edward III's son, was born, who was to become known as the Black Prince. Edward had stipulated, as part of his Edwardian settlement, that 'no Welshman was to be received as a Burgess of Hope on whatever pretext be alleged, nor hold a burgage there, and enjoy its franchise.' Access to the market and trading were also forbidden, the bitterness was greater because it was claimed Welshmen had held burgages in the earlier borough.

Edward, the Black Prince, was invested as the earl of Chester, and Hope was administered by the prince's officials at Chester Castle. In 1335 his surveyors found 'only a place called the castle of Hope, whose walls and towers are largely thrown down and there is no housing there.'

At this time there were five forests in Flintshire, two of which were in Hopedale, the forest of Loidcoid, in the Kinnerton to Shordley area, and the Forest of Rusty, which is believed to have been in the Caergwrle and Cymmau area. These royal hunting forests belonged to Edward, the Black Prince, and were important as a source of revenue, timber, game and a place of recreation. His interests were closely guarded by a forester and even the honey from the wild bees was collected and sold.

At this time Edward III's campaign against France took large numbers of Welshmen — 3,500 — half of whom were archers and half spearmen. These men were paid 6d. a day. Again, Englishmen living in Wales were not recruited.

This was a period of change for the Hundred Years War in France meant many of the men of Hope were away fighting and therefore unable to care for their families. Welsh officials were employed, particularly to raise revenue, but the key posts went to Englishmen. This resulted in many '... feeling that they were outsiders in the governance of their own country' and almost certainly played a prominent role in the build up to the Glyndŵr revolt. The regular departure of men to fight in the war meant that when they returned they had lost their civil rights.

Everyday life

In 1349 the Black Death had affected the county, reaching Ruthin. It is estimated that it killed a third of the population of England and Wales, however, it is not possible to know how many people died in this area. This could only be estimated by the greatly decreased revenues sent to the Exchequer in Chester. Its effect was devastating. The land and the harvesting of crops were neglected and this was not helped by the severe winter of 1352 and a drought in the summer.

The county of Flintshire was required to pay Prince Edward an 'aid' of 1,000 marks, the first subsidy required to maintain the English army overseas.

In 1351, the borough of Hope was created by the grant of a charter which in many ways favoured the English settlers. The burgesses, who were Englishmen, petitioned the Black Prince that they might provide suitable boundaries for their town and paid for the borough of Hope to include the original township of Caergwrle and the newly acquired township of Estyn, 'which was better for agriculture with richer soil and more sunshine.' The burgesses had valuable trading privileges. They had the right to hold fairs in the borough and could claim complete control over the trade of the countryside for three leagues. The Welsh people were expected to bring their produce to the market, which provided the ordinary needs of a household, goods such as eggs, butter, meat, fish, local cloth and locally made tools of wood and earthenware. The annual fair was a great occasion, when merchants from distant places came to sell goods not found locally — silk cloth, ribbons, bars of iron for the blacksmith, gold, silver, salt, spices and steel swords. The poor could not afford to buy goods, but even they would have been fascinated by the displays and the entertainment, including ballad singers, minstrels, storytellers, jugglers and clowns.

Local industry was still developing and it is known that Sir Richard de Stafford erected a fulling mill, or *pandy*, south of the corn mill at Bridge End which increased cloth production. This was rented by Welshmen in 1386. Two Welshmen were recorded as miners of millstones and in 1396 Welshmen rented the flour mills. In 1365 the bridge of Ponterderlloyn (Pont Delyn) was repaired with wood from the forest.

The law and the Welsh

The chartered borough had borough courts of their own convening every three weeks and discharging similar judicial functions to those of the commote courts. There are very few surviving records of the proceedings of the courts during the thirteenth and fourteenth centuries. There were courts at Flint, Rhuddlan, Caerwys, Overton and Hope. The borough court was presided over by the mayor of the borough, assisted by the bailiffs. The 'Sheriff's Turn' took place twice a year, once at Easter time and again about Michaelmas. It was held by the Sheriff in each commote, the purpose being to provide him with full information concerning various offences committed, 'touching the crown and dignity of the King', or in other words the pleas to the crown. Some of the recorded crimes included stealing lead and cattle theft.

The Borough

The boundaries of the new borough appear to have coincided with those of the township of Caergwrle. It was laid out as a planned town with three parallel streets running north–south, with minor connecting streets running east–west. Settlers were given a plot on which to build their own house as well as land in the town field. Burgage plots were 49$\frac{1}{2}$ feet by 33 feet and there is surviving evidence of this system in Caergwrle where the annual rent was 12*d*. The settlement in Hope of tradesmen and craftsmen was encouraged. In the first half of the fourteenth century, the landowners made their money with tolls at the market and tax on the buying and selling of goods. Six Welshmen had to buy a licence to trade. Often people were fined for misbehaviour.

The question arises, 'why did the Borough not develop or grow'? It is thought that as the castle was not repaired or occupied, no lord of the manor was present to defend, employ or buy the local products; no important trading routes passed along the Alyn valley; and lastly, with reference to the agriculture, it was on the wrong side of the River Alyn, where the soil was poor and lay in the shadow of Hope Mountain, which reduced the hours of sunshine.

Charters

The Black Prince died in 1376 and, on the death of his father, Edward III, his son, Richard, became king. In 1380 the lands and lordship of Hope and Hopedale, were granted for life to John de Hollande, knight, of Northwich. He was a violent and cruel man who soon fell out of favour. His lands were forfeited to the King and Henry, Prince of Wales and Earl of Chester, became Lord of Hope.

In 1389 the burgesses of Queen's Hope could:

Only be tried before English jury.

No Welshman could hold market for merchandise or victuals or brew beer to be sold within 3 leagues of the borough. They could only sell goods at the borough market.

No herding or driving flocks or herds by Welshmen in the borough or the area administered by its courts.

RAF reconnaissance photograph of Caergwrle, 1947. The railway line can be clearly seen running from left to right with the castle just left of centre. The Wrexham–Mold road runs diagonally from lower left, passing between the castle and Hope Mountain, to upper right (passing under the railway). [National Assembly for Wales]

Henry IV's parliament had a list of anti Welsh issues to hand when they set to work to draw up new legislation. What is more, during the fourteenth century, many of these discriminatory measures were incorporated into borough charters and used as a pretext for profiteering exercises at the expense and embarrassment of the Welsh. Few borough charters are so vitriolic in their anti Welsh clauses as that issued at Hope in February 1399.

No Welshman can or ought to acquire to himself or his heirs ... any English land for any price, no Burgess was henceforth to be convicted by a Welshman, no Welshman was to hold a market or brew ale within three leagues of the town, all Welshmen of Hopedale were to bring victuals to Hope for sale and Welshmen were prohibited from holding assemblies.

It is from Hope that we get a striking glimpse of how such clauses could be used to exercise ethnic tension. In September 1401, Welshman Roger ab Iorwerth Felinydd (the miller), lost 50 acres of his land which he had purchased, because 'it was English land and had been measured as such at the time of the conquest of Wales.' He had acquired it:

> ... without licence of the lord Prince and contrary to the statutes, provisions and ordinances issued at Caernarvon at the time of the conquest for the burgesses and English boroughs of Wales and observed throughout north Wales. No Welshman can or ought to acquire to himself or his heirs any English land for any price, so long as an English burgess is willing to buy and hold it.

This was anti Welsh prejudice in practice. It is little wonder that this discrimination, exploitation and suppression eventually spilled over into violence.

Owain Glyndŵr

After so much suffering the time was ripe for rebellion and Owain Glyndŵr, a Welsh nobleman who was born c.1354 at Sycharth near Llansilin, would take up the challenge. He became recognised as a symbol of the spirit of Wales and someone who was capable of taking on the challenge against the tyranny of the English.

Henry IV had branded Glyndŵr as a traitor after he failed to respond to a summons to attend an expedition to attack the Scots, a summons, which Lord de Grey, Chief Marcher Lord of north Wales, had failed to deliver in time. In 1400, Owain made an appeal to the English Crown in an attempt to settle this long running dispute between himself and Lord Grey. Receiving no satisfaction, Owain was quick to take revenge. On the 16 September he proclaimed himself Prince of Wales, and on the 20 September 1400 he and his followers attacked Ruthin, then went on to Denbigh, Rhuddlan, Flint, Hawarden, Holt, Oswestry and Welshpool.

His policy was to ' bring all things to waste, that the English should find not strength or resting place in the country.' His main object was to get supplies for a war, and so he seized food, horses, cattle and weapons. These attacks stirred nationalistic feelings amongst the Welsh and during the course of that week hundreds of patriots flocked to join the cause. Henry, Prince of Wales, was sent to Chester to carry out a campaign against Glyndŵr. New Laws were passed which meant that any Welshman living within the vicinity of the English borough would to be held responsible for felonies, robberies or trespasses committed by Glyndŵr's supporters. Tensions mounted as local Welshmen were recruited to Prince Henry's campaign, regardless of their loyalties. In December 1401, three men from Hopedale were imprisoned in Chester as hostages for the good behaviour of their kinsmen.

In July 1402 it was decreed that no one could purchase, or convey out of Chester, bread or ale without a licence. Obviously because of the war, farming activities had been suspended and the people were hungry. In 1402 at Pilleth, Glyndŵr destroyed an English army sent against him and captured, not only Lord Grey, but also Edmund Mortimer, a claimant to the English throne. Glyndŵr received ambassadors from both the King of France and the Pope and established itinerant parliaments at Harlech, Machynlleth and Dolgellau. He and his followers undertook guerrilla warfare, which the English found difficult to control and during 1402 he endeavoured to draw the Irish and Scots into the conflict.

Henry IV, in order to quell this rebellion, reacted quickly and harshly. Parliament was called in January 1402 and passed a series of anti-Welsh laws, amongst which were:

No Welshman was permitted to purchase any land in England. He was not allowed to hold any corporate office, or bear arms within any city, borough or market town.

No Welshman could hold important public office in Wales.

All castles and walled towns were to be garrisoned only by Englishmen.

An Englishmen who married a Welsh woman would lose his right to hold any public office in Wales or the Marches.

No Welsh child is to be brought up as a scholar, nor permitted to be apprenticed to any trade in any town in the Kingdom.

By January 1403 Glyndŵr was posing a more serious threat and infiltrated Flintshire, urging people to openly revolt. The rebels launched raids in the deep winter, deliberately targeting north-east Wales which had, up to now, seen very little trouble. Adopting a scorched earth policy, he burnt the town of Hope on 22 February, the flames being visible as far away as Chester which, at this time, was the centre of English military power. During the next three years, Glyndŵr was at the height of his power and had little to fear as he moved about Wales.

Even so Welshmen were ordered by the Council of the Prince of Wales to set eight day and night watches for Glyndŵr and his followers, one of which was at Trimley Hall above Ffrith and other areas around Hope. It is believed that these Welshmen were more likely to have been looking after their own property.

The Welsh who had sought shelter inside the city of Chester were expelled. If any Welsh person came into the city to trade he had to leave his weapon at the gate. They could not assemble in groups of more than three and the inns were out of bounds. The vicar of Hope, John de Trafford, was granted a licence to buy twelve loaves and two casks of ale each week in Chester for himself and his household. A similar concession made in May suggests defection among the Welsh. The vicar and three Welshmen were to have four loaves of bread and ale — one loaf each — on condition that each submitted a statement every week of what he needed and declared that the provisions were to be only for themselves and their families, 'certain of our faithful lieges with whom they might wish to share, and for no others.' Many of the English burgesses, however, were departing or had gone. Four were allowed to drive their cattle (178 head) out of the lordship of Hope to be sold in England, '... they had been plundered by the rebels and dared not remain there.' Attempts to prevent trade between the earldom of Chester and the rebel forces was in vain. Men from Cheshire and Flintshire were buying large numbers of cattle and horses from the rebels for large sums of money; Welsh forces were buying grain from the Wirral, crossing the Dee fords both by day and night. These were desperate times and risks had to be taken to save themselves from starvation or worse.

Glyndŵr continued to flourish, extending his conquests into south Wales. By 1405, however, support for his cause began to decline, particularly on the north Wales borders. John Talbot, the new Justice for Chester, was fully prepared to offer pardons to rebels and by 1407 about 1,000 rebels had appeared before him to make their peace. The communities of Englefield and Hopedale were fined 1,000 marks as part of their punishment and some rebels lost their lands.

By 1408 the tide had turned in England's favour and Glyndŵr was defeated in open battle and was compelled to return to guerilla warfare. The eventual collapse of the Glyndŵr rebellion did not, however, mean a return to normality. The destruction of the borough of Hope, and the flight of English burgesses to a safer area, meant that it was not until the mid nineteenth century that there was a sizeable community once more on the Caergwrle site. The whole area was depressed, lands forfeited by rebels not occupied and most of Hope deserted. The Flintshire Welsh had submitted to the king by 1410 and were heavily fined for their part in the rebellion.

Very slowly conditions improved and it is apparent from various documents that the Welsh and English were back in business together. When Henry V became king in 1413, he twice offered Glyndŵr a pardon, but there was no response from the Welsh leader who, like all good legendary figures, simply disappeared. Was he dead or in hiding? What happened to him remains a mystery.

In 1418, Henry V gave the lordship of Hope to the eldest son of the former owner, the Duke of Exeter and Earl of Huntingdon.

Large areas of woodland were cleared for pasture in the Kinnerton township, the wood probably being given as fuel to the people of Chester. As both Englishmen and Welshmen had lived off the land, ransacking farms and towns, the effects of this rebellion were devastating. The English parliament imposed a harsh penal system of laws, which remained in force until 1664. Many pardons were granted, but others were heavily fined, bringing about their financial ruin. For the rest of the fifteenth century the country was in economic crisis, made worse by the endemic Black Death and heavy taxation to pay for continuing wars in France. This was a period of dynastic struggle in England between the houses of York and Lancaster, the so-called 'Wars of the Roses'.

War of the Roses, 1455–85

From 1283, the earl of Chester's estates had been held by the royal family or their representatives. In 1484 the manor and lordship of Hope was given to Lord Thomas Stanley by Richard III for 'Singular and faithful service which they have hitherto done us … not only in favouring our right and title but also repressing the treason and malice of our traitors and rebels who have stirred up perfidious commotions.' The Stanleys were a powerful family and the gift of the manor of Hope, Hopedale, castle and several estates, was used to buy their loyalty. Not only did they command considerable forces in Cheshire, but Stanley had also married Margaret Beaufort, the mother of Henry Tudor, Earl of Richmond, chief claimant to the throne of the house of Lancaster, who was waiting in Brittany for a favourable opportunity to make his bid for the Crown.

Both the houses of York and Lancaster were branches of the Plantagenet royal house, tracing their descent from King Edward III. The Battle of Bosworth was fought on 22 August 1485 when Richard III of England, the last of the Plantagenet dynasty, fought a pitched battle with the Lancastrian contender for his crown, Henry Tudor. Henry had landed in Pembrokeshire, the county of his birth, on 7 August, with a small force consisting mainly of French mercenaries, in an attempt to claim the throne of England. He marched north through Wales, drawing support wherever he went. He crossed into England and moved east, through Shrewsbury, to Leicestershire where, at Bosworth Field he faced the army of King Richard III. It was here that the Stanleys betrayed their king. It is said that Lord Stanley and his men waited near the battlefield until the last moment, watching to see who would win, and came in on the side of Henry Tudor. Thomas Stanley is said to have retrieved Richard's lost crown and placed it on the head of his stepson. In gratitude he was created the Earl of Derby.

During a lengthy period of three centuries from 1484 and 1790 the inhabitants of Hope appeared to have achieved a social cohesion which went beyond what could be expected. Welshmen and Englishmen, farmers and tradesmen formed part of a single community, cemented by inter-marriage. Social leadership came from a number of wealthy landowners:

the Lloyds, the Yonges, the Trevors and the Eytons. As these landowners eventually moved away, becoming absentee landlords, the challenges of enclosure and industrialisation were met by the ordinary men, who would find these changes hard to deal with in the next century.

Acts of Union

In 1536 Henry VIII's government enacted a measure that made important changes in the government of Wales. Whereas the Statute of Wales 1284 had *annexed* Wales to the Crown of England, the Acts of Union declared the King's wish to *incorporate* Wales within his realm, becoming part of the English political system. One of the main effects was to secure 'the shiring of the Marches' bringing the numerous marcher lordships within a comprehensive system of counties. Every shire and county town was to send two elected MPs to Parliament. Administration was dependent upon Justices of the Peace who were drawn from the local gentry who were loyal to the Crown. English was to be the language of administration. As a result of these changes, the Act of 1542 assembled Hope, Mold, Maelor Saesneg and the Manor of Marford and Hoseley within the County of Flint, incidentally this was mostly the property of Edward, the third earl of Derby.

It appears that this was a more peaceful time and Flintshire became more stable. Demand grew for corn and timber, and as the local gentry became better educated, they turned their attention to their estates. Conditions in agriculture improved, land was cleared to make way for pasture for sheep and cattle and for growing a variety of crops. As firewood became scarce, there was an increase in the demand for coal, which was abundant in the area. The countryside slowly recuperated.

3. The Civil War

The relationship between Parliament and the King had started to decline in the reign of James I, and continued to deteriorate during the reign of his son, Charles I.

Charles was arrogant, believing in the Divine Right of Kings he preferred to rule alone. He considered Parliament always to be in the wrong, and argued with them over most issues. In 1629 he refused to let Parliament meet and they were locked out for eleven years. He clashed with the Scots by insisting they use a new Prayer book and this, and the introduction of a new tax, led to the complete breakdown of relations between him and Parliament, especially when he decide to arrest five of his biggest critics.

In August 1642 Charles raised his standard at Nottingham and plunged his realm into Civil War.

The majority of Welsh gentry and landowners rallied loyally to the Crown, and paid 'ship money', a tax levied to build up the King's navy. Both Ireland and north Wales were important to the Royalist cause, as they were the most promising recruiting areas. The King hoped to recruit thousands of troops from Ireland and Wales, and we know that there were miners from Flintshire, recruited by Roger Mostyn, amongst the troops from Lancashire and Cheshire.

James, the 7th Earl of Derby, had managed his estates in north Wales personally for some years and spending time in Chester he was acquainted with leading landowners in this area. He was therefore able to rouse a regiment of Foot from the gentry of Flintshire and Denbighshire, whilst others were recruited by the Commissioners of Array*.

Charles I decided to keep a firm hold on Chester, the royalist stronghold, and the Dee estuary and Welsh marches which would provide a safe corridor for the movement of his troops. On 23 September 1642 the King accompanied by the Prince of Wales visited Chester returning on the 24th to Wrexham, where he was greeted enthusiastically by the local inhabitants of the Lordships, who must have been in awe at the sight of their King. He

---

*Commissioners of Array were an obsolete method of raising troops revived by King Charles. From June 1642, commissions were sent by the King to named gentry in every country, empowering them to summon all men aged from 15–60 from whom fit candidates would be chosen for military training in the service of the King. Those appointed as Commissioners of Array formed the nucleus of Royalist county administrators and military organisers.

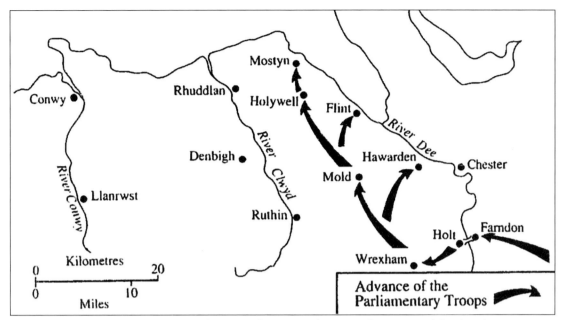

The Parliamentary campaign in north-east Wales, November 1643. [CADW: Welsh Historic Monuments. Crown copyright]

returned to Wrexham again on 7 October for further consultation with those who flocked to his colours.

The first major battle of the Civil War was fought at Edgehill on 23 October 1642. Soldiers wore coloured belts, known as sashes, around their waists to show who they were fighting for. During the battle some Parliamentarians decided to support the King and so changed their sashes. There were few weapons and about 400 of the King's men used wooden sticks or clubs. It is said that the poorly trained Welsh troops were defeated and chased off the battlefield by mounted Parliamentary troops. The outcome of the battle was, however, indecisive and both sides withdrew to consider their future action.

The Parliamentarian Commander-in-Chief Cheshire, Shropshire, Lancashire and Staffordshire, was Sir William Brereton, who regarded Wales as 'the magazine where all his majesty's provisions of victualls and men doe proceed.'

In 1643, Parliamentary forces crossed the River Dee after successfully taking Holt bridge. Led by Brereton they marched to Wrexham where they stayed the night.

Sir William Brereton. [FHS Volume VI]

The following day he led part of his force to Hawarden where the castle was surrendered to them by the Royalist occupants. Within two weeks Parliamentary forces had taken Royalist strongholds in Flintshire including Flint, Mold and Holywell. On 18 November, however, around 2,500 Irish and English Royalist troops landed at Mostyn causing the Parliamentarians to withdraw into Cheshire.

In 1644 Royalists were desperate not to lose ground in north Wales. There was an increase in taxation and a large recruitment drive, which was not very successful. Brereton was desperate to capture Chester but there were constant Royalist challenges.

Although north Wales as a whole was regarded as Royalist territory, there were Parliamentarians in the area, most notably Sir John Trevor (1596–1673) of Plas Teg who had been asked to provide £1,000 to the King's war chest. His negative response to this request resulted in his being stripped of his position as Surveyor of the Navy. Surprisingly, Plas Teg was plundered by a troop of Parliamentarians, possibly the Yorkshire Horse, commanded by Colonel Michael Jones, in April 1645. It is obvious that Jones was ignorant of Sir John's loyalties and the latter submitted a list of the articles taken. Amongst them were '1 faire Bible, 1 crossbow, 1 fowling gun … three pounds in money, 1 great iron rack, divers brass and irons and candlesticks, a cabinet, provisions and sheets.' Some of these items were eventually returned.

The Civil War continued in this area for four years during which small cottages, farms and wooded areas were plundered and stripped bare in order to provide for the armies. Soldiers from both sides stole what they could: money, clothes, food, household goods, cattle, sheep and horses. Doddleston had a small Parliamentarian garrison and was a feeding station where stolen cattle and sheep were kept. The borderlands, within a ten-mile radius of Chester, were denuded of food, men travelling as far as the Berwyn Mountains in order to collect sheep and cattle. Women and children were forced to hide in the countryside and the men were made to enlist. In addition, many soldiers were billeted in farms and cottages, putting an extra strain on the families to eke out their already meagre resources. Churches were ransacked, in Wrexham it is said that the lead organ pipes were made into bullets.

In January 1645, Parliamentarian forces again crossed the Dee, marched to Hawarden and seized Holt, looting and pillaging as they advanced. Once again, Chester began to look vulnerable.

In June the Battle of Naseby was fought and King Charles was beaten. On 3 February 1646, Chester, which was desperately short of food, was surrendered by Lord Byron, allowing Cromwell's forces to freely move into north Wales. Welsh officers and soldiers of the Royalist army were granted safe conduct to go to their own homes, their protection guaranteed for five days. The officers were allowed to take money, clothes and their womenfolk. Amongst the Bodrhydden papers there is a pass dated 9 February 1646 permitting Richard Yonge of Bryn Iorcyn, to travel to his home in Caergurley [sic], issued at Conwy by Lord Byron.

Between 1646 and 1648 the country remained in turmoil and there was much unrest. To make things worse for the people there was a poor harvest in 1647. The Royalists, however, regrouped and they mounted a new offensive in both England and Wales 1648. The effects of this Second Civil War on Flintshire were:

Roads and bridges were neglected

Disruption to local administration

Churches were desecrated

Taxes were imposed on food

The countryside was exhausted by the constant search for food, free quarters, fuel and horses

Ready cash was in short supply in rural areas

A series of poor harvests forced food prices to rise

It is not surprising, therefore, that Parliament was displeased with the activities of staunch Royalist, James, 7th Earl of Derby. He was deprived of his official positions and proclaimed a traitor. Derby was convicted of treason by a Parliamentary court-martial and beheaded at Bolton. His estates being forfeited, Mold and Hope were bought by Captain Andrew Ellis (acting for Sir John Trevor, Colonel Twistleton and himself). Later, Sir John Trevor obtained the manor of Hope. Richard Yonge was one of the witnesses who signed the agreement on 29 June 1657 to the partition of Mold and Hope lands.

The *Calendar of the proceedings of the Committee for Compounding 1645–1660*, edited by M. A. E. Green, summarises the events which followed:

By the recommendation of Lord President Bradshaw and Sir John Trevor, Roger

James, 7th earl of Derby, with his wife, Charlotte, and daughter, Katherine.
[FRO PR/C/201]

Hamner was appointed 23 June 1648 as Steward of the manors of Maylor, Hawarden, Mold and Hope, sequestered from the Earl of Derby.

On 10 June 1651 Andrew Ellis of Althrey was appointed the steward of the Earl of Derby's estates in the county of Flint.

Fortunately the scars of war were quickly healed in a pastoral society. The cattle trade was put on its feet again by the restoration of the English markets and a grant of £3,000 by way of compensation to the drovers by the good office of Sir John Glynne of Hawarden on behalf of Parliament.

4. Religion

The role of the early Church

During the Dark Ages the Christian church took refuge in the mountains of north Wales. This Celtic church, later to be known as the Welsh church, built monasteries which became centres of teaching and learning, with the monks going out to preach. These early Celtic Christian sites dated back to the sixth century. One of the tenets of this early Church was a moral obligation to care for the poor.

Small churches were built of mud and wattle and these humble buildings were the forerunners of the parish churches of today. St Cynfarch's church in Hope is thought to have been founded in the early medieval period and would have been of timber construction. It is thought to be one of the earliest Christian sites in north Wales.

When the Domesday Book was compiled in 1086 there was no reference to a church in Hope. Perhaps the population was too small, or may have been destroyed. The four dioceses of Bangor, St David's, Llandaff and St Asaph were created and a parochial organization was gradually established. The church structure as we know it today was a creation of the Normans, and the bishops who were appointed to Welsh sees owed a professional obedience to

An artist's impression of what the early church may have looked like. [George Scattergood]

Canterbury, although some felt that Wales should have its own archbishop. The first Norman bishop of St Asaph was Gilbert, appointed in 1143. During the twelfth century most of the bishops were French, which caused problems with the Welsh population.

Hope Parish Church is set in a raised circular enclosure, very much in the centre of the village, with streets radiating from it. It is recorded as 'Ecc'a de Estun' in the Norwich Taxation of 1254 at a value of 13s. 4d., and in Pope Nicholas's Taxation of 1291 its value is recorded as £14. The church was damaged during the war between Edward I and Prince Llywelyn, and only a small amount of compensation was paid. Sometime after 1281, it was replaced by a larger stone structure to which, throughout the centuries, there have been many alterations and renovations. The north nave was built *circa* 1500, with the tower being

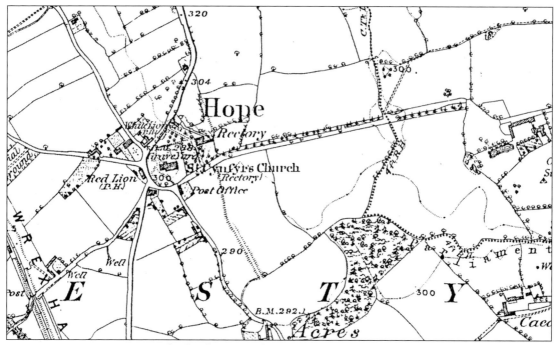

The development of Hope around the Parish Church. Above, OS map, 1871.
Below, photograph [Clwyd Powys Archaeological Trust]

A typical early development of a 'llan' site (George Scattergood) can still be seen in the shape of the present-day church grounds. [Clwyd Powys Archaeological Trust]

added some years later. Even more extensive restoration took place in 1859, and again in 1885.

Hope church became an integral part of everyday life, vital to the community's pastoral care. The work of the Church was seen as the key to improving people's lives, without which many would have starved to death and poverty would have been unbearable. Life was extremely hard in medieval times, and many were only relieved by the work of the Church.

After 1282, Edward I granted to the hospital of St John without [outside] Northgate, Chester, which was for 'poor and sillie persons', not only the rectorial of Hope but also 150 acres of land east of Shordley Green. The value of the to the hospital in 1311 was ten marks and this, along with rents and contributions, totalled £27 4s. 10d., which was used to 'maintain three chaplains, one lamp lit during mass and thirteen beds maintained for thirteen poor and feeble of the City of Chester.' These paupers received daily one loaf of good bread, one large dish full of good vegetables, one 1/2 flask of beer and a pittance of meat or fish as the day and season dictated. By 1347 the hospital had fallen on hard times and Edward III transferred supervision from the Prior of Birkenhead to the Justice of Chester. The building was eventually demolished and in 1660 the site, along with the land, was granted to Colonel Roger Whitely for life.

During the late Middle Ages, a great deal of church rebuilding occurred. Edward I gave £350 (equivalent to £20,000 today) to repair church property which had been damaged during the wars against Llewelyn. St Asaph and Basingwerk Abbey received about £100 each and the remainder was divided between all the parishes including Hope. Not all churches had been damaged, but rectors were paid for loss of due to the destruction of crops and animals during the war. The parish churches in Flintshire were not imposing structures and none have survived their original form. Important people from the parish were allowed to be buried in the walls or under the floor of the church and stained glass windows would

Hope Parish Church, painting by Moses Griffith, late eighteenth century.

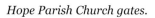

Hope Parish Church gates.

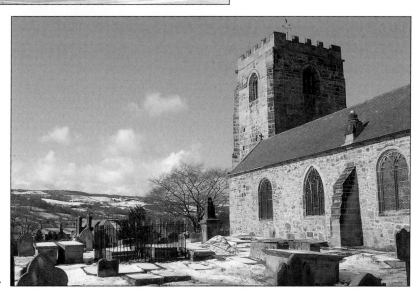

Hope Church.

show knights and their ladies. Not many of these have survived but Hope does have some fragments of these windows.

The parish priest was a rector, a vicar or a chaplain. Little is known about the priests who served in Hope before the Reformation. John de Trafford was vicar in 1440; Thomas Crue in 1503; and Richard Whitford in 1522. The rectors were absentees who took the income while leaving a curate in charge of the parish. To maintain the priest and provide for the work of the Church, money was obtained from various sources, mostly (one tenth of the income of each parishoner, payable in cash or kind). Payments in kind (which could include live animals) were often sold and the money went to the church. Fees were charged for burials, marriages and baptisms and four times a year there were special collections.

Hope Church, drawing by John Witt.

At the end of the sixteenth century, the 'Rectory' stood on the site of the present-day White Lion Inn, which was glebe land. As many as eight services were held in the church every day beginning soon after midnight when the priest celebrated matins, lauds and prime, which were completed by 6am. Mass was usually sung at 9am, followed during the day by tierce, sext, nones and vespers (or evensong), the last service at sunset. People were expected, after careful preparation, to take Holy Communion three times a year, and to attend evensong every Saturday and all the services on Sunday. The services were conducted in Latin except the sermon, the priests wearing cassocks with a hood. They could grow a moustache or beard but heads were shaved into form of tonsure. They were expected to remain unmarried. Not all priests conformed however, for some dressed colourfully, drank and had several wives! The priests were expected to encourage the Welsh and English to live together peacefully, unfortunately the Welsh were usually blamed for any disorder. There was a 'chapel of ease' at Plas y Bwl which was probably the chapel for the Bold family who had built the hall in the sixteenth century. This chapel would have enabled them to avoid the journey to the parish church across the valley, when roads were flooded and dangerous.

Pilgrimages to the Holy Land or Rome were for the rich, whilst the ordinary people of Flintshire visited the local shrines of St Winifred in Holywell, St Asaph and the Holy Rood, Rhuddlan. There were also two places in Chester — the Holy Rood in the Hospital of St John and relics of St Werburgh in the Abbey.

Hope had no manorial hall or castle capable of housing a lord or any important tenants.

Many things remained unchanged after the Stanley family was given the lordship in 1484. Rents were collected and taxes had to be paid, and the Church levied its tithes. Margaret Beaufort, wife of the 1st Earl of Derby, and mother of Henry VII, was famous for her generosity to ecclesiastical and educational institutions. Several churches in north-east Wales benefitted from her many gifts.

Great changes took place with the Reformation of 1517, but the consequent conflict was not resolved until the 1550s. The separation of the church from Rome meant that English became the language of the church instead of Latin, and there was also the introduction of a new liturgy. There is no evidence that the people of Hope, at this time, did anything other than observe the policies and practices laid down by the Crown and the Archbishop of Canterbury. The appointment of rectors and vicars remained the responsibility of the bishop of St Asaph.

Before the Reformation it had always been considered a Christian duty to carry out instructions laid down by Matthew chapter 25 — that all Christians should:

> Feed the hungry
> Give drink to the thirsty
> Welcome the stranger
> Clothe the naked
> Visit the sick
> Visit the prisoner
> Bury the dead.

After the Reformation however, there were changes which meant the poor were left without help. It was obvious that something had to be done to help those who were in desperate need. In 1552 parish registers of the poor were introduced and in 1563 Justices of the Peace were given the power to raise funds to assist them. Categories were drawn up to identify the different types of 'poor' and the beggars that were found in the streets. The 'deserving poor', were those who wanted to work but were unable to find suitable employment. These people were given help in the form of clothes, food or money, known as Outdoor Relief. Those who were too old or too young or ill to work were looked after in

Views of the interior of Hope Church.
Above: The nave and rood screen.
Below left: The altar in the side chapel and the font.
Below left: The Royal Arms, a reminder of when these had to be displayed in every church.
Below right: The memorial to the Trevor family of Plas Teg.

Below left: The Royal Arms, a reminder of when these had to be displayed in every church.

The pulpit.

almshouses, orphanages, workhouses or hospitals. Orphans and children of the poor were to be given an apprenticeship to a tradesman and this was known as Indoor Relief. The 'undeserving poor' were idle beggars, who did not choose to work. They were to be whipped through the town until they learned their lesson! In 1572 it was compulsory for all to pay a local poor tax, the funds being given to the deserving poor. In 1597 it was made law that every district had an Overseer of the Poor, whose job was to work out how much money would be needed by the poor in his district, and to collect the poor rate from property owners. The Overseer was in charge of a township, and at church vestry meetings he would consider applications for relief. Elizabethan Poor Law Act was passed in 1601 was passed which brought together all the measures into one law.

Relief was only offered to people born in the parish or qualified for residency by apprenticeship. The Settlement Act of 1662 allowed Overseers to remove strangers if he or she did not rent a property worth over £10 per annum or had not been able to find work within forty days. Another Settlement Act in 1697 permitted strangers to live in a new parish as long as they had a certificate from their home parish guaranteeing to take them back if they needed to ask for relief.

It was during the reign of Elizabeth I that the Bible was translated into Welsh.

Evangelical Revival

In the seventeenth century puritans such as Rees Pritchard of Llandovery put their message into rhyme. Here is an example of an evangelical and moral verse:

> Advice to the Drunkard;
> If thou'rt a drunkard, fond of ale and wine,
> And smokest vile mundungus without end
> Cry out with speed, to th' pow'r divine,
> To give thee grace, to conquer the foul fiend.

The seventeenth century was a time of many changes and new laws. After the Civil War things were ecclesiastically grim, with many clerics being removed by Parliament, and others, like the vicar of Mold, going into hiding. At the time of the outbreak of war the vicar of Hope was the Rev. John Ellis. In a letter dated 1651 he wrote:

... in Hope and other churches there is no sermon or prayers some times for five, six or seven weeks together ... so that the parishioners when they come to church and finding no minister there fall into the alehouse so that instead of serving God they serve the d[evil].

By the end of the 1650s, following the death of Oliver Cromwell, Charles was called to take his place and, as king, became the head of the Church of England. In 1660 all clergymen who had been ejected by the Act of Propagation in 1652, were restored, the Rev.Henry Jones being one of them. He then began to again record all baptisms, burials and marriages in the parish of Hope.

The Act of Uniformity of 1660 meant that all vicars had to use the Book of Common Prayer and all who preached, which included schoolmasters, had to be licensed by a bishop. Failure to observe the code was punishable by three months in prison for the first offence while the second offence entailed a further three months as well as a £5 fine.

Even though there appeared to be an element of liberty, dissent was still frowned upon. The Baptists, Independents and Quakers continued to meet privately in houses or barns, which was very risky. The 1664 Act of Conventicle, was passed which forbade such meetings and, if five or more people attended a meeting, stiff penalties of imprisonment and fines were imposed. A third offence brought even more severe punishment — seizure of property and seven years transportation. This Act lasted for three years but in 1670 imprisonment was replaced with fines. In Hope in the 1670s, one such group came to light on the Plas Teg estate, possibly at Pant Farm. It is said James Owen, a dissenting minister, was discovered with the tenant of the property, Thomas Fennah, and a small congregation. He was found guilty of allowing a meeting and both Owen and Fennah were imprisoned for three months in Caerwys gaol. Three weeks later, however, both men were released.

Excommunication from the church happened for a variety of reasons. An episode in the church register for 1682 shows that thirteen parishioners were excommunicated, one of whom was Nehemiah Ogden, a Quaker, who had been before the courts in 1672 and 1673.

Flintshire Notitiae
The names of ye excommunicate in ye parish of Estyn in Queen Hope 1681
Nehemiah Ogden of Shordley
The names of them who Baptise not their children after ye form in ye Church of England 1681
Rice of Uwchymynydd Uchaf
Edward Jones of Uwchymynydd Isaf

1682 excommunicates:
Julienus Kendrick de Hope Owen
Johanes Kendrick de Hope Owen
Nehemia Ogden de Shordley, plus 10 others who had died.

The church collected tithes which were one tenth of goods for instance; 1/10 sheaves of corn,

1/10 cocks of hay, a pig from every litter, a goose from every flock, a cock or hen from every flock of poultry, 4*d*. levied on every mare or colt, one in every ten of cattle or sheep. The tithebarns, where the products were collected, were in Sarn Lane Hope, and possibly Castle Street, Caergwrle.The church also owned glebe land which was often farmed by a tenant, such as the White Lion Inn, whose innkeeper was also a farmer.

A small number of parish charities became the responsibility of the vicar and churchwardens. Usually, any bequest of money was invested in land. However some stated how their bequest was to be spent:

1638: John Thomas of Caergwrle gave £10 for the poor of parish with 4*s*. towards the repair of the church.

1642: Richard Lloyd, Fferm who died in 1642, willed £10 to be devoted to purchase of a 'great bell' for Hope Church.

1719: Robert Wynne Rector of the Parish of Estyn bequeathed £120, half of which was to be devoted to teaching twelve poor children as well as the purchase of books for them, the other half was for bread for the poor. He also left a silver flagon and salver for use in the Church valued at £30.

1723: John Price citizen and weaver of London left a piece of land at Colomendy, the rent of which was to provide the poor with white bread, which was a luxury compared to brown and rye varieties, on Sundays, with a yearly sum of 17*s*. 4*d*.

Mrs Elizabeth Sherlock of Ruthin left to the poor a sum of £5.

Mrs Lloyd of Brynyorkin £10.

Mr Ellis Yonge of Brynyorkin £20.

Miss Barbara Yonge £2 12*s*. yearly from 1773

In 1723 it was decided to record benefactors of the poor by erecting a board bearing their names and respective sums donated and placing it within walls of the church where it is still to be found.

There were problems in attracting a 'first class' vicar to Hope for the tithes and glebe land when

The Tithe Barn in Sarn Lane, Hope. Now demolished.

added together were regarded as insufficient. Therefore, in 1732, it was decided to apply to the Queen Anne's Bounty, a fund designed to increase the emoluments (salaries) of the clergy. The fund contributed £100 which equalled the sum raised by the parish. A number of the vicars during the eighteenth century were Oxford graduates and all from the Welsh side of the border. Many were often absentees which provided an opportunity for men such as John Wesley and George Whitfield in England and Howel Harris in Wales, who became itinerant preachers, preaching to crowds outside the church itself. Hope Parish however, did not attract circulating schools, and when evangelical preachers ventured forth they were usually treated with hostility.

It was during this period that influential families and landowners became more involved in the Church and the parish.These included the Yonges, the Glynnes of Hawarden and George Hope, who built a new residence called Hope Hall. The presence of these influential men led to improvements in the church's amenities. In 1762 a new vicarage was built with shippons to house cows attached.

List of the benefactors of the poor, 1723. Hope Church.

At the end of the eighteenth century many social changes were taking place due to industrial development in the area and the 1791 Enclosure Act. This Act changed forever the pattern of land holding which had long been the very fabric of the community.

At this time various sums of money were given outright to people for their services or to help them.

> 1783 Thatching a house 1s. 6d.
> 1784 Paid to Peter Williams for ' crying' a sale 4d.
> 1785 Ringing bell at the quarter 3s.
>   Ale for the sexton when he dug grave 3s.
> 1788 Widow Price to have bed gown and shift

The account books for the Hope Overseers of the Poor during the period 1781–1804, provide a snapshot of how the poorer people of the parish lived during the period, depending on charity for their very basic needs.

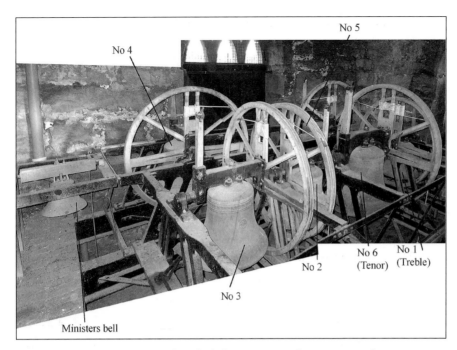

No 5

No 4

No 6
(Tenor)

No 1
(Treble)

No 2

No 3

Ministers bell

The peel of bells at Hope Church.

In 1789 the Overseers decided that a sum of £100 6s. 9d. was necessary for the relief of the poor and to pay the vestry clerk's salary for the next quarter. After the enclosure, July 1800, it was necessary to reassess the rateable value of each property. The church wardens, therefore, decided that 'an application should be made to the Commissioners of the Hope Enclosure for a copy of their book of valuations of the lands within the parish and rates should be made according to the valuations'

The payment of the Poor Rate was very hard on poorer farmers and labourers, who already had to pay rent to a landlord and levies to the church. Some were not able to pay, and for instance in 1791, Timothy Green was summoned to the Quarter Sessions to explain his non-payment.

The basic necessities of daily living for many people were sometimes impossible to obtain without help. There were many genuine reasons why men and women were not able to support themselves and needed assistance from the parish, particularly the elderly, the disabled and widows. Many families were living just above subsistence level which meant that another baby, a death, an accident, a bad harvest or a reduction in working hours could drastically alter the domestic finances for the worse. Some families were given aid intermittently to help them over a difficult period. In 1793 'hard weather' payments were made. If there was a national economic downturn, large numbers had to apply for relief to avoid starvation.

Payments were made to cover rent and a small living allowance, and in addition coal was often delivered in the winter months. In 1795 it is recorded that Widow Maddocks' relief for a year was £2 11s. In rare cases, beds, blankets, stools and other household goods were provided.

The poor had to be clothed and the Overseers paid the weaver for cloth and flannel, and bought cloth, buttons and thread for a tailor. In 1786, the Rev. Warrington, vicar of Hope, ordered the Overseers to pay 'for cloth for shirts, waistcoats and breeches and making them for Harry Tydor 12s. 7d.' They also purchased leather from Chester to be used by John Jones, shoemaker, his charges were — mending shoes 1s. 8d., making a pair of shoes 3s. 6d.

The Overseers were also responsible for the distribution of food, such as butter, potatoes, measures of corn, barley and even herrings in 1801. In 1800 farmers and local landowners, who were subscribers to the relief of the poor, agreed 'to sell our different sorts of grain to the different committees of the parishes of Mold and Hope appointed to purchase the same for the use of the honest labourer at 2s. per bushel under the market price for the time being'

Finding and funding apprenticeships for poor children to give them a good start in life was another task for the Overseers. On 11 February 1801, at the vestry meeting, it was agreed 'that Edward Jones's two boys should be put out as apprentices and to be bound by indenture and to be clothed and the Master to receive £5 for every boy and be bound for five years'. Girls were sent out to service and had clothing bought for them to leave home.

Illegitimacy was a problem within the parish and there was a need to enforce the responsibilities of fathers to make a proper financial provision for the child. A single pregnant woman had to go before a magistrate to be questioned about the paternity of the child. In 1788 'Bolas's maid' was taken to Hartsheath to swear her child, and a warrant was issued to apprehend the father. In 1791, this went a stage further when the father of an illegitimate child was arrested, kept all night at Hope and then 'marriage fees were paid'!

When poor women gave birth their needs were great and so the Overseers gave relief for the 'lying in' period, and for midwifery assistance. Anne Griffiths was paid 7s. 6d. for delivering two babies. If the mother was unable to feed the baby a wet nurse was employed. Some of the absent fathers contributed towards childbirth costs, as in 1793 when Richard Rees gave the parish £1 5s. for Anne Price's confinement.

When men, women and children became in need of relief but were not of Hope parish, they were required to return to their own parish. Removal orders were obtained from the local magistrates and bitter arguments between the expelling parishes and receiving parishes are recorded in the Quarter Sessions records. In 1791 the 'examination of Anne Ellis, removal order, horse hire, meat and drink and removing her to Llanverras' [Llanferres] at a cost of 14s. 6d. People were sometimes removed long distances, as far as Montgomeryshire and Anglesey. It appears from the Hope Overseers' Accounts that Hope parish did pay other parishes to support former Hope residents.

Hope Parish also subscribed £2 2s. annually to Chester Infirmary, which opened in 1755.

Removal order, 1795. [FRO A/30/1/229]

This allowed the Overseers to send sick people there. They were transported by horse (1s.) or horse and cart (8s.). Women were paid to nurse people in their homes and also to help the aged and infirm with household chores. Local healers, doctors and surgeons were consulted, and they all charged for their services. In 1795, £100 was borrowed by the churchwardens, part of which was to pay the doctors' bills. In 1793 the Overseers only agreed to pay 10s. 6d. for a cure for Thomas Pugh 'provided he shall have a cure'. Journeys were made to Wrexham to get medicines and ' Dr Zachary was given 5s. for a receipt [prescription] to cure John Chandler's head'.

Everybody dreaded dying in poverty. But it appears that the Overseers ensured that all had a decent and dignified funeral by paying for shrouds, coffins, crape and even ale! A funeral was arranged for 'a strange pauper who dyed in Caergwrley [sic] and cost 9s.'

In 1795 at the time of the Napoleonic Wars, the vestry agreed a sum of £99 14s. 9d. extra to the poor rate to be used to raise men for His Majesty's Navy and 'to use the utmost of their endeavour to procure and hire such men as speedily as possible'. Edward Jones, a gamekeeper, was paid 14s. 6d. for six days recruiting. Later, the £100 that had been borrowed to pay medical fees, was also used to cover part of the expenses incurred in getting men for the navy. A year later men were recruited for the army.

Sometimes the very infirm, the mentally ill and very destitute families could not be looked after in the parish so they were sent to the workhouse at Wrexham, which was set up in 1737. In 1795 the master of the workhouse charged the parish 2*s.* a week to feed each inmate.

In 1871, Hope Parish joined the Hawarden Union and from then on Hope residents were sent to the workhouse in Broughton. It is said that workhouses were deliberately unpleasant places so as to discourage people applying for assistance. Certainly the thought of being sent to the workhouse filled everyone with fear and dread.

The Overseers of the poor of the Parish in 1864 were:

Thomas Peters, Bryn Yorkin for Cymmau

Watkin Williams, Shordley Green for Shordley

Edward Jones, Cold Chimneys for Hope Owen

John Hughes, Cae Rynallt for Uchmynydd Ucha

Hope parish church was restored in the mid nineteenth century, and here we find a record of the money spent celebrating this event:

A 'do' for opening,

8 policemen, 5*s.* per man

Cleaning church for opening service £2 14*s.*

1st Flintshire (Hope) Engineer Volunteer band 1 day £3

Lassell / Caergwrle brewery for beer £3

Beer for band £1 13*s.*

In 1861 all charities came into hands of vicar. These were not only local charities as we can see by these notes of 1862. A meeting was held to discuss how to raise money for the distressed in Lancashire. This problem had arisen because of a diplomatic incident between Britain and the United States of America. The *Alabama*, a British-built Confederate warship, had done considerable damage to the Union fleet trying to break the Union blockade of the Confederate ports. This interruption of the valuable cotton supply to Lancashire caused great distress and the period was known as the 'cotton famine'. Amounts sent to the relief committee in Manchester included, from workmen at Lassell's brewery, £2, also in 1863 from Gwern Alyn Colliery £1 10*s.* — in total £16 3*s.* 8*d.* was sent.

The 1862 accounts show the expenses involved in the upkeep of the church:

Wine for sacrament £2

Washing supplies £1 12*s.*

Cleaning church £2

Insurance for church £2 4s. 9d.

Coal, oil and candles for church £2 10s

Verger 1 year salary £2

Organist 1 year salary £10

Cleaning parish hearse £1

Winding clock £1

Organ blower 10s

Total £22 16s 9d

In 1864 an organ was installed in the church, donated by a member of the Atcherley family of Cymmau Hall (the harmonium was then sold for £4). There is a plaque on the wall of the church relating to this family.

It is not clear when the *Hope Parish Magazine* was first published. The earliest copy the authors found was dated 1878 when the rector of Hope was the Rev. John Rowlands. In his New Year address he expressed great concern about the indifference of the population towards religion.

I cannot conceal my fears about many of you. I am afraid there is much indifference to religion among us, and that people who ' forget God' in the parish are neither few in number nor far between. Therefore, as your minister, I feel bound to sound a note of warning. Believe me, the end of these things is death.

It is interesting to see how church attendance was influenced by the Church's attitude to sin and war. In 1916, during the First World War, there was a National Mission led by archbishops and bishops, known as the National Mission of Repentance and Hope. Their message was that the war was God's way of punishing people for their sins;

We may be sure that this war is a call to us from God to think seriously of these things and repent. People are saying 'Why does God permit this horrible war?' May it not be because only in this way He can drive home the lessons they need to learn.

The organ at Hope Church.

The cost of repairs at Hope Church, 1852.

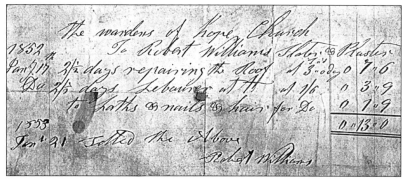

There were many other associations attached to the Church covering most aspects of daily living.

The Temperance Movement was at this time commanding the attention of the whole country. Throughout all the parish magazines there are numerous writings about the evils of drink from every source, police, poets, sailors, employers, church, etc. This very emotive piece appeared in the *Morning Post*:

> Of all the ghastly skeletons that can haunt a house there is none to equal the intemperance of women. Let us guard against it by every reasonable means in our power, as we value the good name and comfort of ourselves, our children and our children's children.

Contributions towards the Church Missionary Society between March 1877 and 1878 amounted to £16 2s. which included donations towards the Society for the Propagation of the Gospel, the British and Foreign Bible Society and the Church Pastoral Aid Society.

Charities aiming to relieve poverty and distress of the community, were many e.g. the Hope Clothing Club, the Hope Parish War Relief Fund, the Girls' Friendly Society (to give moral support to working girls), the Band of Hope (a temperance society), the Mothers' Union, the Blinded Soldiers' Children's Fund, the Church of England Waifs and Strays Society, the Boy Scouts and the Girl Guides.

There was, and still is, an evangelical movement within the Anglican Church namely the Church Army.

The church had endeavoured to become the social conscience of the people. It is interesting, however, to see how the church had changed its views over the previous two centuries.

The poor were just as needy and the tithe

Girls' Friendly Society, 1920s.

payments were still in force, occasionally causing distress and hardship to those who had to pay them. Protests culminated in the so called Tithe War which spread across the Welsh border, and into Flintshire.

There was an excellent account of the villagers reactions, to what could be described as a heavy-handed approach to the problem, in the *Chester Chronicle,* dated 31 March 1888, entitled, 'Caergwrle, Tithe Agitation'.

Caergwrle and neighbourhood has for the last few days been in a state of mild excitement owing to the intelligence that Mr Peterson, of the Peterson and Dodd firm, has been in the district and given five days notice of sale of stock belonging to Mr Swetenham of Stocks Farm (Shordley) valued at £100 and of a cow belonging to Mrs Braithwaite of Caergwrle valued £12 for a tithe of £1 9s. 7d. Mrs Braithwaite offered to pay £1 9s. 7d., this was refused unless costs of 8s was paid. She declined to pay the latter item. She is a widow with eight children one of whom is disabled, and has a good number of sympathisers in the village.

A meeting was held at her home and it was decided to replace her cow with a subscription. On the evening of the sale, an 'indignation' meeting was held at the assembly rooms at the Derby Arms.

Outside her house two effigies have been placed ingeniously constructed representing a parson in full clericals and the auctioneer in attendance upon him with writs in his pocket and specs on his nose. These have caused a great deal of amusement and formed quite an attraction. It is expected there will be a slight demonstration when the auctioneer comes, but nothing more than a little fun is likely to be indulged in.

21 April, 'Tithe War Protest'

One of the most angry districts—for three weeks a feeling of excitement, crowds are reported close to the station to show that they would get a warm reception. Mr Peterson auctioneer travelled from Chester, and was met at Hope by his force of strapping fellows, few under six feet picked from the 2nd Dragoon Guards (Queen's Bays), 2nd Dragoons, the 13th Hussars, 2nd Battalion Scotch [sic] Guards and the 1st Royal Dragoons, under Sgt Major McDougle of 8th Hussars, also a force of police. The whole party was conveyed by wagonette from the Station to the Stocks Farm Hope, Mr Swetenham was not in.

Mr Swetenham on returning home asked if the soldiers were with Mr Peterson and when told this was so said 'I bow to your superior force' The auctioneer Mr Peterson then set out to Caergwrle to see Mrs Braithwaite, however Mr Swetenham got there first and by the time the forces arrived the people of Caergwrle were out in force. They gathered beating tins and blowing horns, in the field nearby was Mrs Braithwaite's black cow.

The crowd assembled, two of them carrying effigies of the vicar and the auctioneer. The one representing the vicar had a placard, which said:

> Dearly beloved brethren —
> it's money I want,
> I must have it now
> If I can't get it
> I'll sell the black cow.

The effigy of Mr Peterson had the words:

Your worship I am authorised by the dearly beloved brethren to sell widows and orphans in order to get my pound of flesh — a Cockney Lawyer.

The hooting and noise in the field was incessant. Mr Peterson and two of the soldiers grabbed the cow's head and led it out of the field. Some shouted 'Lock the gate!' but they were too late. Mrs Braithwaite offered to pay, but not the extra, and this was refused. The crowd tried to stop them and there was lots of laughter and banter — the cow was taken to Rossett market but it could not be arranged to sell it and so it was then taken to Chester market.

This description of Hope parish is taken from *The History of the Diocese of St Asaph*, written by the Ven. D. R. Thomas, 1908.

The parish is divided by the river Alyn into two parts; that above the river called Hope Medachiad, comprises the townships of Uwchmynydd (sub divided into Uwch and Issa), Cymau, Caergwrle and Rhanberfedd; and that below the river those of Hope Owen, Estyn and Shordley. The total area contains 9,171 acres, but a portion was transferred to the daughter parish of Llanfynydd in 1843, leaving to the mother church an area of 5171 acres, with a population of 3,075.

Nonconformity

In the 1851 Religious Census, the vicar of Hope, the Revd. J. V. Lloyd, reported that 'the parish is poor exceedingly. There is only one resident gentleman in the parish. (Col Trevor Roper). Dissent prevails to a great extent.'

Many had abandoned church attendance, while others found it difficult to walk to the church after a hard day's work, along dangerous dark roads. New churches, Methodist, Independent, Welsh Calvinistic, were built and this changed the pattern of worship within the parish. Furthermore, some of the congregations were predominately Welsh speaking,

Dissent had made remarkable headway in the last two decades of the eighteenth century The development of Welsh Christianity was said to have begun in 1735, with the conversion of the zealous Hywel Harris who travelled the country spreading the good news of the gospel. This was the dawn of the Methodist revival, a revival which was to change the shape and feel of Welsh Christianity. It is said that John Wesley visited Chester between 1752 and 1769, visiting Mold three times. It is believed that he stayed at Rackery Farm. His associates and ministers established societies here in 1790. Religious nonconformity continued to progress in the rural areas, not only with the Methodists, but also the Congregationalists and Baptists who were equally impressive in their growth. The main impulse of Nonconformity was evangelicalism, with the emphasis on hearing and preaching the word of God, and laymen becoming more centrally involved.

By the beginning of nineteenth century the Methodist awakening had influenced two other key denominations. The Baptists and the Congregationalists now had their own leaders. As the nineteenth century wore on, Welsh Nonconformist numbers grew and new chapels were built. These often proved to be too small and inconvenient and it became necessary to build larger ones. In the heyday of Nonconformity, if you wished to be sure of a seat, you needed to be in the chapel half an hour early.

The social impact on individuals was tremendous and attitudes changed. Public houses were targeted by holding open-air services in front of them. At the Caergwrle petty sessions in 1888, Amelia Jones who had been drunk was fined 10s. plus costs. If she did not pay she would spend seven days in prison—the judge commented on the evils of drink saying that, 'A man drinking was bad enough, but a woman getting drunk was horrifying'. He also said that Volunteers on drink should not disgrace the Queens uniform. Thousands became teetotal, causing great damage to the beer trade. The crime rate, however, went down and there was more food on the table instead of beer. A Free Church Council was formed in about 1899 and in 1900 the temperance campaign was launched in the district. In 1904 Wales experienced a powerful religious revival that impacted upon both churches and chapels. The result was full chapels, powerful preachers, dramatic conversions and changed lives.

Preaching became the key feature of Welsh worship and hundreds flocked to open air meetings. The preachers were fired with enthusiasm and their personalities attracted people to the churches. One such man was the Rev. John Jones who had been born in Caergwrle — his parents being ordinary, but exceedingly religious people. His early education was in

English but his father taught him to read Welsh. When he grew up he became a weaver for some time. He tells of his early years in Caergwrle, describing it as nearly as 'pagan as India'.

> The district's customs on the Sabbath were, singing and dancing, playing foot and hand ball, pitch and toss, etc., all day. Both old and young, in their hundreds were swearing and fighting with each other; and by night frequenting the taverns until Monday or Tuesday, and often beyond then.

He and his father turned to religion and it seems he was personally 'saved' in the year 1787 when he got married. Soon afterwards he began to preach all over north Wales. For some years he preached on the circuit, travelling a good deal in the six northern counties, sometimes walking and sometimes on horseback. In 1804 he went to Northop and then in 1808 moved to Holywell. Occasionally he travelled as far as Liverpool, Chester, Manchester and south Wales. He was ordained as a full minister in 1820 and is known to have preached at the Presbyterian Chapel in Caergwrle. He died in 1830.

There were nine chapels in Caergwrle, but no record can be found of any in Hope.

The Presbyterian Church (originally Calvinistic Methodist). The first church began around 1770 when Thomas Edwards, who was converted in Coedpoeth, is said to have built a small chapel in Caergwrle on an unknown site. It was here that in 1788 Dorothy Ellis initiated the first Sunday school in the parish. The second chapel was erected in 1809 on the site adjoining Tŷ Cerrig. Originally the services were all in Welsh. As the language declined in the area so did the congregations but when the services were taken in English, attendances steadily grew, and although seating 100 the chapel became too small and a decision was made to build a new bigger one. This third structure, seating 260 people, was built in 1894 of local stone and boasted a Gothic style entrance. Land had been given by two sisters who were members of the chapel. It was built by Mr E. O. Probert from Hope, the original cost being calculated at £1,100, however the final bill was £1,700. The opening ceremony was performed by Colonel MacFie of Hartsheath. Tea was provided in the Drill Hall for 400 and

Presbyterian Church, Caergwrle, 1894.

Wesleyan Methodist Church, High Street, Caergwrle.

the local newspaper reported that 'so large a number of people has not been seen at a religious service in Caergwrle within living memory.' Many gifts and help given to the chapel: Messrs J. P. and H. Griffiths, blacksmiths, gave the iron gates; Mr W. Bowman, Hope Hall, gave the collecting boxes; Mrs Braithwaite helped with the carting. The manse was erected in 1898 and the school room built in 1903. It is recorded that in 1905 there were 220 members. It was a busy church and meetings were held every evening, including singing practices, Bible classes, prayer meetings and the Band of Hope. On Fridays, the United Christian Endeavour Society met there which was for the young people of the church.

The Wesleyan Methodist Church in the High Street, is believed to have been an offshoot of one formed at Rackery Farm, Llay by Richard Williams, who was also the leader at Caergwrle. The origins are obscure but preachers visited Caergwrle well before 1787, meeting in private homes. The first chapel was built in Derby Road in 1823. The attendance in 1851 was recorded as: a.m. 20 plus 10 Sunday School; p.m. 23 school; Evening 50.

As the congregation grew the chapel became inadequate. In 1888 it was decided to build a larger chapel and by 1890, £200 had been raised. The first building to be completed was

Wesleyan Church group, Caergwrle, c.1905.

the schoolroom (in 1899) costing £360 and in the same year the foundation stones were laid for the new church which was opened on 25 May 1900. Mr Probert of Hope built it at a cost of around £1,400.This very fine building of Ruabon brick had a three-panelled window in the chancel as a memorial to George and Sarah Thomas. It was a popular church and in 1905 it is

Wesleyan Sunday School, Caergwrle, c.1903. [FRO PH/12/22]

recorded as having 100 members. There was a Band of Hope which met every Monday. There were many Sunday school outings arranged, in traps and farm wagons to Chester, and by train to New Brighton, Rhyl and Rhydymwyn, followed by a walk to Halkyn for tea. Brakes and covered wagons were used to travel to Llangollen.

The church was closed in 1967 and is now used as a Masonic Hall Lodge.

The Methodist Church in Castle Street was originally a Primitive Methodist church, built in 1859. The original building was replaced in 1914. A bazaar was held to help with fund raising in December 1913 and in April 1914 the ceremony of laying foundation stones (seventeen in all) was held. Mr James Peter, JP, CC, presided over the proceedings and the special opening service took place in December 1914. One of the leading members of the church was John Morris, a local butcher. The 1st Caergwrle Company of the Boys' Brigade used the clubroom for drill, band practice and other activities in the 1940s and also for their meetings. They now attend the service on the third Sunday in the month. During the 1950s and 1960s teas were served to visiting Sunday schools.

Methodist Church, Castle Street, Caergwrle, c.1905.

*Exterior and interior of the methodist Church,
Castle Street, Caergwrle.*

The Bethel Welsh Congregational Church, Mold Road, was first built in 1842 at a cost of £400. There had been earlier meetings which had taken place in private homes. In 1851 the attendance was recorded as: a.m 40; p.m. 41—scholars; Evensong 38.

In 1875 Mr John Morgan Jones, the minister, was paid £22 10s. a month. By 1905 membership had increased to 110, and it was decided the church was too small. A larger church was built in 1908 by Mr Thomas Jones of Wrexham at a cost of over £1,300. There was now room for 350 members with a preaching hall, several classrooms and kitchen, all lit by electricity from the Gwalia Forge owned by Messrs Griffiths who were connected to 'the cause'.

The building debt of £1,050 had to be addressed and so in July 1908 a three-day bazaar was held in Hope School to raise funds with initially £400 to be paid. Buyers were urged to 'purchase largely and your heart will be as light as your purse.'

Competitions were held for the gentlemen — hat trimming and sock darning — and for the ladies — pencil

[DRO DD 6/20/39]

sharpening and a whistling competition. Concerts were held in the evening. Another two-day event was held in 1919 raising a further £300 which apparently paid off the debt.

In the mid twentieth century, as the Welsh speaking congregation became smaller, it became difficult to carry on. It was at this time that they were approached by the Rev. G. Roberts (who had split from the local Presbyterian Church). After some discussion it was agreed that the new Evangelical Church could share the building as they had been meeting in private homes up until then. Following this, the Evangelical Church met at 10.30 a.m. and 6.30p.m. whilst the Welsh congregation met at 2.30 p.m. The first Sunday service was held on 2 April 1972, and in 1974 the church became affiliated with the Evangelical Movement of Wales. In 1980 the ownership of the building was passed to the Evangelical Church.

This church was involved in many ways with the community — Youth Link meetings, Holiday Bible Club for younger children, and monthly ladies meetings. In December 1986 the church produced its first edition of its *Bulletin* which is produced three times a year and distributed to 3,500 homes in the area. In 1990, monthly and bi-monthly services were provided in five residential homes, Bryntirion, Chestnut House, Willowdale, Tŷ Cerrig and also the Glynne. Since November 1997, two members have run a church coffee bar at their homes. Bryn Castell meetings were held on Monday and Friday evenings,

The new Evangelical Church, Mold Road, Caergwrle.

Members of the Caergwrle Evangelical Church, 2005.

United Methodist Free Church, Castle Street.

with as many as sixty to seventy young people attending. In October 2004 due to plans to extend this work this venture became a charity known as 'Rock Salt' which is still supported by the church.

In January 2002 structural problems caused the old church building to be demolished and a new church was constructed on the same site, opening on 1 September 2003.

The United Methodist Free Church in Castle Street had 103 members in 1905. Walter Duke and his son led the chapel and so it was known as Duke's Chapel. It is now the British Legion, but because it was once a chapel, alcohol is not sold on the premises.

Penuel Independent Welsh Chapel, Mold Road, was situated near to Bryntirion Lodge. It was erected in 1828, and had a chapel house for ministers. The average attendance in 1851 was: a.m. 30, plus 60 scholars; p.m. 31, plus 61 scholars; evening 30, plus 50 scholars. The chapel building later became a licensed grocers, but has since been converted into three cottages.

The Congregational Chapel on Station Hill was built in front of the Coronation Terrace. A bungalow now occupies the site.

The Primitive Methodist Chapel on Rhyddyn Hill has now disappeared and a modern house stands on this site. It can be seen on the 1921 OS map.

Capel Horeb y Mynydd/The Horeb Chapel, close to the summit of Hope Mountain.

Open air meetings were held by the Rev. Vavasor Powell who preached here, a little lower down from where the chapel stood. Another excellent preacher,

Members of the Primitive Methodist Chapel, Rhyddyn Hill.

James Owen, also preached here and was arrested, with Thomas Fennah, for holding illegal meetings (see earlier). It is not known when the Calvinistic cause came to Horeb. In 1787 Richard Tibbot of Llanbrynmair converted a young man John Jones of Caergwrle, later to become the Rev. John Jones of Holywell.The chapel was built in 1836 on the spot where he had preached.

Capel Horeb y Mynydd on Hope Mountain.

In 1851 attendance was: a.m 33; p.m.52; evening 40.

Robert Roberts of Tri Thy, Pontblyddyn was an elder. Welsh services were held and it was much later when bi-lingual services were introduced. The chapel land was leased from the Trevor Roper estate, freehold eventually being purchased for £10 in 1972. New coloured glass windows were put in 1981 and a new roof was built in 1983. In 1905 there were 125 members. Unfortunately the chapel was closed at the beginning of the twenty-first century, and is now being converted into a house.

The Plymouth Brethren, twelve in number, met in a room at Bridge End, Caergwrle in 1886. This was a Nonconformist group established in Plymouth in 1830, though with roots in Ireland some years previously. It is difficult to say how they became established in Caergwrle.

The Salvation Army came to Caergwrle in 1882, and held meetings in the Temperance Hall (or Public Hall) until November 1884 when a new Salvation Army Barracks was opened. It has not been possible to find out exactly where this building was located, but it is believed it was on the site of the old Derby Cinema, Castle Street.

In the Salvation Soldier's pocket book of 1884/5, Caergwrle is mentioned, describing a meeting in the Public Hall, which was attended by 150 people. Lieutenant Annie E. Davies noted in the *War Cry*, 8 December 1883,

'Praise God, we are on the move here, and are having the victory. On Sunday we had some good marches in the pouring rain, and we were asking and believing that God would save sinners, and He did not disappoint us. After three-quarters of an hour wrestling with God, three souls came to the feet of Jesus and found mercy, Hallelujah!

The following account of the opening of the new barracks, 26 November 1884, is worth reading as it was written.

The Grand Opening of the New Barracks at Caergwrle

The first Salvation Army Barracks has been erected in Caergwrle, north Wales, and was opened last Saturday night. For two years we have had splendid work going on here, scores of the most depraved characters in and around the neighbourhood, have been brought Low Down by the mighty power of God. Every one was on the tiptoe of expectation; crowds came from miles round, some bringing with them lanterns to help them over the rough roads.

At seven o' clock sharp we found twenty four torches to the front, and the song, 'Jesus, the name high over all', was sung with thrilling determination — and these Welsh Soldiers can sing. After a march, and Several Halts of Testimony.

Round the village, we are back again, and a great ring is formed outside the Barracks, then some prayer and singing. The key was handed to Mrs Wessburg, who spoke of the great honour God had conferred upon her allowing her to be a Soldier in the Salvation Army; and putting the key in the door, she opened it in the name of God and the General of The Salvation Army, for the glory of God, and the salvation of souls, not only in Caergwrle but all Wales.

On the Sunday at the meeting only three souls were saved.

Monday — people flocked from all parts to the opening tea, the Wrexham Brass Band played.

There were many rousing meetings which appear to have been well attended. An appeal was made by the Major for more buildings in north Wales and for donations.

Here is one of the last entries found in the *War Cry*, 4 February 1888:

Three days of bombardment, enthusiastic crowds, truth dealt out with power, waves of blessing rolling over soldiers and sinners; old soldiers and new converts rejoicing together over victories won and devils defeated. All this delighted the blood and fire man. The tea was brewed by the old cook in the Queen's army and everybody enjoyed themselves immensely. The Army is more respected in Caergwrle today than ever before. Go on, comrades, live holy, let your lights shine, be examples of Christ, and victory is yours.'

It is thought that the Army's work may have been misunderstood and viewed with suspicion by the Nonconformists. Their fears were usually allayed when the motives of the organisation were explained. Sadly, however, the Salvation Army appears to have closed in 1892 as no further records of any activity can be found.

Hope Parish Church is still flourishing with the Rev. Martin Snellgrove as the rector. Many charities and associations are connected closely to the church. The chapels in Caergwrle have diminished in number and congregation and there are now only three left: the Presbyterian Church in the High Street; the Methodist Church in Castle Street; and the Evangelical Church on Hawarden Road. These are all active in the community and have good memberships.

Methodist Church Lunch Club, 2006

Presbyterian Church Coffee Morning, 2006

Hope Parish Church 'Pop In' coffee group with the Rev. Martin Snellgrove.

5. Education

Little is known about early education in Hope and Caergwrle for very small snippets of information give only tantalising glimpses of what was available. Over many years the Church played an active role in education and often a small number of boys were taught by the vicar or the curate. When Hope Church was undergoing restoration in 1950, a walled-up entrance to a room above the vestry was discovered which was likely to have been a school room. The Churchwardens' Accounts of 1859 refer to the donation, in 1719, of £60 by the Rev. Robert Wynne, rector of Eastyn the annual interest of which was to be used for teaching and buying books for twelve poor children. In 1789, the parish Overseers paid for Thomas Evans to go to school for one year and in 1790 'schooling a boy out of the Rector's Charity, due ten shillings' was recorded. The following school masters were mentioned in the parish records.

1729	John Reece of Hope village
1780	Edward Jones
1812	Mr Lodge
1800	Revd. R. Smedley, curate of Hope, ran a private boys school

Lewis's *Topographical Dictionary of Wales*, published in 1838, gave information about two day schools:

... one of which contained thirty–five children is partly supported by yearly donations of £3.12.0. from Miss Young (Yonge) and Shipley Conway Esq. And £2 10s. 0d. from the Rector for which seven boys are taught spelling and reading, and partly by payments from the rest of children. The other school appertains to the Methodists and contains fifty pupils paid for by the parents.

A large number of local children were educated in Sunday schools.

During 1846 a number of inspectors travelled around Wales investigating the provision for education.Their findings were published in the *Report of Commissioners of Inquiry into the State of Education in Wales* 1847 (known throughout Wales as 'The Treason of the Blue Books'). One inspector visited two private schools in Hope and in his report noted that Mr

Roberts' school had been established in 1830 in a dwelling house. He had thirty-five children on the books and earned £30 from the school and £8 10s. as a postmaster. He was not trained as a teacher but had been a land surveyor. The building was described as bad and the furniture and apparatus insufficient and in poor repair. The second school was run as a dame school from 1836 in the home of Mrs Barrat, a former publican. There were twelve pupils and she earned £2 12s. from school fees. The building, furniture and apparatus were in poor condition. Both teachers only spoke English.

Hope National School

The National Society for the Education of the Poor in the Principles of the Established Church was formed in 1811, giving grants to set up Church schools. In 1838 the vicar of Hope, the Rev. James Meredith, decided to use such a grant to help build a school in the parish. By a lease and release dated 8 and 9 November the Rt Hon. the Earl of Derby conveyed a piece of land to the Rt Revd The Bishop of St Asaph and the Vicar of Hope. The church paid a nominal five shillings of 'lawful money' for:

> ... that piece or parcel of ground situate lying or being east of the Turnpike road leading from Hope to the Water Corn Mill at Caergwrle Bridge and bounded north by a garden ... paying therefore the rent of one pepper corn per year if demanded. The building erected to be called Hope National School.

The two-roomed school, with girls and boys being taught separately, cost £230 to build with the help of a grant of £20 from the National Society.On the 29 January 1846, John James, the inspector, visited the school and his report is to be found in the commissioners report mentioned earlier. He described the state of the building as, 'indifferent ... the back windows, having been broken by the boys, were closed with shutters. The apparatus is insufficient and the funds are very inadequate.' Although there were seventy children on the books, only forty were present at the time of the inspection. Mr James found that the mistress and master, a former soldier, had not been trained to teach and that the master was 'strict, harsh but produced little discipline.' The children were taught arithmetic, English and scripture, and the girls needlework in the afternoon. Teaching was done through the medium of English, which was spoken incorrectly by both teachers. The inspector was not impressed with the standard of teaching, stating, 'I found only one copybook well written among thirty-seven belonging to the entire school.' The master complained about his inadequate salary of £12, saying he could not live without his army pension of £13. The yearly income of the school was made up of £23 from subscriptions and £10 8s. from fees paid by the pupils.

The National School was inspected by the Rev. Elias Owen, on the 29th of October 1878. The following is his encouraging Report :—

" This School has improved generally during the last year. The teaching is uniformly good in all the classes, and the answering general and intelligent."

Pupil Teachers :—

	Year.	Class in last Examination.	Efficiency in giving Instruction.
F. W. Leggatt,	} 4th	1st	Good.
Sarah J. Edwards,		1st	Good.

Scholars :—

Group II.—Richard Whitehorn.
Sarah E. Dutton.
John C. Jones.
Felicia Dutton.
Group III. Samuel Davies. } All obtained Certificates of merit.
Thomas Edwards.
George Dutton.
Henry Eccleston.

Commended.

Joseph Guest. Eliza Thomas. Emily Savage.

Group IV.—Selina Davies.
Alice Golding.
Albert E. Phœnix. } All obtained Certificates of merit.
Charles E. Jones.
George W. Davies.

Commended.

Harriet A. Davies. Ellen Lewis.
Emily Roberts. Lydia Davies.
Mary Ann Barnes. William Griffiths.

Infants.—

Kitty Arthur.
May Eccleston. } All obtained Certificates of merit.
Caroline Pugh.

Commended.

Polly Roberts. Octavia Davies. William Fidler.

Recommended to the Managers for a book prize, as they have had the highest Certificate, and in this Examination distinguished themselves :—

Andrew Savage. Edward Jones. David Arthur.

GENERAL QUALITY, OF
1. Discipline and tone.—Very good.
2. Repetition.—Good.
3. Religious Education as a whole.—Good.

Results of the religious inspection of 1878.

In 1860 the school was made co-educational with the removal of the partition and a ten foot extension of one room. Funding for the school was very dependent on the generosity of local landowners and residents. In 1862, twenty-one contributors, each giving between £1 and £5, raised £36 6s. In addition, money from concerts, penny readings and fêtes held on the castle grounds was used to buy school equipment. To celebrate the wedding of the Prince of Wales in 1863 a local collection raised £8 to buy medals, wedding rosettes and to pay for a tea for the children.

An increasing school roll meant that the school needed to be enlarged. Another classroom was built in 1878 (costing £125, with a grant of £15 from the National Society). In the Hope *Parish Magazine* dated September 1881, the school managers announced that school fees were to be reduced to 2d., 1½d. and 1d. The improvements to the school, such as putting down boarded flooring, cost £51. A more efficient heating and ventilation system 'will place the school on a par with the more pretentious and costly school buildings which are springing up on all sides.' The managers then listed worthy residents who 'have promised to solicit contributions.'

At the annual school feast, 'prizes for regular attendance, punctuality, industry, sewing and religious knowledge were distributed.' In 1885, Aylmer Frost of Meadowslea, Penyffordd, funded fourteen religious scholarships, giving free schooling for one year. In 1891 legislation was passed to provide free elementary education for all children, which was a great boon for poorer families.

Another room, added in 1894, became a separate infants' department in 1898. In a log book for the infant class, a school inspector wrote of his concerns about poor attendance, the shortage of books and the inefficient heating stove. Even though the attendance officer called regularly, Miss Roberts wrote in December 1903, ' a very wet morning, only seventeen children at school. Very difficult to make progress with continued bad attendance on account of poor weather, sickness and also apathy of the parents in many cases.' At the time there were sixty-one children on the roll.

It became clear that the school buildings were not up to standard and were condemned by the School Board of Education in June 1904. They were too dark and lacked a playground (the children played in the road). However the school was reopened by consent of the Board until a replacement could be built. At one stage a room in the Castle Farm Congregationalist Chapel was used by the school. It was agreed that a new school should be built within easy walking distance from both Hope and Caergwrle villages. One acre of land, owned by Miss Lee, was bought for £200, and the funding of the school was to be divided equally between the

School report, 1899. [FRO E/LB/31/1]

County Council and the Parish of Hope. While the new school was being constructed the winter of 1905-6 proved to be very difficult for children and staff alike, as the old stove smoked so much in the infants' room the school had to be closed.

The new school, called Hope Council School, opened on 24 April 1906, and consisted of six classrooms and a large central hall. There were 154 children in the mixed department and 74 in the infants. The original staff were:

Mr David Price, BA, headmaster.

Mr W.Wass, certified assistant for the mixed department.

Mrs M.Roberts, certified assistant for the infant department.

Miss Florence Tyler, supplementary teacher.

Miss Mary Roberts, supplementary teacher.

Miss Edith Davies, pupil teacher.

Miss Edith Williams, pupil teacher.

Pupil teachers served a five year apprenticeship from the age of thirteen to eighteen

Hope Council School staff, c.1910.

under the direction of the senior teachers. If good enough, at the end of their apprenticeship, they could take an examination to go to a teacher training college.

On 4 May 1906 the headmaster wrote, 'work carried out under unfavourable circumstances for all necessary material has not yet come.' In 1907 an inspector noted the poor state of the playground and the lack of water for drinking and flushing purposes. Later, another concern was raised about the safety of the children who came along Fellows Lane and had to cross the railway line. Representations were made to the managers of the Great Central Railway Co. but they refused to construct a footbridge.

After these teething problems, however, the school went from strength to strength. The inspector's report of 1911 declared ' this large mixed school is doing excellent work. No effort is spared by the capable and enterprising headmaster to keep his school abreast of modern requirements. He is well supported by a loyal and hardworking staff of assistants.'

The need to widen the school curriculum was acknowledged and so history, geography, nature, music, art and Welsh were introduced. By 1912, a school garden had been set up with sixteen plots linking in with the senior classes' science lessons. It was five years later that a kitchen range was installed in

Hope Council School, two classes 25 March 1914.

order to introduce domestic science for the girls. Later, hutted accommodation was provided in the playground for domestic science and woodwork instruction. These facilities were also used by senior pupils from Abermorddu and Penyffordd schools.

Hope National School c.1900.

The teaching in the school continued to be of a high standard. In 1923 an inspector wrote, 'the tone is kind and sympathetic and teachers and pupils cheerfully cooperate with one another in order to accomplish their allotted tasks.'

The First World War affected many children in both villages, with fathers, brothers and uncles leaving for active service in the forces. Mr D. Price, headmaster, was exempted from military service, but male teachers enlisted or joined the Denbighshire Volunteer Regiment, having time off school for training and parades. The shortage of available teachers caused major staffing problems for all schools during this period. In common with many families, teachers also lost loved ones, such as Mrs Roberts' only son who died in 1916.

Courage was recognised when Corporal Robert Williams, who had been awarded the DCM in Gallipoli, 1917, brought his medal to school for the children to admire. The annual 'Kindness to Animals' talk given by the RSPCA drew the children's attention to the suffering and treatment of horses in the field of battle. In 1918 a rationing scheme was set up and the school was used for registration and the issuing of cards and books.

Industrial unrest and strikes also caused problems for families. In 1912 some children were arriving late as they were being given free breakfasts while their fathers were on strike. During the miners lockout of 1921, the new headmaster, Robert Davies, put the

Hope Council School, Standard II, 1924.

Hope Council School, Standard I, 1924.

Provision of Meals Act 1906 into operation. The Act allowed the local Education Authority to provide free meals for children who were unable, by reason of lack of food, to take full advantage of the education provided for them. For example, on 23 May the school provided 126 breakfasts and 132 teas, between forty and fifty percent of the pupils presenting themselves for these meals. In July the headmaster decided to continue to feed those children whose parents had not commenced work.

Discipline was strict and caning on the bottom or hand was the usual punishment. Children, often boys, were caned for trespassing, stone throwing, bullying, lying, being late and running away from school. Another punishment for persistent lateness was to send the children back home!

Fire struck twice at the school. In the first incident, in 1913, extensive damage was done to a classroom and a bookcase and its contents were destroyed. The fire was contained with buckets of water until help arrived. The second fire occurred in 1930 in the roof of an entrance. The children were evacuated and helpers extinguished the fire before the arrival of the Wrexham Fire Brigade.

The childhood diseases of mumps, whooping cough, measles, scarlet fever and diphtheria caused much suffering and in some cases, death. When there was an outbreak the Medical Officer of Health would order the closure of the school until the epidemic had abated. In 1918 influenza raged throughout Britain, affecting all ages, resulting in the school being closed for a month. Medical care in schools began to improve with regular visits from the doctor, the dentist and a nurse. In 1928, the infants were given a cup of Horlicks milk at playtime and in 1934 a third of a pint of milk was available for all pupils at $\frac{1}{2}d$. Later, the doctor could recommend free milk for needy children. From October 1942, school meals were provided at the Hope Church Institute at 4*d*. per head. These proved to be very popular and over 200 children would walk there each schoolday.

School was not all work and no play. Whole-day and half-day holidays were given to celebrate local festivals and the Hope Church Fête. There were national holidays for royal occasions, such as coronations, marriages, jubilees, silver weddings and investitures. When

Hope Council School, cookery class, 1924.

Hope Council School, woodwork class, 1924.

Hope Council School, 1913.

Princess Elizabeth married Prince Philip in November 1947, the children had tea in the afternoon and the following day was a holiday. To commemorate the coronation of Queen Elizabeth II in 1953, trees were planted in the school grounds and two bus loads of children went to see her at the National Eisteddfod held at Rhyl.

During these years the netball and football teams had been winners of the county championships and so all the children were given a half-day holiday to celebrate. Much to the headmaster's annoyance, children also took an unofficial day off school to enjoy the Sunday school outing. In February 1932 thirteen Sunday schools were represented at a meeting and it was agreed that they would all take the same day for the treat or it would be held in the school holidays. This arrangement lasted for many years.

In 1938, when war with Germany became more likely, the school closed for a day for the fitting of gas masks. A year later Mr E. Jones, the headmaster, attended an Air Raid Precautions (ARP) course. In the same year Walter Elliot, Minister of Health, requested local authorities to survey available housing accommodation as part of the government's plans to transfer children and others in an emergency to the homes of those who were willing to take care of them. Such a survey was done in both villages and the headmaster became the billeting officer for the area. The school was closed for an indefinite period as the premises were to be used for evacuation purposes. Householders who were willing to take a child were paid 10s. 6d. a week for lodging, boarding and caring, 8s. 6d. for a second or subsequent child. The school re-opened 11 September 1939 and four days later two schools from Birkenhead arrived. The headmasters, teachers and 200 children were allocated the central hall, woodwork and domestic science huts. On the 18 September a further thirty-two voluntary and thirteen official evacuees from Tollemache, Birkenhead were squeezed into a very overcrowded school. To alleviate the problem twenty-one children under the age of five years were officially excluded. By April, all evacuated teachers had returned to Birkenhead with most of the children. The remaining thirty-nine children were admitted to the school and placed in existing classes.

In 1939 plans were made to protect the children in the event of an air raid. The school managers, responding to a letter of advice from the ARP, suggested that 'in the unlikelihood of the area being subjected to an air raid, the protection of the scholars and staff, in view of the numbers involved, should take the form of trenches supplemented by sand bags in the ground adjoining the school' and an air raid shelter was constructed later. The warning of impending attack was to be the Caergwrle Brewery works whistle. Some nights were spent in the shelters and the children were too tired to attend school the following day.

In 1942 more children came from Liverpool, and an inspector's report of that year noted that the roll of 307 included 50 voluntary and 13 official evacuees. The report concluded that 'the general work of the school cannot but be impeded to some extent by the staffing and accommodation conditions.'

The school yard was used for Home Guard parades and the ARP had a base outside and took classes in the main hall. The teachers' room was used for fire watch duties.

Everybody worked hard during this period. The school

Hope Council School, infants, 1950s

Cricket XI, 1960.

Football XI, 1954–5.

Rounders team, 1947.

Hope Council School sports activities.

Football XI, 1952

Gymnastics, 1930s.

Teaching staff, 1970s.

Hope Council School.

Ancillary staff (with headteacher), 1950s.

managers wrote to Major Rowlands of the Home Guard to ask him to allow Mr Moulton, the school caretaker, to be excused from drill or to have the number of his drills reduced. They explained that in addition to his colliery work he put in 24 hours a week as a cleaner and caretaker.

The National Savings Committee set up schemes to encourage saving to support the war effort. In May 1944 the children went to the cinema in Caergwrle to see the film, *Salute the Soldier*, following which they collected £1,040 in one week and were rewarded for their efforts with a day's holiday.

When hostilities in Europe ended, the 8 and 9 May 1945 were declared national holidays. Four months later, 29 September was recognised as a holiday after the victory over Japan. Married teachers were given two to three weeks leave when their husbands returned from active service and teacher Ceinwen Jones went with a Welsh choir to entertain the troops in the Far East.

After the War school life became easier for everyone. The air raid shelter was put to good use as a store for P.E. equipment and gardening tools. In 1947 reorganisation of schooling took place. Children aged between 11 and 15 years old, who did not pass the examination to go to a grammar school at Mold or Hawarden, were transferred to a secondary modern school at Shotton or Mold and, in 1954, to the new Elfed School, Buckley. In September 1958, Castell Alun Secondary Modern School at Hope opened and local children no longer had to travel to continue their education.

In 1951 Mr E. Jones died and Mr Elfed Roberts was appointed as the new head-teacher. A new dining room and kitchen were completed in 1952, a relief for all those pupils who had to walk to the Church Institute for lunch, regardless of weather conditions. In 1957 a new hall and corridors were built, giving access to the dining

Ysgol Estyn.

room and the heating system was improved. By 1965, with the completion of the headmaster's room and an infants' toilet block, the facilities were up to date.

For many years the school has been at the centre of community life in Hope and Caergwrle. Many local societies have held their meetings there, such as the Women's Institute, the Young Farmers Club and the Poultry Club. The Boys' Brigade used the football field and put on their famous pantomimes in the hall. In the 1960s the plays put on by the Hope Village Players attracted good audiences. The school has also been the venue for evening classes to satisfy every interest: rug making, embroidery, basketry, leatherwork, music appreciation, folk dancing and physical education. Earlier classes of physical culture for girls were spoilt by unruly youths!

As the school roll increased in the early 1970s, the building was further extended. Mr Elfed Roberts retired in 1977 having been the headteacher for twenty-six years. He was a very knowledgeable local historian, who introduced environmental studies into the curriculum. His place was taken by Neville Davies, head from 1977–93, and Philip Monslow took charge from 1993–99.

The children have always been encouraged to widen their horizons with extra-curricular activities and educational visits, sometimes travelling as far as Holland, Belgium and Brittany.

Ysgol Estyn pupils.

Ysgol Estyn pupils and staff, 1997.

Under Mr Ifan Davies' leadership, Ysgol Estyn (as it is now called) continues to be in the forefront of good educational practices, helping children to realise their full potential. In 2006 the present school will be celebrating its centenary, but it should not be forgotten that there has been a school serving children from Hope and Caergwrle for 167 years. A great achievement!

Abermorddu School

The Representation of the People Act, 1867, enfranchised many men who previously had not been able to vote. William Forster when introducing his Education Act to Parliament, argued that, 'now we have given them political power, we must not wait any longer to give them education.' In 1870 this Act became law and so began the transition from a voluntary system to a national system of education.

Under the terms of the Act, the Government instructed the Education Department to set up schools in those areas not adequately served by voluntary schools, such as the Hope National School. Local school boards were to be elected by the ratepayers and members would hold office for three years. Women were allowed to vote for the school boards and also could stand for election. The Boards could commission new schools which would be paid for and maintained by Government grants, local rates and school fees.

No time was wasted and the first Hope School Board was elected in 1871. The election cost £13. John Bury, Clerk to the Wrexham Poor Law Union was the treasurer and clerk. Other board members were: James Sparrow Esq. (chairman); Samuel Poole; Thomas Peters; Rev. T. R. Lloyd; James Rawlins; and William Lassell.

The Board organised schools to be built at Llanfynydd 1874 and Penyffordd 1875. In 1879 a census was made of the children under 14 years of age in the Llanfynydd and Caergwrle districts and after much discussion, it was accepted that a further school was needed and a site at Abermorddu was chosen.

In December 1882 a loan of £2,000 was advanced by the Public Works Loan Board and the Hope School Board agreed a contract with Mr E. O. Probert of Caergwrle to build a school for £1,300, the eventual cost being £1,676.

The construction of the new school aroused considerable local interest. A letter from 'A Ratepayer', published in the *Wrexham Advertiser*, 18 August

Old school, Abermorddu, 1927.

Abermorddu School,
Honours Board.

Abermorddu School,
scholarship winners, 1933.

1883, praised, 'everything in the way of the site and surroundings is in favour of training healthy bodies and the school is neat and airy.' However it raised concerns about the one large classroom viz. ' it is at a heavy disadvantage that teachers perform their tasks when several classes meet in the same resonant hall,' and proposed that the hall should be partitioned. A reply to the letter was published the following week, 25 August 1883, written by 'Nous Verrons', who pointed out that, 'the proximity of the school to the railway was a grave disadvantage to the teacher and the dirty black smoke to the health of the scholars.' The writer criticised 'the stupid … unconvertible and immovable desks, the absence of a lavatory and water connection.' The argument was put forward that the division of the large room, 'would not only cause an outlay of more money, but will compel the Board to increase the teaching staff, and we all know what that means.'

By the time the letter had been published, however, the school had opened on 20 August 1883 with 85 children on the register. The school consisted of a large room to accommodate 144 pupils and a small room for 24 infants. The headmaster was H. D. Davies, who was paid £60 p.a. His wife was the sewing teacher for in order to secure a Government grant, sewing had to be taught to the girls. The other teachers were Cathleen Jones (assistant mistress) and John Griffiths (pupil teacher). A short time later they were joined by John D. Smallwood (assistant teacher) from Llanfynydd Board School.

The new school drew pupils from a wide area, many walking long distances to attend. Some pupils had received little education and few were in the higher standard class, even though school attendance up to the age of 10 had been compulsory since 1880. It is interesting to note that attendance officers from Hope, Wrexham, Gwersyllt, Llay and

Abermorddu School, 1927.

Gresford visited the school, giving some idea of the wide catchment area that it served.

By 1885, 234 children were on the roll and the school was very overcrowded — a problem which continued until 1972! Curtains were put up to divide the large classroom into three parts, replaced in 1896 by a partition. The overcrowding put a great strain on staff, pupils and resources. The inspectors' reports always highlighted the problems. In 1884, 'the Government grant for English barely earned, more books should be had at once.' In 1891, 'the staff too small,' and in 1900, 'managers should face the question boldly in the interest of both teachers and taught who are not getting a fair chance to do their work.' There were 265 children squeezed into a school built for 166. In 1904 a class of 64 older pupils was taught by Mr Smallwood in Abermorddu Chapel.

Inspectors also highlighted other problems, such as the cleanliness of the school. The board members drew up rules for the guidance of the sweeper (cleaner), who was paid 5s. per week. 'The hearth stones must be kept white and the grate black and window sills dusted along with the furniture daily.' Other concerns voiced were the emissions from a defective stove and the need for 'wholesome' drinking water. The inspectors praised good teaching and fair discipline, 'the infants doing very nicely under Miss Roberts' kind care and tuition'(1888). 'The teachers are hard working' (1897) and the discipline is kind (1912) and the school is ably organised and effectively taught (1923).

Legislation in 1891 gave free elementary education and in 1902 Balfour's Education Act laid the responsibility upon local authorities to provide education for children from 5 to 14 years of age. This was to be free and compulsory up to the age of 12. On 1 July 1904, Hope School Board was replaced when the control of the school passed to Flintshire County Council Education Authority. Trained male teachers were now paid £95 per annum, females £75 per annum.

The opening of Hope Council School in 1906 eased the overcrowding a little and some improvements were made to the school building. In 1912, however, John Smallwood, now headmaster, complained it was 'difficult to secure and retain 110 scholars attention in one room.'

Outside improvements were made to the playground, which was gravelled in 1899 and tarred in 1912. Two years later, on land adjoining the school site, a school garden divided into plots was established where the boys were taught horticulture. The rivers Alyn and Cegidog were used to teach the boys to swim, but sadly the river claimed a number of lives.

We discovered a song which must have been sung about this time, and the words appear to underline the inspectors reports about the schools kind and caring nature.

Come tune up your voices and join in the song,
We'll sing of the school house to which we belong.
The object of building was not for display
But for practical use in a practical way.

Chorus
With hearts full of gladness, happy are we,
For our school days are pleasant at Abermorddu.
Each morning of school days we make it a rule
To promptly assemble with neatness at school
The school bell sounds , its cheerful ding dong
Combining our voices with laughter and song.

We study our lessons with diligent care,
To seek out the mysteries we find hidden there,
And should we get stuck and a problem remains,
Our teacher stands ready to make it all plain.

Chorus

The view from the schoolhouse doth beauty fulfil,
The vale of the Alyn and Bryn-y-Gaer hill.
With Caergwrle Castle and Hope Mountain side,
Fills our hearts with emotion, love joy and pride.

Chorus

With loving each other we are happy all day,
With teachers and classmates our partners in play.
Through lifes favoured future, as years roll along
So will remember the school and think of this song.

Childhood diseases caused much suffering even death. The school was often closed for weeks on the orders of the Medical Officer of Health.

For children who misbehaved discipline was strict and the cane was used for truancy, disobedience, impertinence and poor work. One boy, who had been locked in a classroom, broke a window in order to escape and ran home.

The head teachers constantly complained about poor attendance. Children were kept at home to set and raise potatoes, glean after the harvest, pick whinberries and blackberries and help at home. Various methods were used to encourage children to attend school, reward cards, a 'magic lantern show' for good attenders and in 1900 Mr Young, manager of Llay Hall Colliery, offered prize money for good work and punctuality. There were exceptions, when Nancy Lawrence and Walter Wynyard were given 10s. each for eight years of unbroken attendance.

Industrial strikes and unrest had a profound effect on the families, and children were particularly at risk. In 1886 a soup kitchen was set up and entertainment was arranged to raise funds. The colliers' strike of 1893 went on for weeks, with bread and soup distributed at the Drill Hall, Caergwrle, to all needy children. A young boy pupil was smothered picking coal for his family from an old slack bank. Another strike in 1896 meant more emergency feeding and in 1921, 110 children were given dinner and tea during the miners' lockout. These were certainly hard times.

There was very little information about the effects of the First World War in the log books, only that the war savings scheme was established, and a collection made for the 'Jack Cornwell Fund'. (See Scouts) When war was declared in 1939 the managers suggested that trenches should be dug, supplemented by sandbags in the vicinity of the school for use during air raids. Later a request was sent to Shire Hall to supply an air raid shelter. A major concern was that the staff of the school could not hear the air raid siren and only knew once the danger was over! The headmaster and infant teacher went on fire-fighting courses and the school premises were used for fire-watching duties.

Pupils and two teachers from Bidston Avenue Junior and Infant Schools, Birkenhead, were evacuated to the school and billeted in local homes. Both official and private evacuees swelled the number of pupils. However, by 1942, most had returned to their own homes. In 1943 an inspector's report criticized the natural light, ventilation and heating of the school but praised the standard of teaching and discipline of the teachers. There was a national shortage of teachers and the infant department particularly had under qualified teachers. In 1955 the infant and junior schools merged into one school.

In 1934 Mr F. Whittingham of the Farmers' Association had set up the provision of milk for the children.

From 1942 junior children had to walk to the Church Institute for school dinners costing 4d. a day. There were initial difficulties due to lack of accommodation, cutlery and excess noise! These were resolved when the Abermorddu children ate their meals after the Hope school pupils. The infants had their meals brought to the school. This arrangement lasted until 1952 when the meals were carried to the school from a central kitchen at Hope School. This was not very satisfactory as the feeding and kitchen facilities in the school were hopelessly inadequate and the children were eating off sloping desk tops! A dining hall was eventually erected in 1958.

Abermorddu School, 1948–9.

Below left: Abermorddu School, rounders team, 1968.

Abermorddu School, 1960s.

Holidays were given to celebrate royal events, military success, Sunday school treats, friendly societies 'feasts', the circus and fairs at Wrexham. The golden wedding and funeral of Mr Sparrow (the iron and coal master at Ffrwd), were recognized with half-day holidays.

It was inevitable that this overcrowded school had to be replaced. In June 1972 the infants transferred to a new building on the Cymau road. The junior children were later housed in mobile classrooms adjacent to the infant school. Mr R. W. Edwards, headteacher from 1958, retired in 1978 to be replaced by Mr Bryn James, who later took up an appointment at Cartrefle College Wrexham. Mr Ian Swain, then the deputy, became acting head and was appointed headteacher in 1981.

The second building phase was completed in 1983 ,during which the infant school was remodelled and a large extension built to accommodate the junior department.

The school is at the heart of the community and the facilities are used by a number of local clubs and societies. Abermorddu Community Primary School is very popular and successful and its motto 'Happy to learn and learning to be happy' is very apt.

Secondary Education

We now turn our attention to secondary education. The Education Act of 1902 empowered local authorities to provide secondary education. This would not be free and pupils would have to sit a selection examination, so consequently only a small proportion of working class children went into this level.

Sir Henry Hadow's report, *The Education of the Adolescent,* published in 1926, recommended the division of education into;

Primary stage: 5–11 years old
Secondary stage: 11 years and onward

There would be a selection examination to determine whether the child would attend grammar or secondary modern school. With the Education Act 1944, fees were abolished in secondary state education, the leaving age was raised to 15 years, and the system graded into grammar, secondary modern and technical schools. The Government recognized that the steady process of industrialization and technical advancement required an educated workforce to keep Britain an economically strong nation. From 1944 there has been greater equality of opportunity for all children with ability and aptitude to take full advantage of education and this has led to great social change.

Local farmer, County Councillor D. A. Richards, JP, led a campaign for Hope and district to have its own secondary modern school. Many people supported the cause knowing that all children over the age of 11 years travelled by train or bus to schools outside the parish in order to continue their education. The site of the school had been purchased in 1937, but the war years intervened and postwar restrictions on Flintshire Education Authority to build only one school a year, meant that the land was leased to a farmer until the mid 1950s.

Eirene White, MP, and Councillor J. D. Hughes, chairman of the governors, opened the school in 1958. It had been built to accommodate 400–500 pupils, however 294 children were admitted initially, and some first- and second-year entrants transferred from the Elfed School, Buckley and Daniel Owen School, Mold. Mr D. Geraint Williams was the first headteacher, supported by a deputy and ten assistant staff. During the first term teachers worked under great difficulties as building work had not been completed and some practical rooms were not available until the January. There was also a shortage of furniture and equipment. A 'bring and buy' sale was quickly organized, raising £95 to start a school fund. Mr Williams appealed through the press for books to be donated to set up a library; a total of 600 were received.

Mr Williams' vision that the school should be the focal point of the community took a step forward when he organized an adult education programme. By 1959 twenty classes were established, also a school-based youth club. Within a year the school was being used by the community five or six evenings a week. With the lack of suitable P.E. facilities a ramble was organized to climb up Hope Mountain and this continued to be a popular annual event for many years. The dining room was converted into a dance hall for ballroom dancing.

Castell Alun staff, 1958. headteacher Mr Geraint Williams.

In 1960 an outdoor pursuits centre was set up in a small quarrying village near Holyhead, Anglesey. The facilities were basic, the beds being ex War Department double-tier bunks, and the mattresses were straw filled palliasses. It is believed that some of the furniture was made in school in the woodwork class, and parents donated other equipment. The cost of the week end away was 12s. 6d. per head. The headmaster noted that, 'the centre enriched tremendously the corporate life of the school.'

A rural science department was established with greenhouses and a poultry shed; sadly the hens were stolen in October 1961 but were soon replaced. Older boys were encouraged to learn to drive on the yard using the school van. In his report of 1961, Mr Williams pointed out the need for more classrooms and a laboratory. Even so he was proud that the school offered such a wide curriculum, covering practical, technical, commercial and academic subjects.

In 1963 the first edition of the school magazine was launched, entitled *Pont* (Bridge) which emphasized the links between the school, the home and the community. The youth club continued to be very popular and had 102 enrolled members. Older members of the villages were not forgotten when the school entertained a group of senior citizens at Christmas. The inspectors report October 1964 was very encouraging, 'a thriving and purposeful school which has importance for the cultural and social development of the district.' Adult classes went from strength to

Queuing for the toilet at the outdoor pursuit centre near Holyhead.

strength and by 1965 400 people were attending 25 classes.

The next few years proved to be very unsettling for all concerned with the school. At the end of 1966 Flintshire proposed to reorganize secondary education into a comprehensive system. It was decided that Castell Alun would only teach children aged between 11 and 13 after which age they would be transferred to the Elfed School in Buckley to complete their education. Later, the school buildings would become a

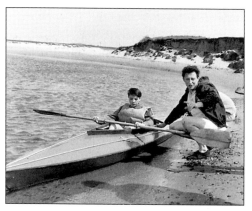

Canoeing activities.

junior school. Hope Parish Council campaigned vigorously to oppose the eventual closure of their senior school. It was argued that the increase in housing in Penyffordd, Kinnerton and other villages in the catchment area meant that the extra children should be accommodated at Castell Alun. However from 1967, the school did become a junior comprehensive and it was not until 1971 that notice was given of plans to enlarge the school to accommodate 660 pupil places changing the character of the school to provide full comprehensive education for pupils aged between 11 and 18. The future of the school was now secure and the campaigners were delighted with the news.

Between 1972 and 1974 a major extension and remodelling of the school was undertaken. The sports centre, youth club, branch library, crèche and an all-weather sports area, including tennis courts, were built for the school and community. The new extension was opened by Frank S. Whittingham and Councillor Thomas Jones, on 29 October 1975. As many as twenty-five voluntary organizations used the school and community centre, sports and other activities could be pursued at all levels.

From the 1970s children were able to go to the outdoor pursuits centre at Bala, with water based activities on Llyn Tegid. There were also opportunities to travel abroad. The school bought four caravans at Barfleur in France, setting up a European centre. Many pupils were able to improve

Girls' gymnastics team.

their French and this led to exchanges with French students. Clwyd County Council developed ties with schools in Wisconsin, USA, and in 1973 the school pioneered the first Clwyd—Wisconsin pupil exchanges. Castell Alun also twinned with a school in Hadston, Denmark, and some pupils were able to visit.

Field study group.

Around 1969, Ash Lea Farm had been purchased to extend the playing fields. A school farm was established and by 1984 it offered practical experience for those pupils who were interested in a career in agriculture.

In July 1985 Geraint Williams, head teacher for twenty-five years, retired and his services to education were recognised by being awarded the OBE. Mr D. Platten was chosen as his successor and he took over a school where the staff and pupils worked together to achieve a high academic standard with excellent examination results. Netball, hockey and football teams were doing well and individual children had notable success in gymnastics, skiing, swimming, ice skating, dance, table tennis and public speaking. The farmhouse was refurbished and an enterprise centre established to help develop links with the local community, especially industry, giving the pupils relevant and practical education in preparation for the world of work. The arts have always been encouraged and for many years the annual school plays, musicals and concerts have been of a high standard attracting large audiences. In 1987 the school gained the prestigious Schools Curriculum Award, having 'established a broad and balanced curriculum enriched by the local community and

Castell Alun pupils, 1960.

Castell Alun School production of My Fair Lady.

School production of Kismet.

*Domestic Science teacher Norma
Evans helps with the costumes.*

Castell Alun School Choir.

Castell Alun teaching staff, 1965.

Celebrating the school's 25th anniversary.

environment'. It was the first school in Clwyd to receive the award.

During the 1990s the school population continued to grow and so did the need for a wider range of specialist teaching facilities. A £2,000,000 building programme was approved to keep Castell Alun at the forefront of educational progress. On the 4 July 1996 there was a celebration to mark the completion of an extension and refurbishment of the school. New facilities included a science block, library, classrooms, dining room, cafeteria, media suite and a remodelled technology suite. The sports centre was also updated to offer excellent facilities for a wide range of activities for use by the school and the community.

Castell Alun School, Year 13, 2004.

Mr D. Platten resigned as headteacher in 1998, Mr John Evans having served as acting headteacher during the previous academic year. Mrs Sandra Maddocks was appointed headteacher in 1998 until her sudden death in 2003. Mr David Mountfort took over the running of the school and became headteacher in March 2004.

Over the years the need to adapt to the changing demands of society has been recognised and the school has gained a number of national and international awards. Pupils and staff work hard and examination results are well above the county and national averages. From 1958 to the present day the school has provided a liberal education, enabling each child to develop to the full, within a caring community.

6. Transport

Roads

Before the Roman invasion of 48 AD, local tribes people would have used a system of paths and trackways. Some of these would have been along the high ground above the dangers lurking in the wooded valleys and lowlands.

Roman dominance over this area was consolidated with the building of the legionary fortress at Deva (Chester), 70–74 AD. This would become the strategic centre of Roman military control of north Wales. Roads were developed to link auxiliary forts often using and improving existing native trackways. Such a road has been identified leaving Chester from the Southgate and bridge through to the Lache and Dodleston to Caergwrle/Hope and on to the Ffrith, (a small Roman settlement). From there the road went south west to Llyn Tegid at Bala and thence to the auxiliary fort of Caer Gai in Gwynedd.

After the departure of the Romans in c.400 AD, their road system deteriorated as the stone surfaces were often robbed for building work. From the medieval period onwards more tracks and pathways were established leading from settlements to the open fields, pastures, woods, quarries, mines, mills, churches and markets. These were often impassable in the winter, with thick mud and water-filled potholes. In dry weather the rutted surface made the roads unfit for wheeled vehicles, so most travellers would be on foot or horseback.

A cheap and reliable way to transport goods, such as corn, ore, coal and cloth was to use packhorses or mules. Each animal carried a load of 250–500lbs in two wicker baskets, or panniers, slung either side of its body. There could be between six to thirty animals in the train and the lead animal had bells on its harness to warn of its approach.

The narrow packhorse bridge spanning the River Alyn at Caergwrle has low parapets

The packhorse bridge on Fellows Lane, c.1910.

which allowed the heavily laden mules to pass easily. The two triangular recesses on the bridge permitted pedestrians to stand to one side as the packhorse train went across. This narrow, stone structure still provides pedestrian access between Fellows Lane and Derby Road. It is Grade II listed and is thought to have been built in the latter quarter of the seventeenth century, perhaps

The packhorse bridge after part of it was washed away after heavy rainfall, November 2000.

after a petition led by Richard Yonge to repair the bridge in 1654. It was an important crossing on the Chester–Bala packhorse trail and linked with another packhorse bridge over the River Cegidog at Ffrith. On 7 November 2000, after a period of heavy rainfall, the River Alyn became very swollen with flood water. The flood overflow arches of the bridge had been allowed to become blocked with silt and debris, consequently the river badly damaged the structure. During the summer of 2001 the bridge was repaired (using original masonry where possible) by F. G. Whitley & Sons, closely monitored by CADW inspectors. Fragments of Ewloe pottery, dating from the fourteenth and fifteenth centuries, were found in silt close to the bridge.

From medieval times until the eighteenth century the inhabitants of each village were expected to contribute towards the work and expense involved in maintaining and repairing roads which passed through their village. Common Law and various authorities enforced these duties, each with a differing amount of success. From very early times, the history of road maintenance appears to be less than satisfactory, with a record of half-hearted and unskilled efforts. Complaints by travellers of the disrepair and neglect, which made travel slow and hazardous, were numerous.

The Highways Act of 1555, which transferred responsibility for the upkeep of the King's Highway to the parishes, remained in force until 1833. It specified that persons holding land, arable or pasture, with an annual value of £50 or more had to supply two men with oxen, a cart and tools to repair the highways for four consecutive days each year. This was increased to six days in 1563.

The Tudor government endeavoured to reorganise the Act of 1555, making provision for each parish to administer and regularise the methods of highway maintenance and authorised the appointment of parish surveyors. Many parishioners were resentful of

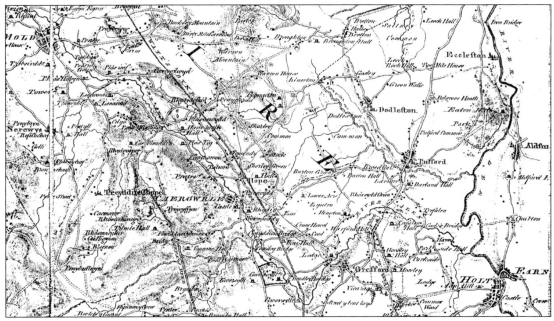

A section of the John Evans map of north Wales, 1795.

having to work and pay to maintain roads used by strangers.

Statute labour, supervised at the Quarter Sessions, was an aspect of the work of a Justice of Peace. In 1654 Richard Yonge of Bryn Iorcyn and fourteen others of the inhabitants of the Parish of Hope petitioned the Justices of the Peace of Flintshire, that steps be taken to repair two bridges, 'Pontcairgurley and Pont y Place Main … both of which are in great decay and ruin'.

In 1735, Justices of the Peace, Richard Wardle and Richard Cratchley, ordered the repair of the 'Higher and Lower' bridges at Caergwrle, at a cost of £10 5s. 6d. Ellis Yonge, JP ordered the repair of the 'Wheatmill Bridge' in 1741. Thomas Griffiths submitted the following estimate to the Quarter Sessions sitting at Easter 1750:

An eastiment of the repairing of Caergurley's bridge.

For making one new pillar and new under working ye oather and for mending ye baffulments on both sides of the bridge, I value there will be just of ye sd. work 20 yards of new stone is for riseing and carring them is £1 0s. 0d.

For lime and sand £1 10s. 0d.

For workmanship £2 5s. 0d.

Total   £4 15s. 0d.

This repair was carried out.

Parishes could be fined for not keeping their roads in good condition. Here are two examples from the Quarter Sessions Minute Book 1788:

> The township of Rhanberfedd fined £50 for not repairing the road from Caergurley to Fferm. The township of Estyn fined £25 for not repairing the road from Caergurley bridge to the Smithy near Colomendy. [Pigeon House Lane]

Sarn Bridge over the River Alyn at Hope.

Money from the county rate was also used to pay for repairing bridges. Pont y Delyn (Fagl Lane) was repaired in 1796 and the Sarn Bridge in 1804, at a cost of £12 0s. 6d.

As wheeled traffic was becoming more common and industrial development advancing, it was recognised that the current system of maintaining roads was totally inadequate. To resolve this problem local landowners and industrialists set up turnpike trusts, which would petition the government for Acts to permit the trustees to take charge of the maintenance of a defined stretch of road. Tolls would be charged on those travelling along it. This money being used for the improvement and upkeep of the road and to build new roads. The revenues also made it possible to employ expert, professional surveyors and road engineers.

The first turnpike Act had been introduced in England in 1663, but it was not until 1752 that the first Welsh turnpike Act was passed — to repair the road from Shrewsbury to Wrexham, via Ellesmere and Overton. An Act for 'amending, widening and keeping in repair the road from the town of Wrexham to Pentre Bridge (Mold)' was passed in 1756–7. This road went through Caergwrle and was an old established routeway, being one of the only four roads in Flintshire surveyed and mapped by John Ogilby in 1675. It formed part of the road from Shrewsbury to St Winifred's Well in Holywell.

On 5 July 1765, Francis Wardle of Hartsheath lent £106 3s. 7d. to the trustees with the tolls collected from the road users to be used as security. In 1818 a further Act allowed an extension to be constructed which branched off at Abermorddu for Caergwrle.

A new road was proposed from Kingsferry to Abermorddu in 1834 for which Mr James Boydell of Hawarden was to be the surveyor. Where necessary, land had to be bought in order to construct new sections, while some existing roads were incorporated into the scheme. At Caergwrle the River Alyn was initially crossed by means of a ford below the weir,

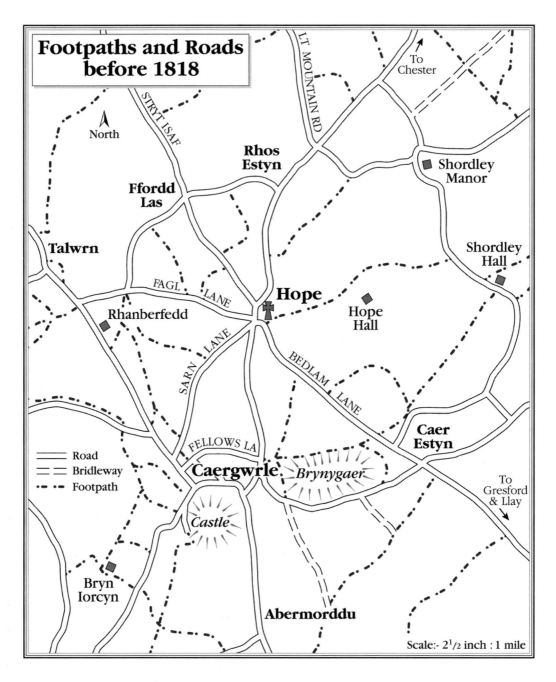

but the above map shows a bridge by the mill. Was it a footbridge? The present stone bridge was built in 1838 when the new road was constructed.

Tollhouses and toll gates were painted white so as to be visible in the dark. They were built where travellers had to pay for using that part of the road. The collection of tolls was usually contracted out to the highest bidder.

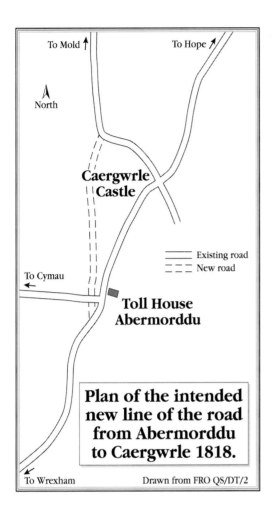

Plan of the intended new line of the road from Abermorddu to Caergwrle 1818.

Drawn from FRO QS/DT/2

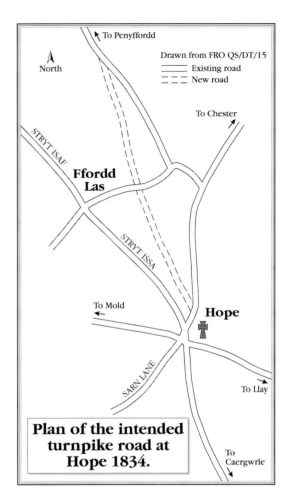

Plan of the intended turnpike road at Hope 1834.

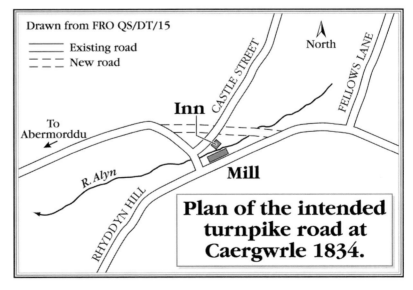

Plan of the intended turnpike road at Caergwrle 1834.

WREXHAM AND MOLD ROAD.

NOTICE IS HEREBY GIVEN,

That a Special Meeting of the Trustees of the Turnpike Road leading from Wrexham, in the County of Denbigh, to Mold, in the County of Flint, called "The Wrexham and Mold Road," will be held pursuant to an Act passed in the Third Year of the Reign of his late Majesty King GEORGE THE FOURTH, and under the Local Act passed in the Fifty-ninth Year of the Reign of his late Majesty King George the Third, at the BLACK LION INN, in MOLD, on Thursday, the 21st day of December next, at Twelve o'Clock at Noon, in order to consult about the propriety of advancing the Tolls by taking the following Tolls instead of those now taken, that is to say—

For every Horse, Mule, or other Beast drawing any Coach, Barouche, Berlin, Landau, Chariot, Chaise, Curricle, Caravan, Chair, Gig, or other such Carriage, Hearse, or Litter, - - - **6d.**

For every Horse, Mule, or other Beast drawing any Waggon, Cart, Wain, Tumbrel, or other such like Carriage, having at the time of using thereof Wheels of the breadth of six inches at the sole or bottom of the Fellies thereof, the sum of - - **4d.**

For every Horse, Mule, or other Beast drawing any Waggon, Cart, Wain, Tumbrel, or other such like Carriage, having at the time of using thereof Wheels of less breadth than six inches at the sole or bottom of the Fellies thereof, the sum of - - - **6d.**

The other Tolls will continue as heretofore, and a Ticket taken at any one Gate will free all the other Gates on the Line.

Dated this Twentieth day of November, One Thousand Eight Hundred and Forty-eight.

Philip Stapleton Humberst

Clerk to the said Trustees.

[FRO D/BC/3137]

• Hope Toll Bar, shown on a property sale map of 1843, had the toll house the left of the road leading to Penyffordd just before the Kinnerton road junction. By 1870 the position of the toll house had been moved to between Caergwrle and Hope, adjacent to the present site of Heulwen Close. In the 1871 census, Edward Davies was the gate keeper and was also employed as a slater.

• The Abermorddu toll house had two rooms and was located on the left of the road to Wrexham, just after the present-day traffic lights.

• Rhanberfedd Toll Chain was on the Caergwrle to Mold road, near to the junction with Fagl Lane.

• Cross Street Toll Gate was close to Oak Alyn, opposite Llay Hall Colliery.

• The position of Rackery Gate is unknown but it is mentioned in 1788.

In January 1845 the tolls charged for using these roads were reduced by half only to be raised again later. The revenues from tolls on the Wrexham to Mold road were, in 1839 — £700 and 1870 — £750. The turnpike gates were finally removed on this road in 1876.

Turnpiked roads had improved but other roads were still in a terrible state, especially in the winter. Many were narrow and low, often serving as drains as well as roads. The Highways Act of 1835 permitted the levying of a highway rate which would pay a labour force to work on the roads. In May 1852 a taxation rate of 2d. in the £1, for one year, made by the surveyor of the township of Caergwrle for repairs to the highway, was approved by two justices of the peace. In 1862, another Highways Act empowered the justices to

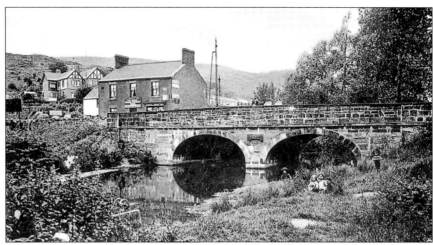

Bridge End, Caergwrle. The bridge was built in 1838.

compulsorily unite parishes into highway authorities. In October 1863 the Hope Church Vestry minute book records the concerns of ratepayers who petitioned not to introduce the new Highway Act in their parish.

> Our township roads are undergoing an improvement generally and we promise that we will appoint surveyors who will expend the money fairly and honestly as the different roads in the township require. For two or three of the last years have pressed heavily upon farmers and though this years harvest is plentiful yet the price of grain is so low that we dread the introduction of a new Act which would add to our burden without offering real benefits.

Above: Flintshire County Council steam lorry.

Above right: A tricycle and a penny farthing bicycle outside the Red Lion, Hope.

Right: A lorry belonging to Crowe of Wrexham in Caergwrle.

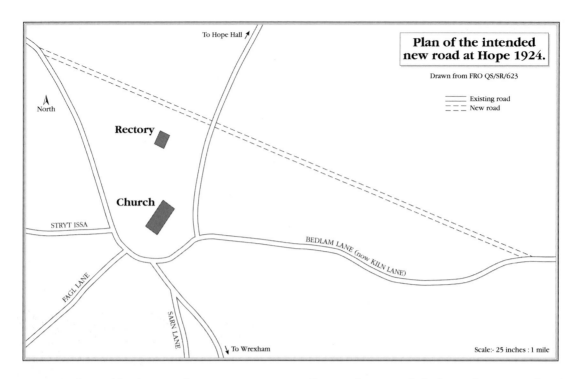

Plan of the intended new road at Hope 1924.

Drawn from FRO QS/SR/623

Existing road
New road

North

Rectory

Church

STRYT ISSA

FAGL LANE

SARN LANE

To Hope Hall

BEDLAM LANE (now KILN LANE)

To Wrexham

Scale:- 25 inches : 1 mile

From the mid nineteenth century, as turnpike roads extended throughout much of southern England, north into Scotland and west into Wales, it was possible to see the beginnings of a fully fledged transport system, with the turnpike roads acting as a means of town and country integration.

The basic idea of local inhabitants being responsible for local roads, organised by parochial officials, remained in force until the late nineteenth century when the Local Government Acts of 1888 and 1894 finally removed all remaining parish authority to the district councils.

In 1924 plans were put forward to divert and stop part of the narrow Bedlam Lane in Hope. A new road was constructed in 1925 paid for by Flintshire County Council.

Traffic congestion, pollution and noise still bedevil both villages. A by-pass has been planned for many years but, as yet, no firm commitment to construct it has been made.

The Railway

The development of steam railways in the nineteenth century brought great changes to travel and communication throughout the British Isles. The effect on industry was enormous, as goods could be transported cheaply and quickly, and people were able to work and visit parts of the country they had never before been able to reach. This was particularly true of Caergwrle, when in the late nineteenth and early twentieth century, many thousands of people enjoyed the pleasures of this once quiet village.

.Kiln Lane (Bedlam Lane), Hope, the road which was the main routeway through the village, became a quiet village lane after the construction of the by-pass.

Gresford Road, looking towards Hope. This by-pass was built in 1925.

Although the railway replaced the long-distance road carriers, there was still a need for the local carriers using a horse and cart to transport goods from the local railhead to the outlying villages, farms and industry. Passengers were also met off the train by pony and trap, taking them to the places where they could stay.

The 1844 Railway Act, proposed by William Gladstone, President of the Board of Trade, required each railway company to operate one passenger train at a charge of 1d. per mile. Carriages provided seats and protection from the weather.

An Act of 14 June 1860 authorised the construction of $5^{1}/_{2}$ miles of single track, running from Buckley to the small port of Connah's Quay on the Dee estuary. In 1861 the scheme for building the Wrexham, Mold & Connah's Quay Railway (WM&CQR), which would run through Hope and Caergwrle, was launched. This next section to be built (incorporated in the Act of 7 August 1862) was $12^{1}/_{2}$ miles long, single-tracked and linked the Buckley Railway to Wrexham. This railway would also be linked to Whitchurch, with branches to Ffrwd, the LNWR Chester–Mold line and to Minera. The building and maintaining of the WM&CQR, was said to be a 'public and local advantage.' There was, however, a great deal of opposition to the railway, 33 men, who were publicans, landowners and farmers in the area, signed a petition, one of whom was Thomas Peters from Bryn Iorcyn.

The line was opened for freight on 1 January 1866 when there was a joint working agreement to work the two sections as one. The main income of the WM&CQR was initially from the mineral traffic. Industry was flourishing and the railway provided the means to carry products overland. Mines, quarries, factories, iron works and brickyards all used the railway, sending their goods to the Dee at Connah's Quay and to all parts of Britain. From the Dee goods were shipped to Birkenhead or Runcorn which enabled them to be put on larger vessels for transportation worldwide.

The local industries developed branch lines, which connected to the main line. In 1877 Llay Hall Colliery opened a branch $1^{1}/_{4}$ miles long, which went as far as the exchange yard in Caergwrle, this branch was worked by its own locomotives and men. Iron ore shipments to Connah's Quay came from the James Sparrow & Sons iron works at Ffrwd and in 1881, 8,940 tons of iron ore were transported by rail. In the first six months of 1885 the *Railway Times* recorded that the railway carried 323,068 tons of minerals, 27, 823 tons of general merchandise and 82,140 passengers.

The stations at this time were called Bridge End (Caergwrle), and Caergwrle (Hope Village). In 1886 James Thomas was the station-master of both stations. There seems to have been some confusion caused by the names of the local railway stations. Readers will recall that the LNWR station on the Mold to Chester line at Penyffordd was called 'Hope and Penyffordd', while the WM&CQR line, Penyffordd

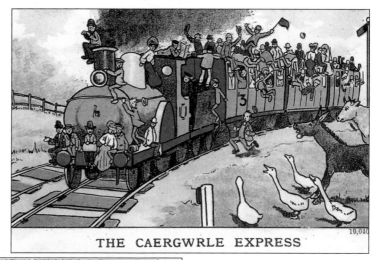

THE CAERGWRLE EXPRESS

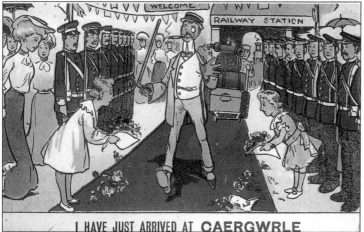

I HAVE JUST ARRIVED AT CAERGWRLE

Two examples of the comic postcards sold at Caergwrle in the early twentieth century.

Views of Caergwrle Castle and Wells Station in the early twentieth century.

for Leeswood, further north up the line was called 'Hope Exchange'.

Hope village station had an impressive water tank, dated 1900, a short siding with a cattle bank (but very little livestock was carried on this line) and a small yard with a wooden goods shed which also served a saw mill. Caergwrle Castle station had no room for a goods yard as it lay between the road and the river Alyn. An unfenced branch line ran to the brewery and was called Sharman's Siding. This was later fenced off by the Great Central Railway, and a gate placed across the single-track line in 1909. During the Second World War the line was used for transporting ammunition from Rhydymwyn and Marchwiel using American locomotives. In the event of an air raid, they were forced to stop under the bridges in order not to attract German aircraft with their sparks and smoke.

There were great celebrations when the railway opened for passengers. Flags and bunting decorated each station. The passenger service opened on 1 May 1866 with three trains per day, and the local newspapers advertised the passenger time-table. At the opening, trains only ran from Wrexham to Buckley, which had a large population and thriving industry. The passenger service to Connah's Quay was not official until later. The trains had 1st, 2nd and 3rd class carriages which were priced accordingly. The lack of carriage space meant that the locomotive's footplate was often used by women on their way to Wrexham Market carrying their baskets. No one was turned away! In 1870, the introduction of one half-day working each week and the Bank Holiday Act increased the opportunities for manual workers to enjoy the delights of our villages. The popularity of the railway was such that extra trains had to be run on Saturdays, leaving Buckley at 2.45pm and Wrexham at 9pm. Only first and second class tickets were issued. Third class was restricted to market days: Mold market on Wednesdays and Saturdays, and Wrexham Market on Thursday and Saturdays.

With the opening of the Hawarden swing bridge over the Dee by Mrs Gladstone 3 August 1889 the Great Central Railway, with the help of the Wirral Railway Committee, was able to extend to Liverpool and Seacombe. Freight started on this part of the line in March 1896, followed by passenger traffic on 18 May and many visitors began to visit Caergwrle by rail, travelling from far and wide to visit the delights of the spa and the castle.

The London & North Eastern Railway (LNER) produced a book *Rambles Around Caergwrle*, written by T. Lloyd Jones, aimed specifically at the railway travelling holidaymakers:

Route of Ramble no. 3
Caergwrle, Castle Hill, Cymmau, Hope Mountain,
Mountain Lake, Horeb and Back.
6½ miles
Cheap Day Return Tickets issued every day by any train to Caergwrle Castle

From	1st Class	3rd Class
Liverpool (Landing Stage)	5s. 7d.	3s. 5d.
Seacombe and Egremont	5s. 5d.	3s. 3d.

There follows an in depth description of the route to be taken over paths and stiles and a descriptive history of the area:

Mountain Lake or Waen Lake as it is sometimes called, is a tiny tarn pleasantly situated amidst heather and bracken on one of the shoulders of Hope Mountain. It is a delightful spot, very popular with many of our wild birds, particularly waders and wild ducks.

The rocky outcrop above the lake is of Carboniferous Limestone, the oldest rock in the district, and is of more than usual interest because of the presence of corals and encrinites, evidence that at one time formed the bed of an ocean.

In 1912 a report in the *Welsh Advertiser* said that a proposal had been made to the Great Western Railway on the Wrexham, Mold & Connah's Quay line to stop the 8.25am train at Hope Village for the convenience of Hawarden County School scholars, and they were also asked to alter the times of trains for the steelworkers at Shotton. This railway line is still used for passengers and occasionally freight.

Omnibus services

February 1914 was the start of a new bus service between Wrexham and Caergwrle which, according to the Hope Parish Council minutes, '... will be augmented during the summer months and should provide an attraction to Wrexhamites and others desirous of enjoying the pure air of Hope and Caergwrle.'

There was also a bus service between Birmingham and the north Wales coast run by the Birmingham and Midland Motor Omnibus Co. whose buses passed through Caergwrle twice a day in each direction. Another good service by the Crosville Motor Omnibus Co. came from Chester via Hawarden. Many other smaller companies ran lighter buses or cars when required. Castle Garage ran seaside and other famous resort tours to Llangollen, Rhyl, Llandudno and Colwyn Bay. A tour of the north Wales coast was not to be missed!

Bridge End, Caergwrle with a Crosville bus half way across the bridge.

Caergwrle High Street, c.1920.

An outing in a charabanc, c.1920.

7. Agriculture

Early history

The structure of land ownership in medieval times meant that the main unit of land division was the manor, held for the crown in return for specific duties and fealties. Prior to the eighteenth century, agriculture was much the same across Europe, and had been since the early Middle Ages. The system in operation was essentially post feudal, with each villager subsistence farming their own strips of land (quillets), as did the burgesses of Hope ad Castrum and Eston. From as early as the twelfth century, however, individually owned fields in Britain were being enclosed.

The corn mills

The Romans were the first to recognise the power of water. Their engineers had learned how to channel water in order to make it run faster, *i.e.* the mill race which provided the power for grinding corn and crushing ore. The River Alyn was the proverbial powerhouse in the Hope area, supporting not only the water corn mills in earlier times, but also the ever expanding industry e.g. saw and paper mills, during the nineteenth century. It is said to have also been used for the transportion of goods.

At the foot of Rhyddyn Hill, Caergwrle.

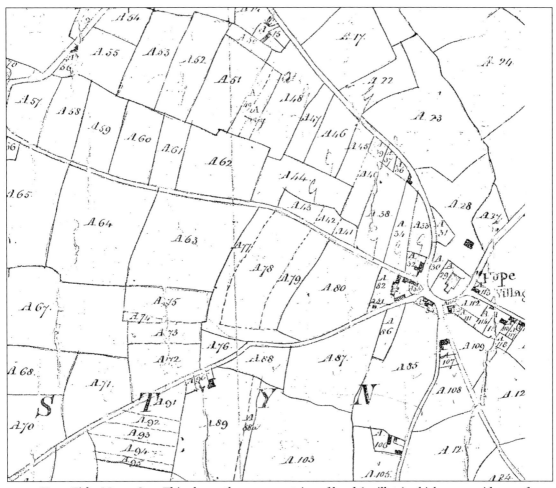

Hope Tithe Map, 1852. This shows the narrow strips of land (quillets) which were evidence of pre-enclosure farming methods. [Castell Alun Resources]

It is impossible to find when the first water-powered corn mills were actually built, but the Normans prohibited domestic querns and everyone was obliged to use the lord's water mill. There were three water-powered corn mills in Caergwrle, as corn was in plentiful supply. The first recorded date is to be found in the Minister's accounts of 1349:

Costs of the Mill — in agreement with one carpenter for one new mill to be constructed there anew by piece work, 60s.

In 113 carts hired to carry timber from the wood to the said mill, 30s. 2d

In iron nails bought for the use of the said mill, 3s. 6d

In felling wood for enclosing pond to hold back the water, 5s. 8d.

In making piles and filling in 18 perches of the dam of the said pond, 6s.

In carrying brushwood for the same pond, 15s. 1^{1}/$_{2}$d.

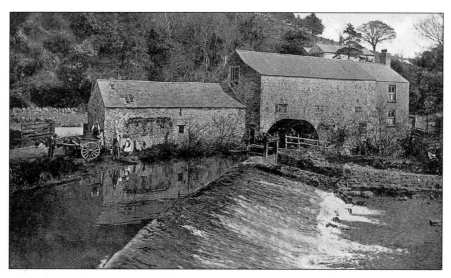

Bridge End Mill showing the sluice gates and water wheel.

In hiring divers workmen for digging and throwing earth upon the dam of the said pond, 4*s.* 4*d*. In collecting broom for the pond, 2*s.* 10*d*.

In carriage of stone for the pond 10*d*.

Total 6*l.* 8*s.* 5^1/$_2$*d*. [£6 8*s* 5^1/$_2$*d*]

Millstones, made from Cefn-y-fedw sandstone, were quarried from the Castle Hill and Hope Mountain. Every windmill and water mill had these large circular and serrated stones to grind corn. Because of the wear and tear brought about by constant use, there was a regular demand for replacement stones. There are still broken and half worked millstones to be found in these quarries. In 1611, there was a legal dispute about the monopoly of the manufacture of millstones between Lewys Yonge of Bryn Iorcyn, and George Hope who worked the Castle Hill quarry. The map will show where the mills were situated. The three water-powered corn mills and lands were worked by George Hope Esq. who rented them at £10 per annum in 1662. A lease dated 24 October 1662, for 'three water corn mills

[DRO DD/G/2936]

on or near the River Alyn and ... [a] parcel of land called Castle Hill or the Quarrey [sic], was signed between John Trevor of Trevalyn and Dorothy Hope of Gwsaney, with an annual rental of £10. A later lease, dated 14 March 1682/3, shows an agreement between Robert Roper on behalf of the Rt Hon.William, earl of Derby, and George Hope Esq. 'Three Water corn mills at Caergurley rent £40 or elsewhere in the Manor of Hope until 2 February 1683/4.'

A field named 'Erw Pandy', by Rhyddyn Hall, gives a clue to the existence of a medieval fulling mill which was later to become part of the corn mill. In 1791 the mill was still owned by the Derby family. The census returns for the period 1861–1901 show the millers to have been the Manley family. In 1861 and 1871, George Manley, and in 1881, 1891 and 1901, Joseph Manley, who was also a grocer. In 1901 there were two corn millers and one traveller who was a miller.

The 1913–14 *Bennetts Business Directory* shows E. J. Manley as the owner of the Tea Rooms at Mill Bank.

Bookers Mill, at Bridge End, Caergwrle went up sale on 21 March 1921. Described as a substantial building, in good order, three storeys high it also had a four-horse stable with loft and other outbuildings. The machinery consisted of three sets of [mill]stones, Eureka wheat cleaner and scourer, small flour dresser with conveyer, small Kibbler and Avery's weighing machine. The owner of the mill, H. G. Webb, who had died in 1921, had taken the flour to Birkenhead, where he had premises which produced 'Millstream Self-Raising Flour', Liverpool Products Co. He apparently bought an old fire engine and removed the top, in order to transport flour (1917). In 1940, a generator, driven by the mill wheel, produced electricity for the pavilion at Rhyddyn Hall, where evening dances took place which lasted as long as water holding pond was able to produce electricity. Mr Jenkins, the miller, was known throughout the area for his amazing strength. It is said that one of his feats was to take a full bag of grain and with one foot under the sack, and pitch it through the ceiling trap door into the mill room eight feet above his head.

The road bridge from Caergwrle to Hope was built in 1838, prior to this the only way traffic crossed the river Alyn was by a ford just below the mill. A small road passed at the side of the Bridge End public house, crossing the river and the mill race, and coming out at the bottom of Rhyddyn Hill near to the entrance to the Rhyddyn estate.

There was also a corn mill at Cefn y Bedd, which was sold in 1915 in the Bryn Iorcyn sale. It was three storeys high, with two water wheels, a loading place, stables for four horses; it also had electric light. The miller at this time was Mr Evan Davies had a lease dated 1910 for twenty-one years at an annual rental of £20. The Mill House (rental £18 per annum), was sold for £630 to the well-known local industrialist, Mr Dyke Dennis. In 1962 Evan Davies & Sons ran the business 'CFB Mill Corn' and the 'Cattle and Poultry' food merchants. This mill was built in 1848 and had two sets of millstones and two overshot iron water wheels of the trough type. It was fed by an artificial stream from the River Cegidog. Each water wheel developed 8–10 horse power. Only one of the mills was used to grind oats, barley and a little wheat for local farmers from their own grain.

An earlier mill, situated a short distance upstream, had been completely demolished sometime before 1848.

Land ownership

As the centuries passed great changes took place in farming and the local population. The fifteenth and sixteenth centuries saw an increase in sheep farming which grew more profitable as new markets opened. This often led to unemployment as villagers lost their land and grazing rights with the continuation of enclosure.

On 12 March 1609, on the Annual Fair Day, it was reported that three men from Caergwrle had objected to paying the Wrexham Market Tolls:

> three yeomen along with three others, from Caergurley [sic] were accused of refusing to pay the due toll on 'diverse cattle,' that is to say oxen, kyne, steers, heifers and horses and also about 500 bushels of grain, namely wheat, malt, barley, oats and passon.

At the end of the seventeenth century there were fewer than six million people throughout the country, however, by the mid nineteenth century, there were seventeen million, half of whom lived in towns.

Throughout the eighteenth century, agriculture continued to be the largest single employer. Even as late as 1811, one third of the labour force was employed in agriculture, forestry and fishing. Here is a brief description of the County of Flintshire in 1720 by Emanuel Bowen:

> The County of Flint is forty miles in circumference, contains about 160,000 acres, and is divided into twelve Hundreds in which are three Market Towns, only Flint the County Town sends a Member to Parliament; has twenty eight Parishes and about 3150 houses. The Air is good but pleasant, somewhat cold by reason of the North Wind. The soil is not so mountainous as in other parts of Wales, for here are many valleys and cornfields, loaden with Wheat, Barley, Pease, Oats etc. Its chief commodities are Cattle, Butter, Cheese, Pit coal, Lead, Millstones, and Honey, with which they make Metheglin.

The 1780s through to the 1850s were difficult times for this country with the Napoleonic

Wars, increased taxation, the 1790s blockade, and the French Revolution of 1789. From 1770 to 1813 the price of foodstuffs had risen, alongside unemployment with the increase of available labour. This resulted in many government acts, which culminated in the General Enclosure Act of 1801.

In the eighteenth century, rights relating to the commons and wastes were recognised in law as being vested in the lord of the manor and in the freeholders. Settlement on the wastes or encroachment upon the commons needed the consent of the landowner, as it infringed on their rights. Even so, because the manorial lords were often remote, as was the case in Hope manor, squatters could take advantage of this by erecting some kind of shelter for themselves.

The manor of Hope had 12,000 acres covering the ecclesiastical parishes of Hope, Llanfynydd and Higher Kinnerton, and had the geographical characteristics of a classic borderland manor, a mixture of Welsh and English cultures. It had first come into the possession of the Stanley family in 1484 when, after centuries of being a part of the Earl of Chester's Welsh estates, Richard III granted it to Lord Thomas Stanley, who became the Earl of Derby, gaining estates and increasing his political influence at court and in the north west. As the years went by, contact with the manor of Hope, however, declined, and it seems that only once in the ensuing centuries was there a personal visit by one of the Stanley family.

There were further changes in the ownership of Hope when Charles II was defeated by Cromwell in the battle of Worcester 1651, the 7th Earl was executed for his part in this battle. It was left to his heir to attempt to raise large sums of money in order to avoid his property being seized. A rise in rents was one way this could be achieved, but, as one might guess, very few of the Hope tenants favoured this arrangement. By 1654, Hope manor, together with all other Stanley property held in Flintshire, passed to other owners. Sir John Trevor 11 (1596–1673) of Trevallin and Plas Teg, became the new owner at a good price and held it until he died. He was a well-respected man of considerable standing with the Commonwealth Government.

At the Restoration, the Stanley's hoped for the return of their property, having sacrificed much in the interests of the Stuarts, but Charles II was unwilling to compensate his namesake, Charles, the 8th Earl of Derby, it being argued that he had freely entered into contracts for the transfer of his former possessions. Derby continued in his efforts and, by means of a private bill in 1678, the 9th Earl was able to revive the legal battle for the restitution of the manor of Hope by arguing that Richard III had granted the manor to the 1st earl of Derby on condition it was inherited through the male line only, and so Earl Charles had had no right to sell the estate in 1651. By 1682 the Stanley claims to Hope, but not to Hawarden or Mold, had been recognised and the Trevor era was at an end.

Edward (12th Earl of Derby), on his marriage to Lady Elizabeth Hamilton, only daughter of the Duke of Hamilton and Brandon, had agreed to the recovery of part of his estate for the provision of 'pin money' for his bride. This included the manor of Hope.

Edward was to become well known as the 'Sporting Earl', founding the two greatest flat horse races, which are still run, the 'Oaks' and the 'Derby'. He had the best studs of racehorses and the best breed of gamecocks in the kingdom. He enjoyed entertaining and gambling for high stakes. The then fashionable sport of cock fighting with his aristocratic friends was the highlight of the first day of the Aintree races.

These activities however put considerable strain on his purse strings and so his agents needed to look for new ways in which to raise his income. They would have been well aware of the significance of the various acts of enclosure which had been passed and of the advantage of replacing small encroachments upon the waste by large, well-rented farms. Furthermore Hope manor was credited with possessing valuable mineral resources, limestone, lead and coal and these could be extracted by adventurers, who could deal directly with the earl's agents rather than with a multiplicity of tenancies. The earl's consent was necessary to implement this bill, and so it is not hard to understand why he agreed and welcomed it.

The enclosure of land in the parish of Hope. [D. G. Evans, FHS Journal, Volume XXXI]

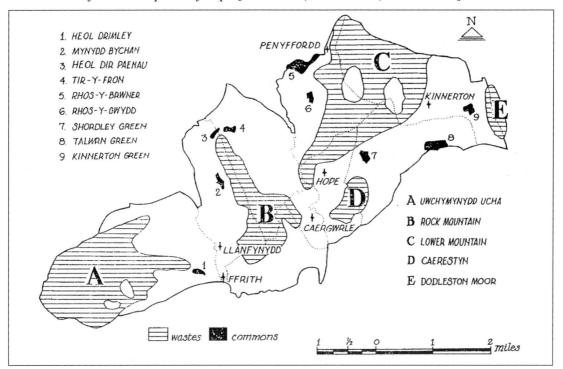

1. HEOL DRIMLEY
2. MYNYDD BYCHAN
3. HEOL DIR PAENAU
4. TIR-Y-FRON
5. RHOS-Y-BAWNER
6. RHOS-Y-GWYDD
7. SHORDLEY GREEN
8. TALWRN GREEN
9. KINNERTON GREEN

A UWCHYMYNYDD UCHA
B ROCK MOUNTAIN
C LOWER MOUNTAIN
D CAERESTYN
E DODLESTON MOOR

wastes commons

The Act of Enclosure, 1791

This Act allowed for the sub-dividision and he enclosure of the common and waste grounds within the manor of Hope in County of Flintshire, in 1791, the 31st year of his reign. It was to make major changes to both the population and the structure of the parish.

At this period in Britain, the poor certainly experienced hard times and many were becoming increasingly dependent on the Poor Law. Outside influences certainly did not help, there were the bad harvests of 1780s, and also rents had risen steeply by fifty per cent during 1780–90. The Seven Years War (1756–63) on the continent, and the American War of Independence (1775–83), meant there was a need for more food to feed our troops and subsidise our allies abroad. There was also a considerable rise in population at the end of eighteenth century.

The industrial and agricultural revolutions meant that agricultural workers struggled to earn a living as new machinery took their place. In 1701 the seed drill was one of the first advancements in agricultural technology, followed by the Rotheram plough (1730) and the threshing machine (1786), thus reducing labour costs and making workers redundant. Many left the land and worked in the new industrial areas of the North and Midlands, creating new markets for agricultural produce. All these factors meant there was a dire need to increase production, and so the commons and wastes were needed to increase the acreage. The supply and demand affected wheat prices, and between 1750 and 1796 they rose from 28s. 10d. per quarter to 78s. 7d.

The countryside was transformed between 1760 and 1830 as the open-field system of cultivation gave way to compact farms and enclosed fields. The rotation of nitrogen fixing and cereal crops obviated the need for leaving a third or half of the land fallow after each planting. With the possibility of more intensive cultivation of farmland, profits from increased food prices could be used by the farmers to invest in improved techniques of production. There were to be many changes in the way the land was used, crop rotation, marling and liming, selective breeding and land drainage, and in order to extend the total acreage of farmland the commons and wastes were taken over. They had to be fenced and redistributed in order to be cultivated in a profitable fashion.

These waste and common lands had been used by poorer people for grazing cattle, sheep and geese, also to obtain fuel, wood and peat, building materials, catch rabbits for food, and possibly squatting which were the beginnings of new settlements. This, in fact, was the only way of life these people knew, therefore to take away this source of livelihood meant deprivation and starvation for many.

They already had to contend with natural disasters such cattle plague which broke out in April 1749 in Cheshire, resulting in the Flintshire magistrates imposing a ban on the movement of cattle between the counties. Because of there precautions it was fourteen months before cattle on the Dodleston Moor had an outbreak. Sir John Glynne and George Hope, local JPs, ordered the lanes and tracks to be closed by fences and gates approving £4 2s. 4d. for this expense. Within the parish of Hope all movement of cattle was suspended for three weeks, strays were impounded and cattle inspectors appointed. Even so between 2 July and 6 August 1750, nine local farms lost cattle to the value of £29 18s.

We can see by this next document the cost of articles, livestock and labour in the year 1787, just prior to the Enclosure Act;

Labour	*Livestock/goods*
Cowmen 10s. 6d.	30 tons limestone at 2s. 6d. a ton = £3 15s.
Fencing 12s. 0d.	candles and oil 2s. 6d.
Labourer 12s. 0d.	200 Quicksets at 6d. (2.5p.) each
Labour 5 days ditching 17s. 0d.	clover seed 2s. 9d. (13.5p) per bag
The mole catcher ¹/₂ year allowance 10s. 6d.	Cow £5
2 months wages £2 10s. labourer	Land Tax £2 11s. 8d.
2 teams 5 days ploughing at 5s. each £2 10s.	Iron for ploughs £5 2s. 2d. wear + tear
Cowmen 10s. 6d.	
2 oxen bought at Ruthin fair £13 16s. 0d.	
by John Lewis who had 3s. 0d. for buying them.	
Team of horses man + boy 4s. 6d.	Black heifer bought at Mold fair £4 10s.
3 men, 3 days carrying kilns out, 12s. each.£9	Sheep x 9 at 10s. 6d. each
Moving + gathering, carrying 2s. 6d.	Tythe hay £4 10s. 0d.

In 1795 a quarter of Flintshire was described as waste or common land. It appears that there were various reasons which made Hope ideally suited for enclosure:

— the community lacked leadership as there was no great landowner present.
— the population could be described as poor, evidence from the church registers showed that ten per cent were on parish relief and ninety per cent were illiterate, and so news was passed by word of mouth
— it was a classic borderland manor, with a total population of 2,000, most of whom worked in agriculture or its related occupations, selling surplus to the markets in Chester or Wrexham.

The Earl of Derby, with his expensive taste in sport and entertaining, saw this as an opportunity to profit from enclosure and agreed to it being implemented. The statutory device of the enclosure bill was an ideal way to increase his income.

The first task was to survey the manor, which was done by James Heys of Knowsley and Richard Smith of Cheadle, each of them employed by the Derby estate office. Their initial duty, after 1 July 1791, was to divide Dodleston Moor by a ditch, leaving two-fifths in the Dodleston parish and the remainder in Hope parish. This ditch apparently still exists and marks the boundary between England and Wales.

The next stage was a requirement by the commissioners: Samuel Weston, of Halewood; Richard Hill, of Staffordshire; John Thomas, of Trevalyn, Denbigh; and Mathew Fletcher, of Clifton. Unfortunately John Thomas died and his place was taken by Thomas Boydell's son, Josiah.

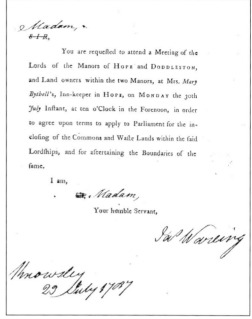

[FRO D/LE/679]

A meeting was held at the home of Mrs Bithell, who lived at the Red Lion, Hope, on 10 August 1791 at 10am. Those with claims to the rights of commons and wastes were to give the commissioners a full true and particular account in writing of such claims, of messuages, lands and hereditments for which claims were made, who was in possession and the quantity of land. Anyone who neglected to deliver such claims at the first or second meeting were to be excluded and debarred from all rights and titles, claims and interest in the commons or wastes. A notice to this effect was pinned to the door of Hope church, three advertisements were also inserted in the Chester newspapers. This first meeting was for Hope only.

The lords of the manors of Hope and Dodleston and the other landowners within the two manors, were included in the meeting which was to agree upon terms for applying to Parliament for the enclosure of the commons and waste lands within the said lordships and ascertaining their boundaries.

There were 81 wide and varied claims, with claimants ranging from Edward O. Wrench to the Mayor of Chester, which held 239 acres of charity land originally devised by Edward I, for St John's Hospital Without the Walls. Claims had to be registered by the end of 1791.

The next task was to allocate commons and wastes and to plan and construct a system of roads by which each plot could be reached. Surveyors were necessary to continue these public works. To raise funds for this work it was decided to sell off pieces of land and they were auctioned at the Red Lion, Dodleston, on 22 June 1792.

In the spring, when the stock was turned out to pasture, conflict between local inhabitants and those who had purchased the commons and wastes was inevitable. The initial conflict began when Thomas Jones, a labourer from Uwchmynydd Isa, 'on 12 April 1793 did wilfully and feloniously pull down a certain fence ... for dividing and inclosing a certain common ... and provided evil example of others in like case'. So read the charge. Eight days later he appeared before two justices to answer his offence, and a warrant of commitment was drawn up. He was then conveyed to the County Gaol in Flint to await the Great Sessions. On the 20 April his relatives and friends began their efforts to secure his release from prison. The leaders of this were Richard Roberts (a yeoman of Uwchmynydd Isa) and John Jones (a labourer of Stryt Isa), Thomas's brother. Support for the gaol break was sought all over Flintshire, from Harwood (Brymbo), Llanfynydd, Shordley and Kinnerton. Early on Monday morning, 22 April, some 200 men had assembled at Pontblyddyn where Richard Roberts was seen giving them ale. Having been regaled in this fashion, the crowd moved off on their ten-mile journey to Flint where they arrived at midday. News of their coming, however, had already reached the gaol and so it was locked and barred. After much negotiating and threats of violence the prisoner was released and the crowd set off home triumphantly. On the return journey, after more refreshment, the day's work not completed, they returned across Buckley Mountain to Penyffordd where at the recently enclosed Rhos y brwyner common, Roberts urged his followers to tear down the fencing and burn it, with the promise that when they got to Caergwrle they would be fed and have a drink at Mrs Jones's. This lady owned the Colomendy estate but resided in Derby Road, Caergwrle, where her brother managed the tannery. She was at Rhos y brwner with her mother and brother, urging the men to destroy the work of the enclosures. To Peter Jones's son she was reported to have said 'Why don't you work like the rest? You are a lusty man and how can you be idler than the others? You shall have none of the bread and cheese and ale if you don't work. There are crocks full of ale at Caergwrle.'

Before the crowd dispersed, fences were torn down at Rhosygwydd (Goose Green at the top of Platts lane, Penyffordd) and at the new enclosure adjoining Platt's Farm, Lower Mountain. They stayed the night in Caergwrle ready for the next day's work.

On Tuesday 23rd a hundred or so men began to assemble at Caergwrle at 10am, drinking ale before setting out to complete the task of tearing down fences. News had evidently leaked out as three magistrates arrived. After an hour of fruitless argument the crowd refusing to disperse resulted in the Revd Williams reading the Riot Act. Ignoring this and all threats, the crowd proceeded to wreck fences. By the end of the day all the commons were available for public use once more. The crowd were satisfied, but underestimated the determination of their opponents. Sir Roger Mostyn visited the War Office 22 May 1793, requesting that the Westmorland and Cumberland troops be stationed in Flintshire until the magistrate thought it was no longer necessary.

At the great sessions, which began in Mold, 15 August 1793, before Justice Mills, the trial of those arrested as a consequence of the public disorders in Hope was heard. A Grand Jury was selected from 32 prominent landowners in Flintshire and a Petty Jury from the 52 empanelled for the occasion.

Before the court were the prisoners Thomas Jones, Richard Roberts, William Jones, Robert Cook and John Jones. They were found guilty of the charges. It was normal procedure for such convicted men to be given hefty sentences, however the clerk of the court wrote on the charge sheets the words, 'Judgement respited',

[FRO D/LE/687]

implying that the judge must have had some doubts about certain aspects of the case. It is apparent that in other areas where there had been disputes the sentences were not harsh. It appears, as can be seen by the letters written at this time, that the gentry did not wish to be too harsh in case this should spark off further unrest. As far as the commissioners were concerned this was an end to the revolt. Twelve judges were of the opinion that:

> ... no judgement could be pronounced against the men imprisoned in Flint gaol for breaking
> down inclosures in the parish of Hope on the proofs given, so it would be prudent to apply for
> pardon immediately to try to prevent further trouble.

Sir Mostyn wrote from London to the Rev. H. W. Eyton, Wrexham, 4 May 1793, to say he was glad that the disturbance in the county had effectively stopped opposition to the enclosure, adding that 'some colour of excuse on the part of the poorer people, but when under the mask of such grievance, they are incited to murmur against all order and to be dissatisfied with their situation—this mischief requires the severest check.'

The provisions of the Enclosure Act involved considerable public works for the 4,053 acres, about 8.5 per cent was devoted to roads and byways, allowing access to the plots allocated to each claimant. Thus for the first time the manor gained an infrastructure of several miles of carriageway, forty feet wide. Today their presence may be detected by their straightness and by the width of their grass verges.

No land was allocated to the poor, or kept for leisure activities, but seven plots were set aside in different parts of the manor to be used by the lord and proprietors of estates for purposes of getting stone, gravel etc. for the repair of the private roads.

By the 23 October 1797, commissioners had completed the allotment of enclosed lands and from the Earl of Derby's accounts we learn that his tenants took possession in the years 1797-9.

During the eighteenth century farm sizes became larger and investment on drainage was required. Some historians argue that enclosure brought about more work, as there was a need to bring the commons under the plough and increase the nation's foodstock, many of the surplus population went to find work in the towns and cities. The result of all these pressures on production meant that changes had to be implemented in the way in which the land was farmed.

One such change was the practise of applying lime to the soil. At one time there were many lime kilns in this area, some are still marked on the map. These kilns formed an integral part of the Industrial Revolution as well as being useful for improving the land, and the lime was used in both the building trade and the iron industry as well as in agriculture. The Minera Lime Company at this time delivered large amounts of lime to various farms. For instance four tons to Plas Teg, and six tons to the Hafod farm. To the west of Bryn Iorcyn lay ample deposits of limestone which could be reduced to quick lime by heating, either in the open or in kilns using a plentiful supply of brushwood as fuel, or occasionally coal.There was a kiln situated on the Bryn Iorcyn site. The heat from these kilns did not go to waste.

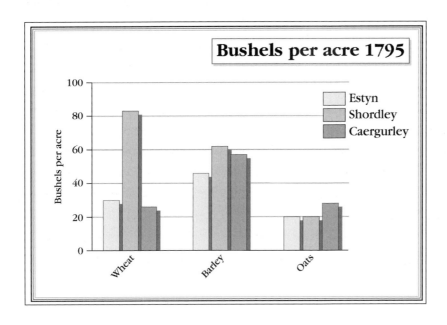

Once the top had been sealed people used it to bake bread, not of wheat, which required yeast, but a flatter bread, probably made from barley flour.

Another method of improving land management was crop rotation which was first mentioned in Roman literature. The three year rotation was practised by farmers in Europe, however, the four year rotation which was pioneered by the Dutch, was popularised in Britain in 1730 by Viscount Charles 'Turnip' Townshend, the eighteenth century agriculturist.

This system of farming was evident in Flintshire, the main crops being wheat, oats or barley, turnips and clover, which meant food for the people and animals. This four field rotation was a key development in agriculture. Turnip was food for both men and animals, clover was an ideal fodder crop and also made the land more fertile, improving the grain yields in the following year.

Animal welfare at this time could be described as rather bizarre, for instance we have the following instructions regarding the pig and the horse:

 If a pig was not growing a full chamber pot was poured along the pig's back. This 'cure' was called to 'Lunt' a pig.
 If a pig was lousy, tobacco was boiled and the juice was poured warm over the infected area
 If a horse was suffering from 'hot feet' he was stood on marshy ground.

An old book *Hints on Agricultural subjects-improving the conditions of the working classes*, written by J. C. Curwen, esq. MP, makes interesting reading. In 1801, because of the failure of the hay crop, and the cost at £8–£10 per ton, there was an attempt to feed working horses with steamed potatoes, mixed with cut straw. Needless to say this did not work.

The following accounts may give you some idea of how agricultural development progressed in the Hope area during the nineteenth century. There appears to have been an increased emphasis on encouraging as well as improving the people's knowledge of farming. Yields were greater in the first half of the nineteenth century. Labourers worked hard, becoming more efficient with the plough and scythe. The farmers' calendar of 1804 shows how different materials were used to improve the soil: soot, coal ash, peat ash, furriers chippings, horn shavings, woollen rags, sheep trotters, pigeon dung and hogs hair. It seems that nothing was wasted. For the larger farms a threshing machine was deemed necessary, this could be loaned out to the smaller farms. There was also an interest shown in what was happening elsewhere in the country and practical advice was given: 'take their nags to see what other people are doing, take a ride for a fortnight — 400–500 miles of country with an eye scrutinising everything.'

In the year 1818 the Flintshire Agricultural Society was formed to encourage both agriculture and industry. Their inaugural meeting was held at the Leeswood Arms, Mold, with Sir Thomas Mostyn, Bart, MP, President. Certificates were awarded for various activities connected to farming, labourers and servants. The candidates had to observe certain conditions, e.g.:

Candidates for the premium of turnips — notice in writing to the secretary before 1 August each year in order to give the judges time to inspect their crops.

Certificates of the qualification of labourers and servants required to be signed by Master or Mistress and by Clergyman of parish or place where service performed.

Claimants for premiums for stock meant that all stock must be on the ground by 11 o' clock and properly secured otherwise they will be disqualified, no stock taken out of field before 2pm.

> **FOR MEN & WOMEN SERVANTS.**
>
> Certificate of Servitude, and Good Character.
>
> We   of the Parish of   in the County of do hereby Certify, that   has lived altogether with   as a Yearly Servant, wholly employed in Husbandry, for the Term of   Years, ending the   Day of   and that Conduct during the whole time has been Honest, Sober, Orderly, and Industrious, and we beg leave to Recommend   as worthy the Reward of the Flintshire Agricultural Society.   Witness our Hands, the   Day of   18
>
> Master or Mistress.}
>
> Officiating Clergyman of the Parish of }
>
> To the Flintshire Agricultural Society. }

[FRO D/GW/1957]

In 1843, Sir Stephen Glynne, owner of the Hawarden estates, conducted a review of his property which included parts of Hope parish, with recommendations for improvements. The vast proportion of the estate consisted of soil of first rate quality, fit not only for wheat and bean husbandry but also for grass and turnips. The report said that although the Hope estate was the least improvable, there were some sound grass and turnip soil around the village of Hope on the banks of the Alyn. Other portions of the estate, lying between the old and new roads to Hawarden on the road leading from the vicarage to Kinnerton, Hope Hall Farm, Shordley Farm and the lands occupied around, were said to be poor, wet, cold soils, lying on a retentive subsoil and probably the least valuable of the district. The soil is described in detail as rich clay loam (*i.e.* fertile soil consisting of sand, clay and silt like organic matter). These farms were said to be in the worst possible order. There were also many smaller tenants on this land who neglected to cultivate their land or property and gardens. Often the tenants found employment in the growing industry around the area, carrying coals to Chester or working in the mines or public works. It was suggested that Shordley Farm should be divided by means of straight ditches and hedges, into 8 to 10 fields. Hope Hall farm was also in need of draining which was crucial to improving the state of the soil in the area. The fields needed to be larger. Most of the houses and cottages in Hope and Caergwrle, belonging to the Glynne Estate, were deemed to be in a state of disrepair and past redemption.

The improvements suggested were a regular course of cropping, alternate husbandry, straightening of the marches, enlargement of fields, improvement of farm steadings, exchanging land with neighbouring properties, reducing in the number of tenants, the demolition of cottages which were in a bad state of disrepair and inconveniently placed or had difficult access or were in the middle of a field, remote from public roads.

Horse ho-ing and weeding was unsatisfactory. Dairy farming was the main activity, no cattle were being produced for fattening for the butcher, only one or two tenants were sheep farming at this time.The Chester market which was only seven miles away had piers and wharfs on the Dee, which was adjacent to Sir Stephen's estate, from where produce was easily transported to Liverpool 30 miles away. From here exports could go to all parts of the UK.

The Drovers

Although there is no evidence in the census returns of any drovers living in either Hope or Caergwrle, they played a vital role in the forging of economic and cultural links between Wales and England in the eighteenth and nineteenth centuries. We know that there was an old drovers' road in the area. Cattle and sheep were taken by drovers to the various markets in Wrexham, Chester and Mold. They received cattle on trust, paying the farmer on the way back from the market. Travellers would often find their path blocked by herds of cattle and sheep. The noise of these animals could be heard for miles, and local farmers locked their cattle up for fear they would be taken with the herds. The reputation of the drovers was not good, and they were often described as a formidable lot with a lack of grace. Twm o'r Nant regarded them as charlatans and recorded this bardic rebuke.

> The old drover sleeps, his term completed
> Throughout his wasted life he cheated
> His world is now a narrow bed
> Fie! Let him cheat her instead.

Droving was still carried out in north-east Wales until rail transport eventually made it obsolete.

The deadly cattle plague of the nineteenth century was rinderpest or contagious typhoid — and it was fatal to the animals. When it broke out in the autumn of 1865, the agricultural industry was ill-equipped to deal with the crisis. Even when the disease was rampant droving continued. The disease was mentioned again in 1872.

The records kept by Mr W.Whittingham at the Hafod Farm show the stock kept on the farm on 1 January 1897:

    1 pony
    31 milking cows
    1 heifer
    8 yearling calves
    12 yearlings
    1 bull
    2 working horses (team)
    1 3 yr. old grey mare, to run milk to station
    4 colts (1 called Charley sold 1898 — £10)
    Horses — Rose, Jessie, Bessie.

The milk from two local farms, Hope Hall (Mr Bowman) and Hafod Farm (Mr Whittingham) was put on the railway at Hope Village station twice a day from 1 May to the end of October, and once a day from 1 November to the end of April. The farmer provided the 15-17 churns of gallons and paid carriage. The milk was sold to individual dairymen in Birkenhead, Seacombe or Liverpool. In April 1892, 24 gallons was sold for 12s. 6d.

Between 1895 and 1908, in order to encourage and pass on his knowledge of farming, Mr Whittingham taught pupils from various places. One such pupil, Eric Keizer was from Liverpool, his parents being glass manufacturers.

There were other activities on the land which attracted competitive meetings. In 1888, the *Chester Chronicle* reported that the Hope and District Ploughing Society held its 5th annual match at Saltney on 10 February. Men from Hope, Tryddyn, Leeswood, Hartsheath, Higher and Lower Kinnerton,

[DRO DD/WY/9061]

Hay making in the fields near Hope.

Llay, Broughton, Hawarden, Saltney and others from distant places took part. Hedging and ditching competitions also took place.

In 1913 the Hope Hall estate was purchased by Flintshire County Council, from the trustees of the will of the late J. H. Bowman, for the sum of £4,400, the property being developed as five smallholdings. By 1950, the poor condition of Hope Hall was considered in a report by the County Architect and it was decided that it would not be economical to repair it. After gaining approval from the Welsh Office, it was decided to demolish the property and build a new four-bedroom farmhouse. This work was carried out in the early 1970s. A sad end to a beautiful building.

Agricultural and Horticultural Shows

The annual Caergwrle Flower Show was held in the grounds of the Glynne Arms, a tent was lit by electric light in August 1906.

In order to show their produce and encourage competition the Hope Horticultural Show was held annually in the school at Penyffordd, the primary object of the show being the exhibition of fruits, vegetables and flowers by cottagers whose rent did not exceed £10 per annum and who had no greenhouses. There is a wonderful description and list of all the produce and entrants. The Royal Buckley Town Band played

Threshing corn in a local farm shortly after the Second World War.

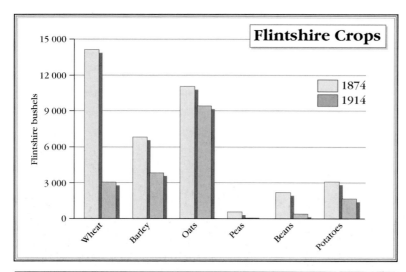

Comparative graphs of arable and livestock farming in Flintshire, 1874 and 1914.

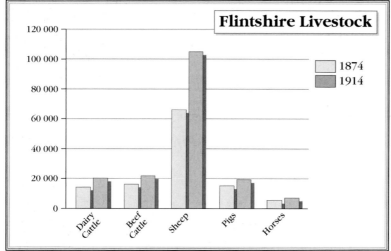

and many dignitaries attended from all over the county. Every known vegetable was entered, including eschalots, turnips, white and red cabbage etc. Fruits included gooseberries, red and black currants, flowers were a hand bouquet, marigolds, sweet william etc Prizes were handed out, some for the best plate of scones made from Coombs 'Eureka' flour, best oven bottomed loaf, best madeira cake made from Allmands Self Raising flour, best butter. There were also Caergwrle Shows and Gymkhanas organised by the Caergwrle branch of the NFU during the 1940s and 1950s. The 1948 Show was held at Hafod Farm on 24 July. The various sections were; Section A Cattle; Shorthorn, Friesian and Ayrshire. Section B; Horses, Section C; Jumping competition. Section D; was the Gymkhana with fourteen races, Section E; Produce which consisted of one dressed chicken, one dressed duck, six brown eggs, six white eggs, 1lb butter. Other shows also included a sheep dog demonstration, Flower arranging, fruit and vegetables.

Sheep being driven down the High Street in Caergwrle. Note the absence of trees on the hill.

Caergwrle Flower Show Committee, 1899/1900.

8. Industry

Before 1750, most men in the parish of Hope were part- or full-time agricultural workers, and some were home-based craftsmen: shoemakers, weavers, tailors, carpenters and blacksmiths. With the industrial development along the rivers Alyn and Cegidog, workers were attracted to the area and the two villages began to grow. By studying the deeds, census returns, maps and trade directories their importance can be fully appreciated. In 1851 Robert Hayes had a wheelwright's shop in Lower Street employing six men. There were wheelwrights in Caergwrle until 1901. Brooms and besoms were manufactured in small workshops until the 1860s. On the 1870 Ordnance Survey map a sawpit is marked at the bottom of Castle Street, where two sawyers, one ('top dog') standing on a trestle above the tree trunk and the other ('under dog') in the pit, would cut through the timber using a long saw. In the 1871 census there were two tailors, six dressmakers, three shoemakers, a knitter and a milliner. Building workers included carpenters, slaters, a thatcher, stone masons, brick makers and layers, plasterers, nail makers, house painters and a wood turner.

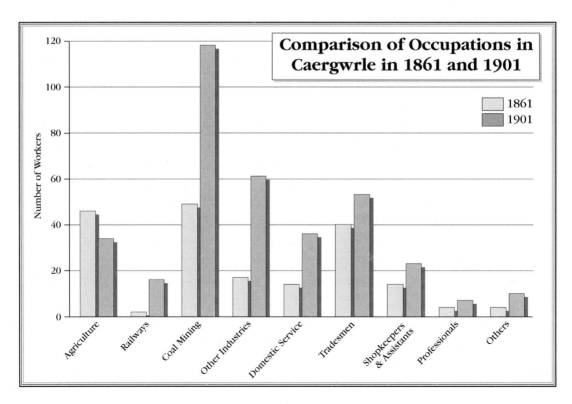

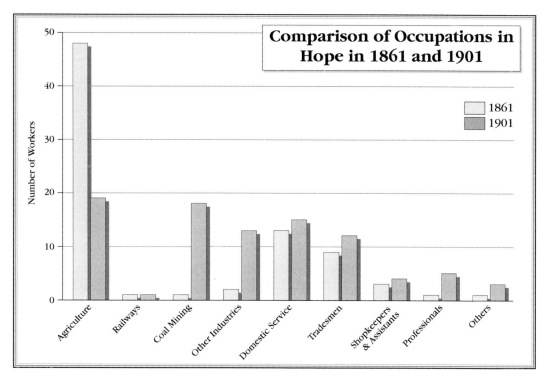

Coal and iron

The coal measures and iron stone beneath Hopedale have been mined for hundreds of years. In 1282 'John the miner' helped to clear the well at Caergwrle Castle, earning 3*d*. a day. In 1351 it was stipulated that the profits from mines in the area were for the Prince's use. His chamberlain also ordered forges to be built in the Forest of Rusty (Yr Estyn) and the Prince be paid 20 marks annually.

Many villagers not only worked in the fields but also dug coal from visible outcrops and shallow shafts known as 'bell pits'. As wood supplies diminished, due to deforestation and enclosure of the land, the need for another fuel encouraged more coal mining in the district. The Industrial Revolution and the development of iron making, meant a greater demand for coal throughout the country. Iron was smelted with charcoal until 1709 when Abraham Darby, from Coalbrookdale, discovered how to use coke for the process. John Wilkinson set up an iron works at Bersham in 1753 and more local iron works were built at Brymbo (1792), Leeswood and Coed Talon (from 1819) and Ffrwd (1824). To meet the demand for coking coal mine shafts were sunk in the valleys of the River Alyn at Hope and Abermorddu and the River Cegidog at Ffrwd.

As Britain's population was steadily increasing, workers and their families came from Welsh speaking rural areas and from English industrial centres to work in the new mines and iron works of north-east Wales.

Mining was very dangerous and noxious gases were a constant hazard, and one such gas was firedamp (methane), which was formed during the decay of vegetable matter and its conversion into coal. The chief danger of firedamp was its explosive properties under certain conditions. Candles were used for lighting until 1815 when Sir Humphrey Davy invented the safety lamp. The introduction of the safety lamp into the north Wales pits was rather slow and some colliery managers were indifferent to the safety issues, whilst colliers and their wives were not convinced that it was safe and the men had to buy their own lamps.

Good ventilation was essential in mining operations. Fresh air helped underground workers and pit ponies by diluting noxious and inflammable gases, carrying away dust and cooling deep working areas. Water had to be pumped out of the mines, so both water and coal were brought to the surface by horse whims or gins, steam engines and later electricity.

Until the nineteenth century coal was mined by the pillar and stall method, where pillars of coal were left to support the roof. Later timber props were used for this purpose, allowing coal to be removed more efficiently along a long working face. In north Wales deep coal measures could not be accessed until new technology made it possible.

In the 1830s and 1840s there were periods of severe depression in the coalfield. Soup kitchens gave relief to miners' families and coal and iron masters faced bankruptcy. In 1831 local miners marched to try to improve their wages to 3s. a day. They worked a twelve hour shift, six days a week. A report of the employment of children in mines was presented to Parliament in 1842. The conditions revealed by this illustrated document were very shocking. As a result an act was passed forbidding the employment underground of women and children under the age of 13. Mr H. H. Jones was the Inspector for North Wales, and he reported that boys as young as seven, but often nine or ten, worked underground, some attending to air doors and others dragging coal wagons containing two to four hundredweight of coal. At the time boys were paid 1s.–1s. 6d. a day, the men earned 13s.–15s. a week. Some girls and women worked on the surface sorting coal and were being paid 6d.–1s. a day. Children were essential workers and adults depended upon them. Colliers took their own children into the mines when they were physically able, and families relied on their financial contribution. The Report also showed that miners lived mostly on bread (of barley or oats), butter, potatoes, milk or broth, sometimes bacon, but very little meat except occasionally on Sundays.

By the mid nineteenth century, the fortunes of the coal industry had begun to improve. The rapid growth of the urban population meant an increased demand for household coal and the development of the railways, steam-powered ships and machin-

A child drawing a coal wagon in a colliery.

The canal at Ffrwd with Caergwrle Castle in the distance. [FRO PR/647]

ery, plus the production of coal gas, opened new markets.

There were times of industrial unrest, but on the whole relations were good in this area, since most men were averse to political radicalisation and some mine owners were willing to work closely with the men to avoid conflict. In 1826 a Coal Miners' Friendly Society was set up and from 1878 the North Wales Permanent Relief Society gave support to injured miners. Edward Hughes and his son Hugh Hughes were trade union pioneers in north Wales covering the period 1878–1932 and both men worked hard to avoid strikes at all costs by getting consensual agreements with mine owners. This did not meet with the approval of all miners, for at a meeting in Wrexham in 1882 local colliers were condemned for not supporting a proposed Alliance of Miners. During the 1890s the Denbighshire and Flintshire Miners Federation was established, earlier attempts having been spasmodic and unsuccessful. Later the National Union of Miners was dominant.

Disused canal bed at Sydallt.

Initially poor roads meant that the carriage of coal was expensive because the roads were often impassable in the winter and coal had to be stockpiled until the weather improved. However roads built by the turnpike trusts in the late eighteenth and early nineteenth centuries did relieve the situation. As the area became more industrialised there was a greater need to be able to transport raw materials and finished goods cheaply and quickly. Two influential local industrialists, John Wilkinson and Richard Kirk, sat on a committee which proposed the building of a canal. In 1796 an Act of Parliament authorised the construction of a series of canals from the Cheshire Plain to Ruabon and then on to Ellesmere, thus linking the rivers Severn, Dee and Mersey. A Western Canal Scheme was planned to have a series of locks at Gwersyllt and from there a small branch canal would be built to pass through Ffrwd and Llanfynydd to Coed Talon. In fact two canal basins were excavated at Gwersyllt and Ffrwd, linked by three miles of canal. This ambitious scheme was abandoned as being too expensive, and part of the canal bed was used to lay the Wrexham, Mold & Connah's Quay Railway which opened on 1 January 1866. There were rail branch lines to the Ffrwd colliery and iron works, Llay Hall Colliery and Brickworks and Caergwrle Brewery. Prior to this, in 1847, a horse-drawn tramway was opened between Ffrwd, Brynmally and Broughton, to facilitate the movement of coal and iron ore.

Ffrwd Ironworks and Colliery

The early history of this colliery is not known but records show that Richard Kirk of Brynmally worked the mine from 1796–1815. In 1824, John Thompson, a coal and ironmaster from Wigan, took over and set up the ironworks by completing the building of furnaces, which had begun in 1820/21. Three years later the miners went on strike, being discontented with their low wages, perceived frauds in the weighing of the coal and the difficult conditions underground. A handbill is mentioned in *Bygones* (1929):

Ffrwd Ironworks, 1889.
[FRO D/WM/283]

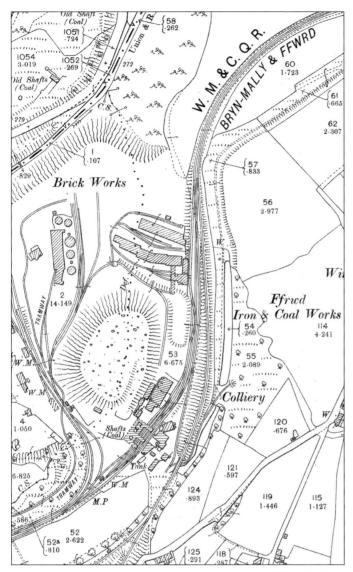

Industrial map of Ffrwd, 1890.

WANTED IMMEDIATELY
200 COLLIERS
Men who will work will receive
2s. 9d. per day.
THE COLLIERS AT THE FROOD
WORKS HAVE REFUSED
TO WORK FOR THE ABOVE
WAGES.
APPLY AT THE FROOD WORKS.

In 1854/5 an engineer named James Sparrow took over the company and was joined in the venture by his sons and Samuel Poole, an experienced ironmaster from Lancashire. Mr Poole, who lived at Rhyddyn Hall, died in 1872 and the Sparrows continued to run this very successful iron-works, coke oven, brickworks and three collieries all in close proximity. By 1880 there were two blast furnaces which used 49 cwts coal and 45 cwts of ore to make a ton of pig iron. Unfortunately in the early 1890s there was an economic depression which resulted in a slump in the iron trade, forcing the Sparrows to close the blast furnaces, and they were not reopened until 1899. This depression also affected the coal market and many pit owners had reduced miners wages causing industrial unrest. The workforce at Ffrwd however decided they had no grievances and continued to work.

On August Bank Holiday 1893, when the mine was closed, a fire broke out above ground. Ffrwd men, neighbouring colliery owners, officials and workmen helped the Wrexham Fire Brigade stop the fire from spreading into the pit workings, but unfortunately there was extensive damage to the surface equipment. An eye witness report in the *Wrexham Advertiser* read:

[FRO D/WM/283]

Confused heaps of charred timbers of the pit bank, remains of pit wagons, screens, etc. half melted cast iron plates, broken pulleys and the broken skeleton of the ventilating fan mark the spot of this large colliery ... At a meeting of Ffrwd workmen and miners held on Tuesday morning it was resolved, in order to show sympathy with their employers in their heavy losses, to work to a man for the week gratis to clear away the debris.

The men realised the need to get the air compressors and pumps working to avoid underground flooding. In a letter to the same newspaper James Sparrow declared that, 'the Ffrwd men are our sincere friends.' He and his son, Major H. Sparrow, felt that they had a responsibility for their workforce and decided to repair and reopen the mine at some financial sacrifice. The damage was estimated have cost at least £3,000. Mr Sparrow who represented the North Wales Coal Owners Association, which was set up in 1875, gave a speech in 1895 saying:

> The masters could not be prosperous if the men were not so too. When I first came to Wales the wages were less than in Lancashire. Forty years have changed all that. Men can now speak English and can move from one part of the country to another.

In 1901, the works had 265 employees of which 241 worked underground. The following year James Sparrow died and in January 1904 the colliery was closed, unable to weather a great depression in the coal trade.

Benjamin Whittingham, born 1824, was furnace manager at the Ffrwd Ironworks for 21 years and was given the above illuminated address on his retirement 14 June 1889. His son William was a blacksmith at the ironworks, he earned £69 *per annum* in 1886.

Pont Plas Maen Colliery (by Ffrwd)

In 1726, four businessmen took the lease of this mine, but by 1759, Sir John Glynne from Hawarden had acquired the site and by 1768 it was a well-established colliery. The hazards of mining at Pont Plas Maen were reported in the *Chester Chronicle* in September 1775: 'four miners were burnt in a sulphurous exhalation', and later in the same month 'one man killed and three badly burnt'. The next year there was a blasting accident, and in 1777 operations were suspended after two major accidents. There is some evidence that mining was restarted on a small scale in the 1800s and James Kyrke of Brymbo had interests in the mine in 1849. A new pit was sunk near to the site of the old workings in 1864, very likely by the Sparrows and Poole of the Ffrwd colliery. The closure date of this mine is unknown.

Llay Hall Colliery

This colliery was situated in Cefn-y-bedd. Before 1873 an iron and wire works, driven by water power from the River Alyn, and a clay works were operating on this site.

In 1873 the Llay Hall Coal, Iron & Firebrick Co. was established, spending £120,000 on buying and developing the site. The sinking of a pit began under the direction of Mr E. Stanley Clark, a mining engineer, and by 1877 the operation was completed. The sinking contractor was John Fidler of Derbyshire. An explosion occurred at the pit killing

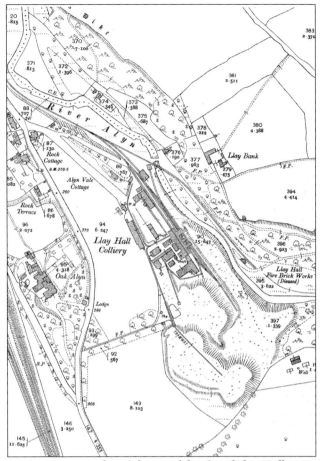

Industrial map of the site of Llay Hall, 1912.

two men and ten horses in 1881, however winding was soon resumed. The company eventually got into financial difficulties, and on 26 October 1881 was sold at a liquidation sale at Chester. The sale catalogue gives us a fascinating insight into the industrial activity on this site:

Colliery: The two pits 255 yards deep accessed main coal seams and had a potential production of 800 tons a day. On the surface there were three pairs of engines, seven boilers, shops for carpenters, smiths and fitters, three hundred wagons and three pit ponies.

The company sold coal to merchants in Birkenhead and had connections with the steam ship and railway companies.

Clayworks: These were equipped to make sanitary pipes, tiles, vases and bricks. There were seven kilns, three for pipe and two for brick production.

Ironworks: These buildings contained six puddling and two heated furnaces also a five ton hammer used to manufacture bars and sheets of pig iron. Power was obtained from a breast

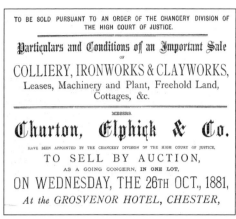

TO BE SOLD PURSUANT TO AN ORDER OF THE CHANCERY DIVISION OF THE HIGH COURT OF JUSTICE.

Particulars and Conditions of an Important Sale

OF

COLLIERY, IRONWORKS & CLAYWORKS,

Leases, Machinery and Plant, Freehold Land, Cottages, &c.

MESSRS.

Churton, Elphick & Co.

HAVE BEEN APPOINTED BY THE CHANCERY DIVISION OF THE HIGH COURT OF JUSTICE,

TO SELL BY AUCTION,

AS A GOING CONCERN, IN ONE LOT,

ON WEDNESDAY, THE 26TH OCT., 1881,

At the GROSVENOR HOTEL, CHESTER,

[FRO D/C/110]

water wheel turned by the River Alyn as well as a steam engine.

Railway: A light railway line, one and a quarter miles in length, had been built to link the site to the Wrexham, Mold & Connah's Quay Railway, later taken-over as part of the LNER. There was a locomotive shed on site as well as a depot at Wrexham, used to supply that town with coal and clay goods.

Workers Cottages: There were thirty cottages accessed behind the New Inn, let at 4/- per week.

After further financial difficulties the company was taken over by Mr E. Stanley Clark in 1885. He proved to be a remarkable businessman and the company prospered under his direction. As with other collieries, the economic depression of the 1890s affected Llay Hall, and in line with other owners Mr Clark felt it was necessary to call for a 17 per cent reduction in wages. The miners felt aggrieved and a newspaper report described how on:

> Friday 12 August 1893 an organised raid on the colliery took place at 9.30pm. Throughout the afternoon men, women and children assembled in the vicinity. Bodies of men, some 400 strong marched five deep towards the colliery. Some sixty or seventy youths with sticks and stones rushed forward destroying all the glass. One large water barrel and a trolley tub were thrown down the shafts. One miner was injured.

Mr Clark later received £39 'for damage caused by a riotous crowd'.

The strike continued for some months and the local community rallied to help the

Llay Hall Colliery workers.

View of Llay Hall Colliery.

The de-railed locomotive Welshman operated at Llay Hall, 1891–1949.

Llay Hall Colliery, 1947. Edward Huxley working as a banksman.

STATEMENT OF ACCOUNTS
OF THE
Llay Hall Colliery Accident and Superannuation Fund,
FOR THE YEAR ENDING JUNE 30th, 1899.

RECEIPTS.	£ s. d.	PAYMENTS.	£ s. d.
Member's Contributions	349 7 8	Payments to Injured Members as per list below	87 8 0
Proprietor's Contributions	198 2 6	Secretary's Salary	10 0 0
Balance owing to Treasurer...	2 9 5	Treasurer's Salary	5 0 0
Interest allowed by Bankers	1 12 8	Committeemen's Fees	10 19 0
		Auditing Books	0 15 0
		Treasurer's Expenses to Wrexham ...	0 8 6
		Returned to A. Shelbourne	0 2 0
		Stamps	0 1 0
		Carriage of Rule Books	0 2 0
		Cheque Book	0 5 0
		Expenses of J. E. Fidler and S. J. Young to Wrexham County Court, re Thomas Griffiths' case	1 0 0
		Cash in Bank	485 16 9
Total...£551 12 3		Total...£551 12 3	

Total worth of Funds £435 16s. 9d.

We the undersigned have examined the foregoing Accounts with the Books and Vouchers and we certify the same to be correct.

Signed on behalf of the Employer & Workmen.

Birmingham,   C. A. HARRISON, BARRATT, WEST & Co., Auditors.
25th Sept., 1899.

This Statement has been Audited and found correct.

July 12th, 1899.   THOS. O. YOUNG, PETER GEO. ROGERS, } Auditors.

It is with great pleasure we submit to you (the Workmen of the Llay Hall Colliery) a report of the Auditing of the Accidental Fund of the above. We have Audited the Books and found them in every respect clean and correct, and much credit given to the Secretary in the manner the Books are kept. Also to the Committee in the duty they have had to perform. Trusting this will meet the approval of all concerned in the above-mentioned Fund.

We remain,

Your obedient Servants,

THOS. O. YOUNG, PETER GEO. ROGERS, } Auditors.

JAMES ELLIOT FIDLER, Secretary.   SAML. J. YOUNG, President.

July 14th, 1899.

➤ PAYMENTS TO INJURED MEMBERS. ◄

	Wks.	Amount £ s. d.		Wks.	Amount £ s. d.		Wks.	Amount £ s. d.
Wm. Edwards, 64	3	1 16 0	Brought forward	29	8 0	Brought forward	65	6 0
E. J. Lewis	2	1 4 0	Phil Woolliams	2	1 4 0	Robt. Roberts	1	0 12 0
Jas. Bigig	2	1 4 0	Rd. Williams, 56	2	1 4 0	J. T. Jones, Fairy	1	0 10 0
Robt. Jones, boy	5	1 10 0	Watkin W. Williams	3	0 18 0	Dd. Jones, Bridge End	4	2 8 0
T. H. Griffiths	1	0 12 0	Robt. E. Roberts	7	4 4 0	W. H. Garston	1	0 12 0
G. S. Davies	2	1 4 0	Jno. Lewis	2	1 4 0	Jno. Crewe	1	0 12 0
Ed. Tudor	3	1 16 0	Robt. Edwards	1	0 6 0	W. Rigby	2	1 4 0
W. Davies (Fierce)	3	1 16 0	A. Shelbourne	1	0 6 0	Hugh Rogers	1	0 12 0
Ed. Lamb	2	1 4 0	Robt. Jones	1	0 12 0	Ed. Humphries	1	0 12 0
Jno. Edwards, Deputy	2	1 4 0	Jno. Challoner	2	1 4 0	M. Wynne	5	3 0 0
T. Wright, Deputy	3	1 16 0	J. E. Jones	2	0 12 0	Noah Griffiths	5	3 0 0
Jno. T. Jones, collier	3	1 16 0	Jno. Lloyd	8	1 16 0	J. L. Davies	1	0 12 0
Chas. Pridden	3	1 16 0	Ed. Jones	4	2 8 0	Jno. Ellis	6	3 12 0
Chas. Pridden	1	0 6 0	Jas. Jones	1	0 12 0	Ed. Roberts	2	1 4 0
Josiah Jones	5	3 0 0	T. Griffiths, Mold	6	3 12 0	Thos. Wynne	1	0 12 0
Ed. Peters	1	0 12 0	Wm. Jones, Caergwrle	4	2 8 0	Saml. Wright	1	0 12 0
Mk. Baugh	2	1 4 0	Robt. Griffiths, killed Nov. 28th, 1898	10	0 0	Geo. Griffiths	2	1 4 0
Geo. Bannister	2	0 12 0	Chas. Thomas, grant by Committee	1	0 0	Albert Johnson	1	0 12 0
Wm. Baugh	2	1 4 0	Saml. Pridden	4	2 8 0	Ed. Williams	1	0 12 0
Jas. Jones, bricklayer	3	1 16 0						
Carried forward	29	8 0	Carried forward	65	6 0		£87	8 0

▼ Printed by Edwin Jones, " Argus " Office, 50, Chester Street, Wrexham.

[FRO D/BC/2382]

impoverished miners. The landlord of the Red Lion, Ffrwd, gave 100 loaves of bread and there were collections in the chapels for families affected by the strike. A soup kitchen was established at the Drill Hall, Caergwrle by Mrs Trevor Roper of Plas Teg and Mrs Kyrke of Nantyffrith Hall. In October 70 families were receiving relief twice weekly (3d. for an adult and 1½d. for a child) from the local relief committee.

By the end of 1893 the strike was over, the men agreeing to return to work on the old terms pending a general settlement. Mining was a dangerous occupation and accidents often happened. In November 1895 the workers subscribed 2s. each to purchase a horse drawn ambulance van and Mr Clark gave a new harness. To comply with the Workers Compensation Act 1897 the Llay Hall Colliery Works Accident and Superannuation Fund was set up. Workers earning 2s. 6d. per day contributed 4d. per week to the fund, those earning less gave 2d. The money would be used to compensate workers for loss by reason of accident occurring to them while employed at the works and to superannuate aged workmen no longer able to work, they would receive a pension of 5s. per week.

When Mr Clark died in 1900 his eldest son, E. Stuart Clark, took charge of the company and proved to be as successful as his father, winning a major contract to supply coal to the Wrexham Gas Co. The colliery was electrified in 1902/3 and in 1914 a modern brickmaking concern was established on the site of the old clay works. Some coal seams were becoming exhausted and number two shaft was deepened to reach Queen Coal seams.

During the First World War colliers contributed 3d. and boys 1d. a week to aid war funds. Some men also attended mining classes held at Abermorddu School, their ages ranging from 15 to 50 years, and 11 of them sat examinations in 1914.

Llay Hall colliery continued to do well and was a major employer.

1901 460 employed   374 worked underground

1938 505 employed   380 worked underground

The colliery was nationalised on 1 January 1947, the Government paying £38,000 in compensation to the owners. Eight days later, there was a major explosion in which five men were badly burned and some underground workings damaged. The mine closed in 1949 with the miners transferring to other collieries in the area.

Thomas G. Lewis, born in 1905, was a miner for 47 years, starting work at Llay Hall pit aged 13. Too young to go underground, he worked on the surface picking dirt from coal as it passed on the conveyor for which he was paid 11s. 9d. per week. Aged 14, he went underground, his first job being to work with a horse pulling full tubs for 12s. 6d. a week. In 1921 he went to work at Llay Main Colliery.

Hope Colliery

Hope Colliery, also known as Gwern Alyn, was situated near to Cefn-y-bedd railway station. It was established before the construction of the railway in 1866 and consisted of two main shafts and a smaller one reaching the Brassy and Main Coal seams, which dipped south-south-east.

Parish records for 1863 show that the workmen from this colliery donated £1 10s. 0d. to the Lancashire Cotton Workers Distress fund. In 1875 the Lilleshall Coal & Iron Co. took over the colliery and developed it further by taking a lease on an area to the east. By the early 1880s the company decided to concentrate on their Shropshire business and abandoned the colliery.

Cefn-y-bedd Colliery

This colliery was established in 1913 near to the New Inn. Two tunnels were constructed under Windy Hill to reach the Droughy seams. In 1914, 43 men were employed, of whom 25 worked underground. This colliery was very productive and was worked entirely by electric power from Llay Hall Colliery. It closed in 1934.

Silver and Lead Mining

In 1881, Thomas Evans and Joshua Williams of Caergwrle sank a shaft on land belonging to Edward Smallwood of Caeglas, Cymau, to 'search for lead or any other mineral'. They agreed to pay a rent of 15s. and a royalty of £1 out of every £10 earned. In 1881 there were 12 men employed underground, in 1882, 9 men and in 1883 10 men. Between 1884 and 1887 the mining operation was suspended and nothing is known of any further activities.

Brickmaking

Two types of clay are found in this area: boulder clay and fireclay. Boulder clay was left behind on the surface of the land as the glaciers melted, and is rather like plasticene in texture and can be used to make pottery. Fireclay deposits are found within the coal measures. It is hard and gritty and is used to make bricks, tiles, pipes, chimney pots and pottery. Small brickworks were set up to serve the local rural area, the clay being dug from the pits close by. With industrial development the demand for bricks grew and larger brickworks were established in close proximity to the collieries.

Hope Tilery

This was at Rhos Estyn making some bricks but mainly drain pipes. It was put up for sale in 1855 by Mr G. C. Goodwin and was again on the market in 1875, but had closed by 1900.

Hope Hall Estate Brickyard

The bricks were machine made and stamped 'Hope Hall'. They were used in the construction of Hope Hall in the 1750s and on the estate. The works had closed by 1871.

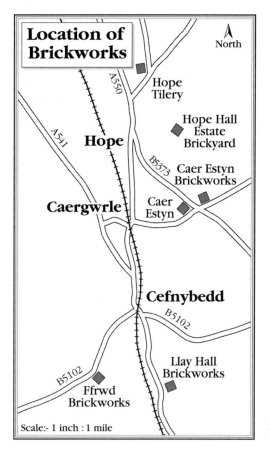

Scale:- 1 inch : 1 mile

Caer Estyn Brickworks

These had been set up by 1872 but closed later. In 1909 a 'new', but short lived venture was established making wire cut bricks.

Caer Estyn

This was an older brickyard where the clay was dug from the base of the rising land nearby. It was functioning in 1864 but had probably closed by the late 1870s.

Golly Brickworks

The brickworks were near Golly Farm. In the 1871 and 1881 census the occupants of the cottage were described as brick makers, employing men and boys. Ten years later the family were farming for a living.

Llay Hall Brickworks (see also Llay Hall Colliery)

Map based on information from Life in the Victorian Brickyards of Flintshire and Denbighshire'.

Llay Hall Brickworks.

The brickworks were established in the 1850s, the fireclay being readily accessible to make house bricks, fire bricks, floor and roof tiles, chimney and drain pots. The company experienced difficulties and eventually closed in 1871. Two years later the Llay Hall Coal, Iron & Firebrick Co. was set up and the chief engineer, Mr E. Stanley Clark, modernised and extended the brickworks. Unfortunately further financial difficulties beset the company during the early 1880s. Then in 1885 Mr Clark took over the running of the company. The brickworks did not do as well as the colliery. In 1914 Llay Main Colliery had begun to sink a new pit shaft and Mr Clark agreed to supply them with bricks. He updated the old site by building two new mills, an 18 chambered continuous kiln and re laid the railway siding. Work on the sinking of the pit stopped due to the outbreak of the First world War but the works continued producing bricks for the Ministry of Munitions. For the next 60 years the company was very successful but in June 1975, due to changes in the building industry, it closed with the loss of 20 jobs. The site of the old colliery, iron foundry and brickworks is now the Llay Hall Industrial Estate.

Ffrwd Brickworks
This brickyard, with two kilns, is shown on the 1879 Ordnance Survey map and the company advertised bricks for sale in the local paper. Brick making went on here until the early 1900s.

Paper making
This stone built mill was on the bank of the River Alyn between Cefnybedd and Abermorddu with a mill race 100 yards upstream. The water was directed into the building along a narrow concrete channel forcing it to flow faster onto the internal water wheel. Later, a steam boiler was installed to help power the machinery.

The earliest reference to paper making at Hope was in 1811 and five years later Samuel Price was the paper maker. In 1842 a 'new' paper mill was listed operated by R. C. and J. H. Rawlins until the late 1880s. Both these men resided in Caergwrle. Small, hand, fine and unglazed papers were produced as well as blue and brown paper for bags. In 1843, a female paper glazier earned 2*s*. a week and a paper sorter 3*s*. In 1880, an agreement was reached between the proprietors of Llay Hall Colliery and the paper mill for the use of the branch railway line to carry raw materials and finished goods. The mill was sold in November 1890 for £1,050 and the contents and machinery were sold separately, realising low prices as the machinery was by then antiquated.

The production of 'Vim'

By 1903 another business had been set up in the old works, where Flint & Silica Millers (run by L. W. Carder) was producing materials to make 'Vim', a white, gritty cleaning powder. Mr Carder, who was working with the Lever brothers, secured a lease to extract silica from Minera to be used in the process. In 1915 a sale catalogue of local properties showed that the mill was no longer in use.

Wire Mill

The wire mill was built downstream from the Cefnybedd corn mill on the River Cegidog. It was known as the C.F.B. Wire Mill, producing winding ropes for the local collieries. In the parish records of 1782 the Overseers of the Poor Law paid 6*s*. to the mill, probably to sponsor a pauper boy apprentice. The closure date of this mill is unknown.

Blacksmiths and toolmakers

The earliest reference to a smith was in the Chancery Miscellanea, a long and detailed account of the expenditure incurred in the repair of Hope Castle 1282: 'Walter, a smith dwelling in Hope' was paid 7*d*. a day for himself, his mate and their tools. Iron was bought for him from Chester to make hinges and other fittings.

Throughout the centuries blacksmiths were important craftsmen, shoeing horses also making and repairing agricultural, domestic, industrial and military items. In the 1891 census there were forges at:

Talwrn	smith	William Humphries
Caer Estyn	"	James Griffiths
Hope	"	Charles Martin
Caergwrle	"	Thomas Davies

Also in Caergwrle were the following skilled edged tool makers:

Jonathon Griffiths	Philip Griffiths
Joseph Griffiths	Robert Griffiths
John Griffiths	John Edwards

Caergwrle became an important centre for the manufacture of spades, shovels, scythes, shears and other edged tools. In both the 1851 and 1861 census John and Edward Davies were described as edged tool makers, working a forge by the Packhorse Bridge. By 1871 Joseph and Jonathon Griffiths had set up a business at a forge in the Gwalia, employing ten men. In 1890 John and Philip Griffiths worked the smithy by the Packhorse Bridge and were trading as Caergwrle Manufacturing Co. Both forges used steam power. The demand for edged tools and other industrial and agricultural goods was constant and so business flourished. In 1894 the family presented tools as prizes to the Ploughing Society.

The following advertisement appeared in the *Bennetts Business Directory* 1913–14

The Gwalia Forge Co. Manufacturer of Spades, Bill, Brushing and Danse Hooks, also Steel Colliery Tubs, Angle Bars, Suck Moulds and general forging of all description or made to customers own samples.

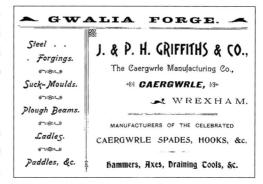

In 1915 the forge was bought by R. W. Lea, a mining engineer, and in 1925 he moved the business to larger premises on the Wrexham road. The forge specialised in the manufacture of mining equipment such as pit cages, tubs and colliers' baskets. During the Second World War orders were completed for local and overseas contracts including Russia. After Mr Lea's death in 1947, his son W. L. Lea took over the business. As the coal mining industry declined the company diversified making items such as fire escapes, snow ploughs, railings and gates. The railings around Mold Church were made at the Gwalia Forge. After Mr W. L. Lea's death his daughter, Mrs G. Leaney, her father-in-law and Mr Arthur Williams, the blacksmith, endeavoured to keep the business going. In the 1970s a decision was made to sell to Bostock Builders of Gwersyllt who continued to run the forge for a while. They in turn sold to Deva Forge of Chester who carried on the manufacture of wrought iron goods until the Gwalia Forge eventually closed.

Timber merchants

The old saw mill at Caergwrle was situated on the bank of the Alyn downstream from the Packhorse Bridge. A mill race 150 yards upstream channelled water to the mill wheel. Access to the mill was difficult, down the steep, narrow Fellows Lane. The large timber wagons, drawn by four to six horses, were challenging to control and accidents were not uncommon.

Two views of the water-driven saw mill on the banks of the River Alyn at Caergwrle.

The saw mill was originally owned by Lord Derby and then by William Whittingham and rented by Thomas Evans. The 1871 census shows that he and his three sons were running a very successful timber business, employing 16 men amongst them woodcutters, sawyers and timber measurers. They made fencing, gates, wheelbarrows, agricultural items and pit props for the local mines.

The Evans's timber business continued to prosper and in the 1930s the decision was made to move to a new site by Hope railway station where timber could be brought to the works by rail. John Evans died in 1944 at the age of 90, having built up this flourishing business. As an employer he was remembered as quick to discern a good honest workman and was known as a firm but appreciative master. During the Second World War Frank Evans and his men worked hard to meet the demand for pit props, which were sent all over the country. After the war Thomas Derrick Evans, and later his son John, continued to run the business diversifying into the manufacture of pallets. The continuing decline of the coal industry affected the need for pit props, and the business closed in the 1990s.

Brewing – 'Caergwrle Ales the best in Wales'
In 1860/1 Mr Lassell, a brewer, set up a brewery in Caergwrle utilising a good supply of spring water on the site. When extra water was required it was piped from a small reservoir on the hillside above the Gwalia, known as the Mountain Pool water.

An oveview of Caergwrle showing the brewery buildings on the right.

The business prospered and the pale, mild and bitter ales sold well, as did the invalid stout. In 1866 the Wrexham, Mold & Connah's Quay Railway was built with a short branch line to the brewery. Shunting was carried out by the railway company but the brewery's internal shunting was done by means of a horse.

The 1871 census shows the number of men employed: a manager brewer, four cellar men, three coopers, two clerks, a waggoner, seven labourers, an engine driver, a watchman and an errand boy.

By 1874 Septimus A. Sharman was manager and also a partner, and was living in the Brewery House adjacent to the works. In December 1878 he issued the following:

LASSELL AND SHARMAN
Rules and regulations of the
Brewery

Caergwrle brewery steam lorry laden with beer barrels.

Caergwrle brewery with the railway line coming right to the buildings. Wagons were shunted by horse power.

1. I have appointed Edward Roberts as my foreman, and in my absence I shall expect all orders given by him in the Brewery to be cheerfully and promptly obeyed.

2. Mr Povey will remain in the office, and in my absence will have sole control over the carters, who must yield implicit obedience to his orders.

3. No person (unless employed on the premises) to enter the Brewery.

4. No man will (under any pretence) be allowed to remain on the premises after hours.

5. Each man must provide himself with a jar and will receive at six o'clock every day in the office three pints of ale, if any man is discovered drinking other ale, or giving it away, he will be instantly dismissed.

6. No tools, or anything belonging to the Brewery to be lent to anyone upon any consideration, without leave from Edward Roberts, Mr Povey or myself.

7. No man to leave the premises during working hours without permission.

All men, whether carters or others, will be expected cheerfully to help at any work to which they may be set.

Any man who is not willing to strictly abide by these rules will be kind enough to give notice of his intention by Friday next. The rules will come into force on Monday next, 16 December 1878

Caergwrle brewery workers

The brewery kept abreast of the times installing a gas making plant to provide gas for all the buildings, including the workshops of the engineer, blacksmith and cooper. Part of the large cellar provided stabling for the delivery horses. Beer was taken by railway to Shotton, where a depot had been set up in Bridge Street.

In 1894 the business was registered as a limited company and beer sales continued to rise. Many public houses in the area sold these beers and there was an off-licence at the brewery. The Sharman family took a keen interest in all village activities and were generous benefactors.

In 1937 Lassell and Sharman's brewery was one of the first breweries to offer beer in a can. An unopened can of Caergwrle Ale was sold at auction in 2001 for £25. In 1945 the brewery was taken over by Burtonwood Brewery of Warrington and closed a few years later.

Paint making

When a fire in 1950 destroyed the London factory of Messrs C. R. Averil Ltd., graphite refiners and industrial paint manufacturers, the firm moved to Caergwrle where it had acquired the old brewery site. The firm found the buildings to be ideal. The main production plant was on the ground floor where three refining mills were situated. The oils, mediums and pigments were stored on the first floor and on the second floor the large, thick slate ale fermenting tanks were ideal for storage of raw materials.

The company had been refining graphite and making industrial paint for specialised applications since 1920. It was decided that new paints should be developed for the domestic market and in 1957 a one-coat enamel paint and an emulsion paint were being produced. Demand for the 'Alyn' products was such that production was increased to 200 gallons a day. At one time there were 18 people employed at the works, most recruited locally, working in the laboratories, offices and in the production plant.

When the company closed c.1970 the site was left derelict for a while before being cleared to build houses.

Quarrying

Carboniferous limestone is found to the west of Caergwrle and has been quarried for hundreds of years for building stone, road construction and lime making. Lime was produced by either burning the limestone in the open or in limekilns using brushwood and later coal as fuel. Liming land was encouraged to improve the soil's fertility. In July 1621 Alice, the dowager countess of Derby, appointed Lewys Yonge of Bryn Iorcyn, 'viewer, surveyor, director and overseer of limestone quarries in the Lordship of Hope'. Lime was also used to make mortar. From the eighteenth century there was a rapid expansion in the use of lime as a flux in iron making and small quarries and limekilns supplied local iron foundries. On the Ordnance Survey Map of 1879 there are seven lime kilns to be found on the eastern slopes of Hope Mountain.

Cefn-y-fedw sandstone is to be found on Hope Mountain (named Rock Mountain on the Enclosure Map), Castle Hill and Bryn-y-gaer. It has been used for building stone, road foundations, in glass making and millstones. There are two quarries where broken and half worked millstones can still be found. The first is on the slopes of Hope Mountain, this was owned by the Yonge family of Bryn Iorcyn. The second is on Castle Hill and was rented by the Hope family. In 1611 there was a legal dispute between the two families as to whom had the monopoly of making and selling the millstones. The very best millstones came from France but were very costly and during the Napoleonic Wars impossible to get. Another source was Anglesey but if the miller was working on a tight profit margin he was happy to have the cheaper Caergwrle stones, even though they were not as good as the others.

The quarry at Bryn-y-gaer has destroyed 25 per cent of the Caer Estyn hill fort. Over the years various companies have quarried stone from there. An area known as the Parish Rock, was allocated to the local inhabitants by Lord Derby, giving them the right to take stone. Alun Edwards, builder, used the quarry until the 1960s when it was taken over by Caird Environmental who operated it until the 1990s.

Sand and gravel

At the close of the last glacial period the ice began to melt and outwashes of sand and gravel were deposited in the valley of the River Alyn. In the 1851 census there were recorded three sand merchants (one of whom was a woman) and two sand carriers. Sandpits were at Fellows Lane and Kiln Wood with gravel pits either side of Pontdelyn Bridge, Fagl Lane.

In 1900, William Whittingham detailed deliveries to Lassell and Sharman's Brewery, Llay Hall Colliery, Hope Paper Mill, farmers and other residents as far as Chester. W. Piercey & Son of the Glynne Arms, Caergwrle were sand and gravel merchants in 1928.

Large scale commercial extraction began from the Fagl Lane sand and gravel pit. By 1986 the company, already working 54 acres was allowed to extend the workings a further 35 acres over a period of 15 years. One of the conditions of permission was the creation of a nature conservation area of at least one hectare in size. In 1993 the company was granted a further seven acre extension to allow the dredger to move into other areas without damaging the boundary land. In that year it was estimated that the current reserves were in excess of six million tonnes and the average extraction was 255,000 tonnes annually.

In 2002 permission was again sought to extend the site by another ten hectares

A millstone built into one of the walls of Hope Church.

and to dredge the existing working area to a greater depth.This would mean a life of between 10 and 15 years for the operation, which employed 30 people. This was not to be, as dredging operations stopped and the quarry closed in April 2004. Hanson's the owners explained, 'we have had some real problems of getting the material out of the ground'. Local inhabitants were affected by wind blown and wheel borne sand, also by the noise of heavy machinery. The large scale extraction of aggregates has had significant environmental impact on the Alyn Valley at Hope, where there is now a 30-acre lake which is attracting wildlife. The owners of the quarry stated on 10 March 2004, ' We will not be closing down and leaving. Restoration plans will have to be completed and we are looking to work closely with environmental groups'. It is hoped that the site could be used for water amenity and nature conservation purposes.

9. Utilities

Water and Sewerage

In the early years of the nineteenth century Edwin Chadwick shocked the establishment with his sanitation report. As a result of his findings the Public Health Act of 1875 was passed by Gladstone's government which obliged all authorities to install drainage and sewerage systems. It was realised how essential it was to clean up the water supplies and improve drainage, having identifying its devastating effect on health and the environment. Chadwick's research put forward the following recommendations:

Good and perfect drainage was essential.

Ample supplies of water free from the contamination of sewers, cesspools and housedrains.

Habits of personal cleanliness and domestic cleanliness to be encouraged.

There were open sewers in both Hope and Caergwrle and in 1909 there were meetings to discuss the sewerage scheme. Despite the opposition of ratepayers, the Local Government Board approved £7,000, which was to be funded by the whole of the parish. In Pystill Lane, a new sewer, consisting of 9 inch earthenware socket pipes about 100 yards long, was laid. There was still much to do in Caergwrle with regard to the sewers, but the council did recognise the need to replace them. In Lower Street the privies and ashpits of four houses belonging to Thomas Vaughan were deemed unfit for use and were to be replaced. In 1914 the condition of the open sewer in

SUMMARY of Sanitary Work done in the Rural Sanitary Districts of Hawarden Union.	1898.	1899.
(1.) INSPECTIONS.—	451	577
(2.) NUISANCES ABATED.—		
Drains cleaned and repaired	18	16
Drains reconstructed	29	31
Drains trapped	34	44
Waste pipes disconnected	6	3
Waste pipes provided		8
Cesspools abolished	1	1
Privies and ashpits repaired and covered	19	43
New privies and ashpits provided	18	36
Ashpits cleansed	21	35
Offensive accumulations removed	6	8
Houses cleansed and limewashed	7	8
Yards paved		11
Roofs and eaves troughs repaired	5	9
Overcrowding		5
Animals improperly kept		12
Houses disinhabited		5
Houses made fit for habitation		3
(3.) ACTION TAKEN RE ABATEMENT OF NUISANCES.-		
Letters written		108
Informal notices issued		42
Legal notices issued		31
Prosecutions		4
Orders granted		3
(4.) WATER SUPPLY.—		
New houses supplied and certificates granted	90	75
Old houses supplied	79	15
Samples taken for analysis	5	7
Samples condemned as unfit	3	4

Summary of the sanitary work carried out by the Rural District of Hawarden Union.
[FRO D/DM/661/6]

Fellows Lane was seen as a danger to public health, but it was not until the mid 1920s that a sewerage works finally came to Caergwrle.

The provision of water to both villages was initially supplied by wells. In Edward Lhwyd's book *Archaeologia Cambrensis Parochialia Queries* (1699) the following wells are mentioned:

Ffynnon Gyngar, within a field of ye church.

Ffynnon Baris in Hob Owen, this well boils up ... [Pigeon House Lane]

Ffynnon Ffragle, a great stream ... This was below Fron near Llanfynydd and was said to drive a water wheel.

Ffynon Deg. There's a place below Kaer Gwrle on ye bank of the Alyn which affords a Salt Water. Said to be below Rhyddyn Hall.

Ffynnon Goetiau; in a field opposite the Celyn.

Ffynnon Goch; below Bryn Iorcyn.

Ffynnon Garreg; below Cymau.

Ffynnon y Cyff; in Shordley.

According to Ellis Davies (writing about Fynon Gyngar) 'the water of the well was at one time used for baptisms'. It is said to have been near the church, at the end of Kiln Wood, close to Wat's Dyke.

The Pystyll (spring) in Caergwrle is a stone-lined outlet for spring water (Grade II listing). The Pystill provided a continuous flow of water, and was possibly the water supply for the early settlement.

The Pistyll in Hope Street, Caergwrle.

Infectious diseases such as typhoid and enteric fever were caused by unclean well water, resulting in deaths and illness in the parish. In Talwrn, Hope, one of these cases a man was 'ill for two days but went to work the third day'. All the wells had to be tested by the County Analyst in the 1890s

At the top of the Gwalia there were water-holding tanks which supplied Caergwrle with mountain water. One local resident recalls the well which was at the top of Kiln Lane and kept by a cantankerous lady who would only allow water to be collected at certain times of the day.

The scheme for providing Hope and Caergwrle with water from the Wrexham water works was passed by the Hawarden District Council in 1907. There were many strong objections from local people who believed that the supply should be from local sources. The Wrexham & East Denbighshire Water Company eventually supplied about 75 per cent of the houses, the remainder relied on the mountain supply which was believed to be of unquestionable purity.

Electricity

In 1909 a company of local gentlemen, including Arthur Owen Griffiths, set up the Caergwrle Electric Light Company with a generating station on part of the Gwalia Forge site. The company was one of the first in the British Isles to generate its own current. There was a great need for street lighting as was demonstrated in 1912 when a lady visitor from Liverpool fell over the embankment in Castle Street on her way to the railway station, and was 'severely shocked'. It was felt that lighting would ' encourage a better class of people to come and reside in the district.' The cost of setting up street lighting by the Caergwrle Electric Light Company was estimated at £27, with an annual charge of £15.

The company is mentioned in *Bennett's Business Directory* for 1913–14, with D. I. Price as Secretary. Many private concerns,including collieries, had their own supply. The Electric Supply Act of 1926 completely reorganised the industry and provided for the construction of the National Grid. More reliable supplies led to an increasing use of electricity for power in industry. In 1940 a generator, driven by the mill wheel provided electricity for the evening dances at Rhyddyn Hall. The responsibility of providing electricity was eventually taken over by the North Wales Power Co. until the industry was nationalised in 1948.

The Post Office in Caergwrle, c.1905.

10. Law and Punishment

The earliest reference to a legal establishment in the parish of Hope is 1351 when it was hoped to use the tower of the castle as a prison. No further action was taken however.

Prior to the building of the new police station at Caergwrle prisoners were held in a round building, at the foot of Castle Hill. Inside there was a stone slab, raised a foot off the ground, where the prisoners sat or lay down.

Plans for a police station and a magistrates' courtroom were drawn up and approved in 1902. On the ground floor there would be living accommodation for a policeman, three cells and an exercise yard. On the first floor, accessed by a staircase, was the courtroom and magistrates retiring room. Another staircase led to three bedrooms. In 1968 plans were drawn up for three police houses and a section station, to include two detention cells, which were later built.

The local magistrate played an important part in the enforcement of law. As well as administering local justice, the magistrate possessed the power to call upon the regular army and local militia to deal with social unrest. Magistrates were chosen by the Crown, on

The Roundhouse gaol opposite the Castle Inn, Caergwrle, c. 1840. Drawn by Henri Gastineau

Caergwrle village viewed from the Castle. Bottom left-hand corner, the back of the Police Station and, centre left the animal pound.

Caergwrle Police Station and Magistrates' Court.

the recommendation of the lord lieutenant of the county. Men could only be magistrates if they had an income of £100 from free-hold land. This system meant that they came from the established, land-owning families, rather than those who made their money in the industrial revolution. There was a magistrate's room at the Crane Inn in Hope which was later transferred to the Glynne Arms in Caergwrle.

The Enclosure Act at the end of the late eighteenth century caused great disturbances and the Riot Act was read on numerous occasions throughout the county. This was meant to strengthen the power of the civil authorities when threatened with riotous behaviour. The act made it a serious crime for a crowd of twelve or more people to refuse to disperse within an hour of being ordered to do so by a magistrate. On 23 April 1793, the Riot Act was read at the Red Lion Hope in order to break up the unlawful gathering of people protesting against the enclosure of the common land in the parish.

The system of parish constables was introduced into Wales in the sixteenth century, for the maintenance of law and order. In the eighteenth century these constables were elected by the Church Vestry, and held office for one year. Hope had eight of these 'petty' officers. The Vestry executed warrants, prepared lists of jurors and levied rates. Wages were also fixed by them. Self protection associations, financed by leading tradesmen and farmers, were established in rural areas in the late eighteenth and nineteenth centuries, to act as law enforcing bodies in addition to the parish constables. The *Chester Chronicle* of 26 March 1790 recorded the Hope Association's articles of agreement to prosecute offender or offenders who are guilty of stealing and, if necessary, 'to ride one hundred miles in order to catch the culprit, especially the theft of mares, horses or geldings.' The following were the rewards paid to any person who 'shall by evidence convict the guilty person:

Vestry minutes, 1850–63. [FRO D/WM/209]

For burglary £4 4s.

Stealing any mare horse or gelding £2 2s.

Stealing pigs or poultry 10s. 6d.

Stealing leather 10s. 6d.

Breaking or stealing gates or hedges or stealing posts rails 5s.

Robbing an orchard, garden or fish pond £1 1s.

Barking or cutting trees £1 1s.

Stealing corn or grain out of field, threshed or unthreshed £1 1s.

Stealing any corn, grain, hay, potatoes or turnips, or carts ploughs or other implements of husbandry 10s. 6d.

As the nineteenth century progressed it was felt that crime was on the increase, being associated with the growth of industrial activity. It became clear that the old system was ineffective. The Rural Constabulary Act of 1839 provided the justices of the peace of each county, through the powers of the Quarter Sessions, to establish a paid police officer for every thousand head of population. Flintshire however, decided to keep the parish constables, and it was not until the passing of the County and Borough Police Act in 1856 that they decided to change and appoint a force of 30 men, including two superintendents and three sergeants. The county appointed Peter Browne of Plas yn Cwm, St Asaph, as its first Chief Constable on 15 January 1857 and the new constabulary started operations on 21 March under a Police Committee set up by the Quarter Sessions and financed by a 1d.

rate.There were three divisions, Holywell, Overton and Mold. Caergwrle was in the Mold Division, headed by Superintendent William Thomas.

The duties of the constables were varied: in addition to catching thieves and criminals they served summonses, looked out for army deserters, impounded stray cattle and supervised elections. Constables were also available for hire at special events such as weddings, coming-of-age celebrations (21 years), bazaars and agricultural shows. Uniforms were provided by a Chester tailor for £3 13s. 6d. each, consisting of a frock coat, which had the Flintshire Constabulary badge in white metal, and the Prince of Wales' feathers on the collars. They also were given a pair of trousers, a hat, a cape, a belt, a stock (which was worn around the neck) and clasps.

The Flintshire Constabulary continued to operate until 1967 when it merged with the Gwynedd Constabulary, eventually becoming part of the North Wales Police Force.
There were two or three punishment stocks in the vicinity, one at the cross roads near to Stock Farm, Shordley and the other near the White Lion, Hope, by the old vicarage. Repairing the stocks in Caergwrle cost 6s. in 1793; we do not know where these were situated. In 1792, John Fenix was paid 1s. 6d. for moving the stocks, but again there is no record of where they were moved to. In 1787, Thomas Griffiths was placed in the stocks as a punishment for a petty crime. Offenders were also often whipped publicly and made to pay a fine before release.

In the gaol files of the Court of Great Sessions for 1784, there is a reference to Edward Rees, labourer of Hope parish, having been found guilty of stealing a gelding valued at £10, the property of William Edwards. He apparently was not executed although it was a capital offence. At this time the practice was to commute the sentence of those found guilty and then transport them to the colonies. He apparently received a sentence of seven years transportation. This does not seem to have been carried out and he appears to have remained in Flint gaol, possibly because the loss of the American colonies made transportation impossible and the government had not yet begun to send convicts to Botany Bay in Australia.

One famous trial which took place in 1734 was reported in *Read's Weekly Journal* on 25 June 1734. When an election was held in Flint a bitter campaign was fought with landowners coercing tenants into voting for their candidate. Feelings were running high and, following 'the rejoicings on the news of Wynne being declared elected, a riot and disorder happened in which a voter lost his life. The Coroner's Inquest returned a verdict of wilful murder.' Thomas Eyton and Richard Lloyd were two magistrates who took the evidence concerning the riot in Caergwrle between the rival groups of supporters which had resulted in the death of William Roberts. Samuel Davies of Caergwrle declared that he had been standing in his own doorway when he saw Edward Jones, who threatened to kill him. With that he shut the door. When he opened the door again Edward Jones aimed a blow at him and he quickly wihdrew into the house, but William Roberts was struck with a piece of wood. Margaret Prichard of Caergwrle told how when she was walking home past Bridge End she went to Samuel Davies's house where she saw the wife of William Roberts, holding her husband in her arms, he had been wounded. She heard Edward Jones saying, 'By the Devil that he would kill both men and women that would shout out a Glynne.' This was heard by others. Elizabeth Davies said she heard Edward Jones shout that they would kill everyone who came out of the houses. Edward Jones, a black-smith of Hope, was found guilty of manslaughter by the jury. The punishment for this was branding, and so he was branded on the hand and bound over for £100 for three years.

Witness statements for the trial of Edward Jones, 1734. [FRO D/BJ/381]

11. The Brave Men and Women of Hope and Caergwrle

The men of Hope and Caergwrle have been involved in warfare throughout the centuries. From the battles of the thirteenth century to the wars of the twentieth century, there had always been military activity in this area.

One of the earliest pieces of evidence we found of military training and activity was of the local military volunteer company, which started in 1830. At this time, between 1770 and 1830 the Tories were the dominant force in the House of Commons. They were opposed to increasing numbers of people who could vote, and so there was a great deal of unrest and many reform riots took place in the towns.

In the 1830s as a result of these disturbances throughout England, Scotland and Wales the Flintshire Yeomanry Cavalry was formed. They were commanded by Major, the Earl Grosvenor, and set up in the winter of 1830 as a result of the malicious burning and destruction of buildings. Several troops were formed viz.: Border, Hawarden, Mold and Holywell.

The Flintshire Yeomanry Cavalry was discussed at a meeting of gentlemen of the county at Hawarden Castle, 30 December 1830, and it was founded in January 1831. The Hawarden Troop was commissioned in 1831 with Sir Stephen Richard Glynne, Bart, as captain. Each troop had commissioned officers, non commissioned officers and private troopers. In the Hawarden Troop there were several privates from Hope and Caergwrle:

> Thomas Huxley (1833), Hope
> Griffith Jones (1833), Caergwrle
> John Jones (1835), Hope
> Thomas Parry (1836), Hope
> George Rhoden (1833), Hope Mountain
> John Simpson (1831), Stryt Isa Hope

At first the men drilled in their normal attire with their horses in their 'rough state'. Their first drill was in deep snow in the February and they continued throughout March and June until uniforms were supplied by the army clothiers. Their first day in permanent uniform was 31 July 1831 when they paraded in Mold. Their clothing was designed in compliance with the wishes of his late majesty King William IV, i.e. scarlet and silver. Undress uniform was a dark Oxford grey with stripe of red to the cap and trousers. Dress uniform for the non commissioned officers and privates was a scarlet jacket with three rows of plated $^1/_2$ ball buttons without lace and a very small skirt. Trousers were of dark Oxford grey with a $1^1/_2$ inch-wide scarlet stripe. A pistol and a sword were supplied by the government. They wore a black beaver shako with brass chin bands, and a brass maltese cross with plated Prince of Wales's feathers in centre topped off with a brass crown and a plume socket. The plume was of black horse hair.

All the men provided their own horses which restricted membership of the Yeomanry to prosperous farmers or businessmen. They trained regularly and were called out for camps, great public occasions and at times of civil unrest. Unlike the Denbighshire Yeomanry, the Flintshire corps did not survive long and, as an economy measure, was disbanded in 1838/39.

In the 1860s Volunteer units were raised throughout England and Wales as a home defence reserve force against a fear of invasion from France. The Flintshire Volunteers, originally based at Hope, moved to Buckley in the 1870s. According to the *Worrall's Directory* (1874) the Flintshire Rifle Volunteers (Caergwrle) No. 6 Company was led by Captain T. Broughton (Caergwrle) and Lieutenant Dashwood Parry (Caergwrle). The Drill Instructor was a regular soldier, Sergeant John Welch. Both the Hawarden and Caergwrle volunteers used the rifle range at Barracks Lane, Ffrwd.

There are records of local men fighting in the South African wars.

In the Hope *Parish Magazine* of 1879, there is a record of the departure of soldiers to South Africa during the last

Castell Alun School Resources.

"F" CO. (Caergwrle) 2nd V.B. R.W.F.

The Members of the above Company and Friends,

WILL ENTERTAIN
Lance-Corporal WILLIAM ROBERTS, Private EDWIN WRIGHT, Private JOHN GALLIER and Private TREVOR PARRY,

Selected for Active Service in

SOUTH AFRICA, AT A FAREWELL SMOKING CONCERT

In the Drill Hall, Caergwrle, On Friday Evening, February 2nd, 1900

Commencing at 6-30 p.m. Sharp.

All Volunteers, Friends, and Well-wishers are cordially invited to be present, so that we may give them such a send off as they will always remember,

Admission Free, on presentation of an introduction ticket. Each person pays for what he orders.

Tickets can be had, free, from:—
Captain A. H. Sparrow, Grey Holt; Sergt.-Instructor Claridge, Drill Hall; Armourer-Sergeant J. Cooper, Col.-Sergeant T. Davies, Sergeant Piercey, Corporal Sam Jones, Corporal Wm. Roberts, Mr. J. Wilbraham, and Mr. W. R. Savage, Caergwrle. Lce.-Sergeant Pryce Lewis and Mr. H. D. Davies, Abermorddu. Sergeant Ed. Griffiths, Ffrwd. Sergeant James, Llanfynydd. Lce.-Corporal Taylor, and Lce.-Corporal Bickley, Brymbo. Private T. H. Jones, New Inn.

W. Potter, Printer, 18 & 19, High Street, Wrexham.

Parade in Caergwrle during the Anglo-Boer War.

Sgt Sam Eccleston, c.1900.

Local soldiers at the time of the Anglo-Boer War.

*Illuminated address commemorating the service of
Private E. Wright in the Anglo-Boer War.*

week in February, exciting 'deep public interest'. Religious societies provided each man with portions of Scripture and other literature. A Farewell concert was held for those departing to South Africa, 'F' Co.(Caergwrle) 2nd Volunteer Battalion. R.W.F., Patriotic songs were sung for example 'Home Sweet Home' and 'Rolling Home'.

The Hope and Caergwrle Volunteers fought in the Boer War. Here we see a photograph of them returning from the front in South Africa. They were to receive 'illuminated addresses' and silver pins on which to display their medals at the Drill Hall. The men receiving this honour were Corp. W. Roberts, Ptes. W. H. Jones, John Crewe, G. Guage, J. C. Williams and E. Wright.

The Ambulance Corps was also highly praised:

> Col. Sgt Selby rose amidst great cheering and said he had belonged to the RWF for 18 years, a regiment second to none in the country. The Ambulance Corps. in the army was the finest in the world. He had seen deeds done by them that would have won the VC over and over again in South Africa—but they were not recognised.

The audience responded with a toast.

In the early years of the twentieth century there appears to have been a Volunteer Company in Caergwrle. It was reported in the *Western Advertiser* that, 'The local company of 2nd Volunteers Battalion Royal Welsh Fusiliers journeyed to Mostyn Park for their annual drill … The Sgt Instructor, Noel Ridings, retired on 17 March 1906, and was presented with a marble clock and illuminated address.'

The First World War 1914–18

When the First World War broke out in the summer of 1914, for many people it was yet another war, which would be over by Christmas, certainly a feeling which was encouraged by the newspapers. This was understandable as since the 1850s the wars fought in Europe had been over in less than ten months. The events of 1914 however, marked a decisive turning point in the lives of thousands of people, after which the world was never to appear the same again.

The loss of life of so many of our young men touched most families and also the community. Both wars affected us, not only changing the way we lived but also changed the way many women lived. They were to become more active in different occupations which were often associated with the male population.

Recruitment

There were many reasons why men joined the 'Colours'. At the beginning there was a great deal of patriotism, and for many there was a sense of adventure and an escape from everyday life, which sometimes included unemployment.

A great deal of pressure was subsequently put on our men to join and recruitment meetings were held at various venues throughout the county which included a lantern show which showed several Caergwrle contingents joining the colours, also warships, aeroplanes and pictures of King George V and Queen Mary.

One of the first to join the Welsh Regiment in London was Mr David Livingstone Jones, Plas Newydd Farm, in November 1914. A large number of the Territorials, the 5th Battalion of the RWF came home after training, to say goodbye to relatives and friends, before embarking on 'foreign service'. 'They left on the 2.30pm train in the best of spirits with a hearty send off from a large crowd'.

A recruitment meeting, reported in the *Western Advertiser*, was held in Caergwrle 1915, appealing to young men in the audience to join the colours, 'Corporal Frost's speech was most convincing. Alderman R. Allen JP also spoke and expressed his willingness to join, provided six young men there and then volunteered to join with him. Lt King (of Hope) 5th RWF also spoke, four recruits ascended the platform.' It was expected that several young men would join, and patriotic songs were sung. In November 1915 the district was divided into six divisions, canvassers were appointed and were handed authority cards signed by Lord Derby and Mr H. N. Gladstone, Lord Lieutenant of the County. A 'patriotic treat' was given in February 1915 by the local branch of the North Wales Temperance Union for relatives and dependants of soldiers who had joined the colours. 'This excellent tea was followed by a lantern view of the war.'

As the war progressed recruitment appears to have became more difficult. A meeting was held on 31 March 1917 considering the matter of National Service. It was decided to divide the parish into ten districts and canvassers, mostly women, were appointed to each district, calling upon young men of military age. A large number of men and women, however, considered their work, in the munitions factory, on the farms and in the mines, to be of national importance.

One recruitment drive included a contingent from the Mold 5th Reserve Battalion Royal Welsh Fusiliers who paraded in the district. This was considered to be a good 'muster,' the majority of men in khaki, some in plain clothes. It had the desired effect of recruiting several men from Caergwrle and other villages in the parish. Nurses were also called up for service, Miss H. Marston who had trained at Liverpool Royal Infirmary, also joined up.

Voluntary Training Corps (VTC)

During the First World War, those men and boys who were either too old or too young for war joined the Volunteer Training Corps, an unofficial group which, until 1918, had no official uniform or rifles. They were the 1914–18 equivalent of the Second World War's Home Guard. According to the newspapers, a local company was formed in Caergwrle and Hope in 1915, although the numbers were not as large as expected. Drills took place in Hope Council School yard. The object of the corps was to train men for the defence of our Britain against invasion. It had been hoped to form a battalion of approximately 1,000 men in the Wrexham District which would be affiliated to the central association of the VTC and thus be recognised by the War Office. Men over the age of 38 were urged to join as well as youths aged between 16 and 18.

Rolls of Honour and Casualties of the Great War

Those who went to war would change, and for them it would be an experience never to be forgotten. Both local newspapers and the Hope *Parish Magazine* recorded 'Rolls of Honour' naming men who were on leave or had been injured or killed on active service. Here are just a few of the stories and comments recorded, a poignant reminder for us all:

1914

A number of the 5th Battalion home on leave to wish farewell before embarking for foreign service—hearty send off.

November. John Thomas, Private in the Royal Welsh Regiment [sic] killed in battle of the Yser. Information from a colleague who was with him in the trenches.

1916

Pte Sydney Pugh, 5th Battalion RWF killed in action on 2nd day after arrival of the battalion in the Dardanelles (Gallipoli)—Memorial service.

June. Cpl. Bert Savage home on leave, friends pleased to see him looking so well.

Pte. William J. Savage, Highland Battalion, Royal Scots, gazetted to 2nd Lt Black Watch, Royal Highlanders. He is the older brother of Bert Savage.

Pte William Jones Roberts, 10th RWF killed in France. The Commanding Officer wrote to his mother at Rhanberfedd Farm, saying 'he was a splendid soldier and beloved by all'. His brother has been wounded but is recovering in Ramsgate hospital.'

Pte Hadley Crewe has been recommended for a MM for his conspicuous bravery in France.

Pte Frank Evans, Liverpool Scottish, home on leave after 'stiff fighting'.

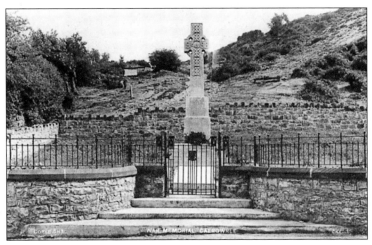

The War Memorial at the foot of Castle Hill, Caergwrle.

July. Bert Savage Signal Co. Divisional Engineers Royal Naval Division received Certificate of Merit for his service in the Dardanelles (Gallipoli)— specially mentioned by his commanding officer for zeal and devotion to duty while in active service. A letter he wrote to his father read:

I had to go along the trenches at 11pm up to my waist in ice cold water to repair a telephone wire which had been cut by a Turkish rifle bullet, and all the time I was at work bullets were whizzing over my head, which I had to keep low.

In another letter to his father Bert tells of his experiences in Greece. Riding donkeys, he and his friend travelled through small villages enjoying the peace and talking to the Greek people, being careful not to divulge any information about their movements.

Cpl W. F. Maddocks, RWF, killed in action in France, from Derby Road, Caergwrle.
November, Cpl Jos Gerrard, home on leave from Egypt.
December, Pte Ralph Henshaw, 10th RWF, died in Bethnal Green Hospital from wounds
  he received in France. Formerly of the Denbighshire Yeomanry.
Pte Edward Roberts, RWF, in France, reported missing, killed in action.
Wireless Officer Hugh Piercey home on short leave. Son of Mr W. Piercey, Glynne Arms

1917
January Pte Frank Evans wounded, son of timber merchant.
Pte Harold Parker promotion for valiant service, Battle of the Somme
Sgt W. Ellis on short leave from Egypt
Pte W. Jones, RAMC, on sick leave, congestion of the lungs.
Captain Robert Davies, RWF, on leave, numerous friends welcomed him home.
  Decorated with the DCM, presented with a wristlet watch.

February Pte Marford, RAMC, who joined colours early stages of the war, on leave.

March Cpl Cecil Oliver RWF killed in action*
Sgt Bert Savage promoted in Royal Engineers Signal section, now in France.
2nd Lt. Frank Savage RM Royal naval division 'killed instantly, whilst nobly leading his
  men'*
Frank Morris, RAMC, on leave from France after 18 months away.
Mr Cooksley, Flying Corps also on leave (Hope).
Pte W. Davies, wounded in 'eastern theatre of war' Erw Cottage, Caergwrle.

April   Pte Jos Rogers wounded in Mesopotania, had already been invalided home with frost bite, then sent back.

Lt Richard Allen (JP, Alderman), RWF, on leave.

August Pte. Fred Williams, Kings Royal Rifles ,wounded, died in September.

Signaller Rogers, Liverpool Scottish, wounded in France.

Lt H.Kilvert 8th RWF, killed in action in France

Capt. C. Trevor Roper, owner of Plas Teg, killed in France. 'He was a kind considerate landlord and highly respected by his tenants. He leaves a widow and two daughters. Son of the late George Trevor Roper.' Memorial service, 1 September 1917.

September Pte Tom Evans, MM, Welsh Guards, died of wounds in France. 'He had a quiet amiable disposition and was highly respected in the district.' Bryn Alyn Bridgend.

Pte Bert Jones, L/Cpl.Welsh Guards killed in action, Alyn Bank, Caergwrle

Sgt Thomas Rowlands, 10th RWF, Cefn-y-bedd, presented with Military Medal in the field.

November Pte James Dudds, RAMC, MM.

Pte Jos Roberts Evison, 9th RWF, MM.

Pte Geoffrey Trevor Roper, 32nd Royal Fusiliers, killed in action.

December Pte W. Davies, wounded—died

Dispatch rider Harold Eccleston, RE, of Hope Road, home on leave, looks well.

Sgt A. Martin, RWF, also on leave, to bury one of his children, has to return.

Lt Savage, Black Watch, discharged, returning as a chemist.

Lt Eric Edwards (Rhyddyn Hill). South Wales Borderers. killed in France, had joined the North Wales 'Pals'.

1918

January   Pte James Kendrick South Wales Borderers on 14 days leave looks well worked on the Great Central Railway before joining the colours.

NB. When leave was granted it was very short, in fact, soldiers from Australia spent their leave in north Wales on local farms.

Lt Cpl. W. A. Stuart, Linesman Signaller, East Lancashire Regiment (Caer Estyn), awarded Military Medal— ' He did fine work under heavy artillery and machine gun fire, and he showed a fine example of devotion to duty. He enlisted in September

1914 and has been in France and Egypt over two and a half years. His elder brother was awarded a medal eleven months ago.'

May Pte W. Arnold Huson, Cheshire Regiment, killed in France. 'Only there for three weeks. Spoken of highly by officers, age 19 years,' Mrs Griffiths, mother, of Queens Café.

June   Pte James Scott, RWF, Hope, missing believed to be POW.
Gunner Edward, son of Mr Thomas Edward, Castle Dining Rooms, killed.
Cpl Joseph Neeson, on leave, 'been on active service since beginning of war.'

Local distinction—'Not generally known that one of our brave boys, Samuel Douglas Grouge. RN had the proud distinction of being chosen as one of a force of picked volunteers in the daring raid on Zeebruge last month. Lead Stoker on the *Vindictive* the old battleship which was afterwards filled with concrete and sunk to block the entrance to Ostend harbour. We all congratulate him most heartily and are proud of him.'

August, Brigade Instructer T. W. Wilbraham, Florence Cottage, wounded.

October, Gunner Willie Jones, son of Alfred Jones, Hope, killed in France.

'Shortly after the signing of the Armistice Pte Arthur Price died of wounds. He had been awarded the MM for conspicuous bravery. One of four brothers serving plus his brother-in-law.'

A memorial service was held for W. A. Jones, W. A. Griffiths. M. Peters, Walter Williams, Fred Williams, R. Lewis, A. Edward, W. A. Huson, J. W. Roberts and W. Davies, all had fallen in the war.

1919
February. Seven POWs returned, each given a sovereign in gold.

May. Pte. Albert Davies died of pneumonia in France.
Sgt Albert Edward Roberts died as a result of severe wounds received in France. Military funeral.

---

* Names not on the War Memorial in Caergwrle are Cecil Oliver and Frank Savage.

The army had to be supplied with great amounts of food, clothing, equipment, armaments and ammunition. In 1918 there were three million men and 500,000 horses to feed. The static nature of the front lines on the western front however meant that a network of railways could be built to transport not only equipment etc. but also the soldiers.

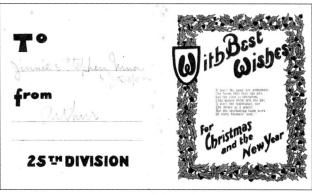

Christmas card from the Western Front, 1917.

One such journey is described by F. S. Whittingham who joined the 13th Hussars of 3rd Res. Cavalry, No. 1 Troop, C Squadron, on 7 June 1918, and was based at the East Cavalry Barracks Aldershot He was then transferred to the Tank Corps. There is an interesting description of his training, he learned about compasses and magnetism, also the workings of the tank and the parts of the 6lb gun and Hotchkiss .303 light machine gun. Before his transfer to the front he was given a list of French words to learn such as 'bread, water, soldier, wounded, German etc'. He kept a notebook describing his journey through France to the front line:

Few remarks on my journey to France 25/10/1918.

Leaving Wareham 7.15am on troop train, about 560 of Res. Unit we come through into Shaincliffe arriving about 3.30am, we disembarked and marched to Folkestone and put up in empty houses(kept for that purpose) until morning. We washed had breakfast, paraded at 8am to march to boat. We sailed off at 10 each wearing a life belt and were escorted by airships and submarine and torpedo boat. We arrived at Boulogne 12.15 marched through the town to the rest camp up a VERY steep hill. We were medically examined there and given a blanket and posted to tents 12-13 in each and got settled down there for the night. We drew our rations for the following day (each day we carried our own rations, enough for all day, composed of chiefly a piece of bread (loaf to three) jam, tinned butter, bully beef, beans and a piece of cheese.

On Sunday am 27th we lined up about 10 and marched to another rest camp about 1¹/₂ miles away called St Martins (both being outside Boulogne). We drew 2 blankets there and got 10 to a tent. Had some tea at 4pm. Went to the Sal.Army service hut at night and stayed till morning, we drew rations at 8.30am paraded and marched through St Martins Boulogne to the station. A French troop train came up just tranship vans and we were put 36 in each truck. We had something to eat at (EFP) and left at about 11.45 arriving at Le Treport 4.45pm having travelled very slow. We passed through St Jasse, Etaples, Conchere le temples. Chippy valines, waen court Le Treport. On arrival we marched to camp situated on the top of a hill very steep walk

from town. We got onto the square and were divided into sections. I in P, after tea we were
issued with 2 blankets and ground sheet and shewed our tents, 7 in each one.

Reveille next at 5.30am—issued with helmet gave particulars and had a bath.'

Here the description ends, one can only imagine the thoughts of these men arriving at
the battle front. The horrors of which must have been known to them through friends and
newspapers.

The casualties, as we see by the War Memorial and lists in the churches and chapels,
were many. The local newspapers when reporting the casualties gave us a taste of the action
and bravery of so many men. As a memorial to those who had fallen in the Great War, the
church bells were melted down to provide a new peal. One of these bells bore the inscription
'Jesus be our Speed' dated 1623.

A number of refugees from Belgian arrived at Plas Teg in 1914. Fund raising and
entertainment at the Presbyterian Hall was organised by the Band of Hope workers. Some
refugees took part. There were four living at Plas Teg, however two were taken ill with
typhoid and taken to the isolation hospital in Dobshill.

During this conflict women became very involved in the war effort. A local register was
kept of women prepared to work on the farms, including those who would milk cows, help
with the harvest or become general workers. A War Agricultural Committee was set up as
food produced abroad became difficult to bring to our shores, causing great hardship. Every
effort was made for communities to grow their own food, cultivating gardens and
allotments. 18,000 acres of grassland in Flintshire was ploughed for crops in 1918. An 'egg
and poultry' demonstration toured the country to educate people about the production of
table poultry and eggs. Shooting parties were arranged to will wood pigeons, sparrows and
rooks which damaged crops. There was also an application for German POWs to be emplyed
to work the land.

The villages seem to have become a closer knit community during these long terrible
years. Donations to the Hope Parish War Relief Fund were collected monthly. Various ways
of raising funds were encouraged from a whist drive to the sale of a donkey! In May 1916 the
total amount paid into the bank of Liverpool was £102 0s. 6d. The officers of the Soldiers
Comforts Committee dispatched a large parcel of mufflers, socks, mitts cuffs and shirts for
the Welsh troops (March 1916). The Girls Knitting club also made garments which were sent
to RWF wherever they were needed. In 1917, 271 parcels were sent to men in the forces at
various fronts as well as 16 parcels for wounded soldiers.

Names on the War Memorial — First world War 1914–19

L/Cpl H. T. Astbury, RE, died 1/2/1919, aged 36
2nd Lt G. B. Bate, RFC, 18 Squadron, died France 29/4/1917, buried Queant Road Cemetery, Buissy
Pte T. J. Bunnel, 10 RWF, died France 16/8/1916, buried Guillemont Road Cemetery
Capt H. S. Collins, Egyptian Labour Corps, died Egypt 17/11/1917, buried Alexandria (Hadra) Memorial Cemetery
Pte Albert Davies, RE, died of pneumonia in France.
Pte D. Davies, 1/5 RWF, killed in action Gallipoli 10/8/1915, Helles Memorial
Pte G. Davies, 2/5 RWF, killed in action in Mesopotamia, 1916
Gnr G. V. Davies, RFA, died of wounds, France, aged 21
Pte M. Davies, 17 RWF, killed in action, France, aged 25
Pte W. Davies, RAMC
Lt Eric Edwards, 12 SWB, killed in action, France
Pte D. Edwards, RGA
Pte T. Evans, MM, Welsh Guards, died of wounds, France
Pte A. Griffiths, 1 North Staffs, killed in action, France
Pte F. Griffiths, 8 North Staffs
Pte T. J. Griffiths, 1/5 RWF, killed in action Palestine 26/3/1917, Jerusalem Memorial
Pte Walter Griffiths, 8 RWF, died of wounds, Mesopotamia, 1917, aged 20
Pte W. A. Griffiths, 15 Welsh, died of wounds, France 4/10/1918, Terlincthun British Cemetery, Wimille
Midshipman J. A. Hamilton, RN, died HMS *Vicnor* 13/1/1915 west of Donegal, Portsmouth Naval Memorial
Dvr G. Harley, RFA, killed in action, France, 1917.
Pte A. Hemmings, 1/5 RWF, killed in action Palestine 26/3/1918, Jerusalem Memorial
Pte R. Henshaw, 10 RWF, died of wounds 18/11/1916, aged 20, Hope Cemetery
L/Sgt J. L. Howell, 1 South African Infantry, killed in action, France 16/7/1916, Delville Wood Cemetery
Pte W. A. Huson, 15 Cheshire Regt, killed in action France 23/4/1918, Pozieres Memorial
Pte J. W. Ithell, 11 East Lancs, killed in action France 6/11/1918, Terlincthun British Cemetery, Wimille
Pte T. Ithell, 3 Lancashire Fusiliers
Pte W. E. Jenkins, 9 RWF, killed in action France 3/7/1916, Thiepval Memorial
L/Cpl. Bert Jones, Welsh Guards, killed in action
Pte C. E. Jones, 4 Grenadier Guards, died France 16/10/1915, Loos Memorial
Pte J. W. Jones, 2/5 RWF
Dvr W. A. Jones, RFA, died of wounds France 26/9/1918, aged 29, Faubourg D'Amiens Cemetery, Arras
Pte W. H. Jones, 10 RWF, killed in action France 13/11/1916, aged 35, Thiepval Memorial
Pte J. Kendrick, 66 Labour Corps (Training Reserve), died 2/11/1918, buried Hope cemetery
2/Lt H. Kilvert, 9 RWF, killed in action France 1/8/1917, Bailleul Cemetery Extension (Nord)
Sgt R. Lewis, SWB
Cpl W. F. Maddock, 17 RWF, killed in action France 9/7/1916, Thiepval Memorial
L/Cpl J. P. Messham, 16 RWF, killed in action France 23/8/1916, Essex Farm Cemetery
L/Cpl R. Morris, 8 RWF, killed Mesopotamia 15/2/1917, aged 19, Basra Memorial, Iraq
Cpl A. Martin, 4 RWF
Pte T. O. Parry, 5 SWB, killed France 20/10/1918, aged 19, Romeries Communal Cemetery Extension
Cpl M. Peters, MM, 10 RWF, killed Mesopotamia, 1917, aged 24
Pte R. Poole, Liverpool Scottish H
Cpl A. Price, MM, 10 RSF
Pte S. Pugh, 1/5 RWF, killed Gallipoli 11/8/1915, aged 23, Helles Memorial
Pte A. E. Roberts, 3 RWF, died of wounds
Pte L. D. Roberts, 13 RWF, died of wounds France 5/6/1916, aged 22, Merville Communal Cemetery
L/Cpl E. T. Roberts, 2 RWF, killed in action France 3/11/1916, Thiepval Memorial
Pte J. W. Roberts, 5 Connaught Rangers, died Palestine 10 March 1918, buried Ramleh War Cemetery
Sgt R. Rowlands, 10 RWF, killed Belgium 17/2/1916, Ypres (Menin Gate) Memorial
Pte W. J. Roberts, 10 RWF, killed in action France 18/6/1917, Arras Memorial
Pte J. E. Speed, 1 RWF, killed in action France 21/10/1914, aged 25, Ypres (Menin Gate) Memorial
Pte W. Thomas, 1/5 RWF, killed in action Gallipoli 17/8/1915, Helles Memorial
Capt. C. C. Trevor-Roper, 14 Hampshire Regt, died Belgium 3/8/1917, aged 33, Duhallow A.D.S. Cemetery
Pte G. Trevor-Roper, 32 RF, killed in action Belgium 20/9/1917, aged 31, Tync Cot Memorial

Pte J. T. Tydd, 2 RWF, killed in action France 3/11/1914, Pont-du-Hem Military Cemetery, La Gorgue
Pte G. J. Vaughan, Canadian Infantry (West Ontario Regiment), killed in action France 18/10/1918, aged 36, Vred Communal Cemetery
Pte S. Wilcock, 10 RWF, killed in action France 16/8/1916, Thiepval Memorial
Pte F. Williams, 12 King's Liverpool Regt, died of wounds France 26/8/1918, Aubigny Communal Cemetery Extension
Pte T. E. Williams, 9 RWF, killed in action France 3/7/1916, Thiepval Memorial
Pte W. Williams, RGA

The Second World War, 1939–45

This war was very different from the First World War. Conscription had been introduced before the outbreak of hostilities and there was therefore no reliance on men and women volunteering for military service. This war was brought to everyone's doorstep in the guise of bombs.

Roll of Honour

1941

December — William Parsonage, Stoker 2nd class, on HMS *Prince of Wales*, Royal Navy killed. According to the newspaper 'He was a well known and extremely popular local boy, he was formerly employed at Llay Main Colliery. Until a few years ago he was keenly interested in the Caergwrle Boys' Brigade ... became Lieutenant in the company.'

1942

January — Charles Maurice Watmore, Stoker 1st class on the destroyer HMS *Thanet*. The ship was sunk on 27 January 1942 by Japanese destroyers while attacking Japanese transport ships. All hands were lost.

April — A number of men were reported missing.

June — John Symans, 2nd Lieutenant, Royal Indian Army Service Corps, died 11 June.

July — Eric Ernest Barlow, Petty Officer Royal Navy, serving on the HMS *Niger*

Ronald, Kenneth and Geoffrey Evans, of Bryn Celyn, Caergwrle.

posted missing at sea 6 July. He had been a popular NCO in the Caergwrle Boys' Brigade. HMS *Niger*, a minesweeper, was mined off Iceland along with six merchant ships.

1943

August — announced in the *London Gazette*: Surgeon Lieutenant P. R. C. Evans (Wrexham) received the George Medal and Surgeon Lieutenant Robert H. Jones of Highfield, Hope the DSO.

' They were on a ship which had fought in close action with an enemy patrol. A shell killed or wounded all on the upper bridge. Most casualties were too serious to be moved but with the aid of a pocket torch, Lt Jones carried out emergency treatment among the wreckage, with a skill that saved the lives of at least three officers and one rating. His father Captain Jones served in the Great War and won the MC with bar and was twice mentioned in dispatches.'

1944

February — Colin Pickering, Trooper, Royal Armoured Corps, 2nd Lothians and Border Horse, killed 8 February.

March — Richard D. Trevor Roper DFC, DFM, Flight Lieutenant, Royal Air Force Volunteer Reserve, 97 Squadron. Killed. He was awarded the Distinguished Flying Medal in 1943 as the tail-gunner of Wing Commander Guy Gibson's aircraft which, on 16 May 1943 led 617 Squadron, nicknamed the 'Dambusters', to Germany, on a mission that was to become one of the most famous episodes of this war. The raid has been written about and a film made recording their daring exploits.

The crew of Lancaster bomber 'G for George' of No 617 Squadron board for the famous 'Dambusters' mission. Richard Trevor-Roper of Plas Teg is on the extreme left. Wing-Commander Guy Gibson is standing in the doorway of the aeroplane.

August — Revd F. W. Musgrave killed in action on 2 August, while serving as chaplain to the forces. Rev. Musgrave and his batman had driven into a farm yard when enemy shelling commenced and he was killed by shrapnel. He was a curate of the parish.

1945

April — Frank E. Tudor, Signalman, Royal Corps of Signals, killed 23 April. As can be seen from the War Memorial there are many more names, not just from Hope and Caergwrle, but the surrounding area, who will never be forgotten. See Appendix for more detail of those men listed.

Air Raid Precaution/ Home Guards

Men who were in reserved occupations such as farmers, aircraft workers, ship builders and miners volunteered to join the Air Raid Precaution services which included the Auxiliary Fire Service, Fire Brigade Reserve and Air Raid Wardens. The Air Raid Precaution Act of 1937 forced local authorities to protect and make provision for the public in the event of war reaching our country.

The duties of the ARP were varied from blackout checking to fire watching. As much as 30s. fine could be imposed for leaving a light on during the black out. Betty and Dennis Bulmer and John Griffiths were motor-cycle dispatch riders during this time, assisting with communications. Fire watching at the Exchange Station meant 3s. a night for volunteers.

Even the children became involved in war work. A list was made of those boys or girls who were willing to do farm work. Abermorddu School was given two fire buckets and a stirrup pump. Staff went to Coed Talon to learn how to use them for fire-fighting. There was a three-tier bunk at the school for use by people on fire watching duties.

During air raids some residents sheltered in the brewery cellars or underground at Llay Hall Colliery. Air raid shelters were built in the villages.

Anti-gas training was given under the auspices of Flintshire County Council. Gas masks were issued to everyone, both adults and children, with instructions pointing out the need to practise wearing them as 'Hitler will send no warning'.

Careless talk, i.e. telling someone about shipping movements, realised a £5 fine plus £7.7s costs!

The Observer Corps had been set up during the 1930s to watch out for and report on enemy aircraft. The nearest HQ to Caergwrle was in Coedpoeth.

Advice was given in the form of leaflets for instance how to use your home as an air raid shelter, also First aid booklets.

In 1940, following the Battle of Britain, the *Luftwaffe* switched to night attacks against

Members of the Hope and Caergwrle Home Guard, c.1943. Members would march through the village meeting the Pontblyddyn Platoon half way along the Mold Road. They also went up Hope Mountain to watch out for German parachutists. The men in the photograph who wore ribbons had fought in the First World War. [Mr H. E. Griffiths]

Police Sergeant Albert Griffith with members of the Hope and Caergwrle Civil Defence. Sgt Griffiths served in the police force for 33 years, starting in Connah's Quay. [Mr H. E. Griffiths]

British cities and in 1941 over-flew Flintshire on their way to and from Liverpool and Manchester. Many of the bombs dropped on north Wales were the result of poor navigation, the setting up of decoy targets by the British or perhaps German airmen getting rid of the bombs before returning home. A searchlight, sited at Hope Hall was linked to the anti aircraft in the area.

On 31 August 1940 at 8.15pm a delayed action bomb exploded at Cefn y Bedd and several houses were damaged. Three hours later hundreds of incendiary bombs were dropped in the Caer Estyn area and a barn containing ten tons of hay was set on fire.

The Local Defence Volunteers (known locally as Look, Duck and Vanish!) were formed early in the war with a view to providing defences against any invasion of the British Isles. Their name was later changed to the Home Guard. Members were made of men who were either too young or too old for regular military service or whose occupation excluded them from being called-up. The television programme *Dad's Army* illustrates the lighter moments. The Caergwrle contingent was formed in May 1940 and wore denim at first until they had their uniform of khaki in mid 1941.

In June 1938, the Women's Voluntary service for Air Raid Precaution (to give it its original name) was formed. The membership was essentially middle class, dressed in bottle-green coats and conspicuous hats, for which the volunteers had to pay.

In February 1939, with the role of the Women's Voluntary Service for ARP ever expanding, the name changed to the Women's Voluntary Service for Civil Defence, although to most they were simply the WVS. Much of the wartime duties focussed on the aftermath of air raids in some areas.

In 1939 approximately 300 evacuees arrived in Caergwrle. On arrival they were taken to Hope Council School and given refreshment, accommodation was organised prior to their arrival. The WVS which was based in Caergwrle, was also largely responsible for organising a recreation room and crèche for mothers and very young children who had been evacuated to the village from Liverpool, Birkenhead or even as far away as London, and were 'now our guests'. It was somewhere for the mothers to meet, rest and shelter on wet days.

With even more mouths to feed, shortages meant a need for rationing which began in January 1940 and had a profound effect on the eating habits of the nation. The lowest weekly food allowance in 1940 was:

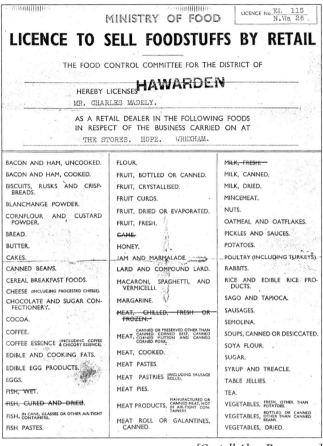

[Castell Alun Resources]

4oz bacon or ham
2oz butter
8oz sugar
2oz tea
1oz cheese
4oz margarine
1 pkt dried eggs per week
Oranges limited to expectant mothers
Sweets rationed

4oz hard soap
3oz toilet soap or flakes
6oz soap powder

Mrs Gabriel (right) of Hope Hall as a Land Girl during the Second World War. She is wearing protective clothing for spraying operations.

To the girl who is being 'demobbed'

SOME ADVICE
FROM BROWNS OF CHESTER

Suggested outfit

	Price	Coupons
Coat - tweed or plain cloth	£5-2-10	18
Frock - Art Crepe	£2-13-7	7
Stockings, 2prs	8-4	6
Vests, 2	7-2	6
Corset	10-9	3
Art Silk Knickers	6-7	3
Shoes (1 pair)	£1-19-0	7
Nightdress	15-9	6
	£12-4-0	56

Women were also conscripted into the armed forces and into industry, many working the aircraft factory in Broughton and the Royal Ordnance factories at Rhydymwyn and Marchwiel where they replaced those men who had gone to war.

The Women's Land Army in Flintshire was actually formed on 1 June 1939. In December there were ten landgirls, however by 1943 the number had risen to 602. These were volunteers from all walks of life, not only from Flintshire but from Yorkshire, Lancashire and Fleetwood. They were trained in many aspects of agriculture in Wrexham. They chose what they would like to do from general farmwork, milking, muck spreading, harvest and hay making, even water divining. Mrs Gabriel from Hope Hall Farm, Hope, was a Land Girl and trained at Coedpoeth, learning how to milk by hand and machine. She was also involved in general farming activities and specialised in the pruning and spraying of fruit trees. Based at hostels in Ruthin, Coed y Glyn (Wrexham), or Gresford there were forty in each hostel. She also worked at Bellis' in Holt, picking fruit and vegetables. There were five in a team and a van was used to transport them to and from work.

Another specialist job for the Land Army was that of pest control which was an essential aspect of farming. Killing rats, rabbits and moles was not for the faint-hearted, but it was vital work as we had to grow our own food. The

[FRO D/WM/252]

rats were either caught in iron traps or chased by a terrier dog into their hole where they were gassed whilst someone stood by the bolt hole and killed them with sticks. In Flintshire there was a pest control group of four who killed vermin. Between February 1941 and April 1942 they destroyed 3,545 rabbits, 7,689 rats and 1,901 moles which were skinned and sold for 1s. Rats tails were sold to the government for 1d. each. (We don't know why!)

The Ladies' Football Team which raised funds for the Welcome Home Fund, 1946.

Their uniform consisted of a brown slouch hat, greatcoat, cream shirts, green pullover and a pair of brown corduroy breeches. There was no official way to wear the uniform, as was noted in the local papers: 'No one can do more extraordinary things with a uniform than a Land girl who has put her mind to it.' Headscarves and turbans were standard wear for work in the fields. To save on clothing coupons and overcome shortages, arm slings were bought from the chemist at 2s 6d, dyed and utilised as turbans.

There were of course those women who joined the services, one or two from Caergwrle joined the Womens' Auxilliary Air Force (WAAF).

There were Italian and German prisoners of war accommodated in the area, who were put to work on local farms. One resident remembers Italian POW's potato picking in Hope, where the council houses are now built.

After the war there were many changes, women had become more independent and men who had been away from home for some time sometimes found it difficult to settle back into pre war mode.

The Royal British Legion

The Royal British Legion is a national organisation which was set up in 1921 to help ex-servicemen and women. A branch was established in Caergwrle after the Second World War, meeting in the former United Methodist Free Church in Castle Street. There is now only a small membership in both the men's and women's sections but they are determined to continue with the organisation which includes collecting for the very successful annual Poppy appeal(which raised £1900 locally in 2005), the organiser being Mr Tony Hughes. The Remembrance Day parade in November, which includes both the Boys' and the Girls' Brigade congregates at the Halfway Inn in Caergwrle, then marches to the War Memorial led by the band of the Boys' Brigade. Here wreaths are laid and after prayers they march to Hope Parish Church where the service is taken by the chaplain to the British Legion, the Revd. Martin Snellgrove.

Names on the War Memorial — Second World War, 1939-45

L/AC Frederick John Bradshaw, RAF, killed 8/2/46, aged 39, buried Bristol
L/S (Supply Assistant) Eric Ernest Barlow, RN, HMS *Niger*, died 6/7/42 off Iceland, aged 22, Chatham Naval Memorial
A/B Percy Norman Clarke, RN, HMS *Midge*, died 1/5/43, aged 19, buried Hope
F/Sgt/Pilot Frederick Ronald Duxbury, RAFVR, 542 Squadron, killed France 6/3/43, aged 21, buried Bayeux War Cemetery
Gnr Vincent Davies, RA, killed Italy 11/9/44, aged 31, buried Gradara War Cemetery
Gnr T. Davies, RA
Fus Glyn Edwards, RF (City of London Regiment), died Italy 24/2/44, aged 24, Cassino Memorial
Tpr Thomas Handley Edwards, RAC Anti-tank Regt, died France 4/6/40, aged 21, Dunkirk Memorial
Pte T. Edwards, RASC, died Tripoli 29/5/43, Tripoli War Cemetery
Gnr James Ellis, RA, 6 HAA Regt, died Thailand 9/5/43 (POW), buried Kanchanaburi War Cemetery
Cpl Derek Hugh Ellis, RAFVR, died India 5/12/45, buried Rawalpindi War Cemetery
S/Ldr James Hobbs, RAF, 156 Squadron, died 15/10/42, aged 30, Runnymede Memorial
Pte C. Humphries, Royal Marines
F/Sgt W. H. Johnson, RAF
L/AC Bernard Jones, RAFVR, died 1/1/45, burieed Brussels Town Cemetery
Rev. F. W. Musgrove, Chaplain to HM Forces, killed 2/8/44, aged 29
F/Sgt/Pilot Francis Richard Morris, RAFVR, died 8/8/43, aged 23, buried Hope
Fus. Joseph Price, 2 RWF, died Madagasgar 5/5/42, aged 29, buried Diego Suarez War Cemetery
Tpr Colin Pickering, 2 Lothian & Border Horse, RAC, died Algeria 8/2/44, aged 20, buried Bone War Cemetery, Annaba
Stoker William Parsonage, RN, HMS *Prince of Wales*, died east of Malaya 10/12/41, Portsmouth Naval Memorial
Pte Hector Parry, 1 KSLI, died France 22/5/40, aged 25, Dunkirk Memorial
L/Cpl Richard M. A. Ridge, RASC, died Belgium 10/4/45, aged 21, buried Turnhout Communal Cemetery
L/Sjt Sydney Robert Ridge, 1 Welsh Guards, died Germany 8/4/45, aged 25, buried Rheinberg War Cemetery
Fus. W. Roberts, RWF
Pte Joseph Edward Reynolds,1 Monmouthshire Regt, died Normandy 17/8/44, aged 28, buried Banneville-la-Campagne War Cemetery
F/Lt Richard Dacre Trevor-Roper, DFC, DFM, RAFVR, 97 Squadron, killed Germany 31/3/44, buried Dumbach War Cemetery
Lt John Patrick Symons, RIASC, died India 11/6/42, buried Delhi War Cemetery
Sgmn Frank Edward Tudor, RCS, died Italy 23/4/45, aged 24, buried Argenta Gap War Cemetery
Tpr Richard Sowery, RAVC, died Greece between 25–30/4/41, aged 21, Athens Memorial
Cpl John Williams, 6 Parachute Regt (10 RWF), died France 15/8/44, aged 24, buried Mazargues War Cemetry Marseilles
Stoker Charles Maurice Watmore, RN, HMS *Thanet,* died 27/1/42 east of Malaya, aged 21, Plymouth Naval Memorial
Stoker A. Williams? Alun, RN, HMS *Curacoa*, died 2/10/42 River Clyde in collision with RMS *Queen Mary*, aged 24, Chatham Naval Memorial
P/O/Pilot Glyn Williams, RAAF, 464 Squadron, killed Germany 3/12/44, aged 21, buried Reichswald Forest War Cemetery
Cpl Stephen Williams, 1 KOYLI, died Italy 8/3/44, aged 26, buried Beach Head War Cemetery, Anzio
F/Sgt/Pilot John Charles Willis, RAFVR, died 8/3/44, aged 26, buried Tripoli War Cemetery
Tpr William Wright, RAC, Royal Tank Regt, died France 11/8/44, aged 26, buried Ryes War Cemetery, Bazenville.

12. Social Life

There were a number of shops, businesses and inns in the villages of Hope and Caergwrle, as listed in the various business directories. Below are details of those businesses that existed in 1936 which will be remembered by some members of today's community. At that time there was certainly no need to go to shopping to Mold or Wrexham, as most things were available locally.

Bennett's Business Directory:
HOPE—Population 4806 (including Penyffordd and Penymynydd)
Post/money order/telegraph office, Mrs Shone.
Grocer, G. Braithwaite.
Motor & cycle agent, W. Crosbie.
Grocer, E. A. Davies.
Grocer, A. E. Hill (Lion Store).
Motor Garage, H. Hooley.
Grocer, Mrs E. Jones.
Coal merchant and haulage contractor, S. Lawrence.
Joiner, L. Rogers.
Coal merchant, A.Underwood.
Smith, A. Williams.
Tailor, P. P. Williams.
Drapers, D. & W. Winters.

CAERGWRLE, Population 2,200 (including Cefnybedd & Abermorddu)
Grocer, Bells Stores, High St.
Paint stores, T. Bulmer, Station Rd.
Caergwrle & District Electricity Supply Co. Ltd.
Caergwrle National Mineral Table Water Co.
Boot stores, L. Conde, High St.
Cosy Cinema, Castle St.

Surgeon, R. R. Dalling.

Watchmaker, A. L. Davies, Castle St.

Confectioner, O. Davies, High St.

Chemist, T. W. Davies, High St.

Hairdresser, T. Dove, Castle St.

Fried fish saloon, K. Duke, Hawarden Rd.

Fishmonger, H. Eccleston, Castle St.

Confectioner, A. Edwards, Pystill Lane.

Draper, H.Edwards, Bee Hive.

Butchers, J. Edwards & Son, High St.

Grocer, T. Edwards, Castle Dining Rooms.

Monumental mason, W. Edwards

Boot maker, J. W. Edwards, High St. (opposite station)

Timber merchant, J. Evans, Bryn Alyn.

Draper, Miss Evans, (Vera's) Castle St.

General stores, R. Fisher & Sons, High St.

Butcher, P. Griffiths, Derby Rd. & Penyffordd.

Apartments, Mrs J. Griffiths, Queens Café.

Grosvenor Commercial Café, Mrs Thomas, Castle St.

Gwalia Forge Co., engineers.

Conde's Shoe Shop, 1930s.

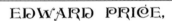

Motor engineer, E. T. Henshaw.

Ladies hairdresser, Miss Hesketh, Castle St.

Grocer & baker, J. Hopwood, Castle Stores.

High class grocer, baker & confectioner, J. Hurst, Castle St.

General & fancy draper, A. S. Jones, High St.

Cycle dealer, J. S. Jones, High St.

Confectioner, Hawarden Rd.

Tea rooms, Mrs Lamb.

Lassell & Sharman Ltd, brewers & mineral water manufacturers.

Confectioner, W. R. Lee, High St.

Castle Garage, W. R. Lee.

General dealer, F.J.Lewis, Bridge Stores.

The Hughes family ran the bicycle shop.

House decoration, F. J. Lewis, Bridge Stores.

Grocers, W. Lewis, High St.

Fruiterer, Lloyd, High St.

Fried fish saloon, M. Martin, Castle St.

Newsagent and Post Office, C. E. M. Mayland.

Midland Bank.

Butchers, J. Morris & Sons, Castle St.

Baker & grocer, T. Myddleton, Lower St.

National Provincial Bank Ltd, Castle St.

Newsagent, Mrs Noble, Hawarden Rd.

OK Boot Stores, Castle St.

Coal merchants & haulage contractors, R. J. Parry & Co., White House.

Fish & chip saloon, Parry's, Castle St.

Motor haulage contractors, Piercy & Son.

Grocer, E. Price & Sons, High St.

Building contractor & undertaker, electric saw mills, Hawarden Rd. Tel. 37.

Funerals, Harry Pugh.

Confectioner, D. Roberts, Station Rd.

Painter/paperhanger & dealer in all kinds of fancy goods, toys, hardware,wallpapers, mixed paints, etc., E. Roberts, Castle St.

Butchers, L & Roberts Son, Lower St.

Newsagent, Mrs A. Vaughan, High St.

Fried fish saloon, T. Vaughan, Lower St.

Victoria Café, B. Ryder, High St.

Joiner, C. Williams, Lower St.

Confectioner, F. Williams, High St.

Tobacconist, H. Williams, High St.

The Hurst grocery shop.

The Village Inns

For many men the public house was a refuge from family life in small, overcrowded houses; a place where they could socialise with friends, conduct business, join friendly societies and hold political meetings.

Early in the nineteenth century the increase in drunkenness amongst the lower classes, caused by gin drinking, was causing great concern and so in 1830 the Beer House Act was passed enabling any ratepayer, on payment of £2 2s. p.a., to get a licence from the excise to sell beer on or off the premises. The Government hoped that this would divert the demand away from spirits to beer, which was considered to be a more healthy drink. Beer drinking was further encouraged that year when duty on beer was abolished in the budget, reducing the price by 20 per cent. Not surprisingly, beer houses opened everywhere, and by 1869 the setting up of all new beer houses had to have the approval of the local magistrates in an attempt to curtail their growth. Three years later Bruce's Licensing Act placed all drinking places, public houses and beer houses, under the control of the licensing justices. Sunday drinking hours had already been reduced to six hours in 1854, divided into two blocks with a dry period in between. The Act of 1872 extended the hours to $8^1/_2$ and introduced a statutory weekday closing time. In 1916, Lloyd George introduced divided drinking sessions to the rest of the weekdays, citing the need to have sober munitions workers.

The Halfway Inn, Caergwrle

This public house is marked on the 1846 map of Caergwrle. Over the years the landlords relied on their wives to run the business as they undertook another full-time job. In 1871 H. Griffiths was a coal miner, 1881 John Graham a labourer and in 1901 John Edwards was a butcher. Lodgers were taken in and on the census night in 1881 there were seven staying, most of them working in the local coal mines and paper works. As late as 1903, two bedrooms were available for rent. This inn was supplied with beer by the Albion Brewery, Wrexham.

The Crown, Caergwrle

The Crown was sold in Chester in 1863 and by 1871 was run by John Williams, a slaterer and plasterer.

Business adverts from the local trade directory.

The Glynne Arms, High Street, Caergwrle.

His wife was described in the census as a beer seller, so it was very likely just a beer house. By 1903, it still offered limited facilities other than those for 'drinking purposes only'. During the next thirty years the need to meet the demand of the many visitors to Caergwrle encouraged the landlords to improve the inn and by 1932 'board residence and apartments' were advertised and Wrexham-brewed Island Green Ales were for sale.

The Glynne Arms, Caergwrle

The first documentation of this inn was in 1852 when it was sold along with four acres. The Piercey family have been connected with the Glynne Arms, a free house, for generations. John Piercey became the landlord in the late 1860s/early 1870s, and by the time of the 1881 census Martha, his widow, was the innkeeper as well as a farmer. She also took in lodgers and on the census night there were five woodcutters staying at the inn. She was a very well known and influential resident of the village and eventually her son, William, took over the running of the business which was described in 1903 as 'a good commercial house.' The large building to the right of the main building was used as a magistrate's room and, it was said, as a barracks for

The Derby Arms in Derby Street, Caergwrle.

The Bridge End Inn on the right, the Temperance Tearooms on the left and, in the distance, Hope National School.

the local Militia. In 1975, Mrs Margaret Piercey decided to retire and the Glynne Arms was sold for £18,000 and became a residential home for older people.

The Derby Arms, caergwrle

The early history of this inn is not known but it is thought that it could date from the seventeenth century. We do know for certain that in 1861 and 1871 Sarah Jones was the landlady. Around 1880, Henry Eccleston, an engine fitter, bought the inn which was a free house. In 1881 his wife was described as the innkeeper, assisted by her three daughters. Mr Eccleston had a large extension built at the back of the inn which was an ideal assembly room in which political, social, musical and sporting occasions could be held. In 1903 the inn had, 'good accommodation' and by 1932 apartments were available for visitors and parties could be catered for. The inn was very popular for works, clubs and church outings from Liverpool where a dinner could be laid on to complete a day's outing to the village.

The Bridge End Inn, Caergwrle

There has been an inn at the crossing point of the River Alyn for many years, in fact it could be the oldest in Caergwrle. In 1800 the Bridge End public house was up for sale with the adjoining ten acres. In the 1871 and 1881 census, John Jones was the innkeeper and also a master joiner. John Usher, pattern maker, followed him with his wife, Elizabeth the innkeeper, helped by her daughters and two servants. The inn, a free house, was very

The Castle Inn, High Street, Caergwrle on the left.

popular with visitors being very close to the railway station and the spa. It offered overnight accommodation and in 1912 was described as 'an Hotel.'

Ye Olde Castle Inn , Caergwrle

This inn can be clearly seen in Henri Gastineau's 1840 picture of Caergwrle. The roof is thatched and the building opposite is the round lock-up or small gaol. The building has a date stone of '1732' with the initials 'RI EI'. From around 1871, John Moore and later his widow Sarah, were landlords for over 30 years. He supplemented his income by farming 14 acres. Mrs Moore's claim to fame was that she catered for Mr and Mrs Gladstone when they visited the village. The inn has always been popular with travellers and visitors and the

advertisement (right) describes what could be obtained. The small room at the end of the building may have originally been for farm use, before being converted into a tea room, and latterly as a visitors' centre for the Caergwrle Historical Festival.

"Ye Olde Castle Inn," Caergwrle.

Wines & Spirits of the best quality.

Bass' Pale Ale in Bottle.

Dinners & Teas on the shortest notice.

Favourite house for Cyclists.

Birkenhead Brewery Co.'s Celebrated Ales.

Guinness' Stout in Bottle.

Pic-nic Parties Catered for

Splendid New Stables.

Within 5 minutes walk of the famed Rhyddyn Hall Spa.

Close to Caergwrle Castle

W. MOSES, Proprietor.

Advert for the Castle Inn.

A view of Caergwrle High Street in the early 1900s.

Lassell & Sharman Brewery, Caergwrle
Caergwrle brewed ales were available from an off-licence at the brewery.

Two other public houses existed in Caergwrle during the nineteenth century. One was thought to have been in the row of stone cottages in Castle Street, name unknown. The other, the Split Eagle, also known as the Split Crow, was documented in 1841 in Lower Street and on the 1846 map it was shown to be on the left-hand corner going down to the Packhorse Bridge.

The Red Lion, Hope
The modest thatched building was demolished and the present Red Lion built in the 1920s. During the latter part of the eighteenth century, during the unrest following the Enclosure Act, the Red Lion is mentioned as a meeting place with Mrs Bithell living there. However it is not clear if she was the landlady.

The earliest recorded landlord was John Dutton in 1861. In the latter years of the nineteenth century, John and

The old Red Lion, Hope, with Goodwin Terrace in the distance.

The old Red Lion Hope, c.1910.
The gates on the left lead into the
churchyard.

The new Red Lion, Hope.

Elizabeth Moses were running the inn and the brewery supplying their needs was C. Bates & Son, Wrexham. In 1903 the inn was described as having 'fair accommodation'. The new Red Lion is a very impressive building and in 1932 an advertisement stated 'catering a speciality, garage and filling station for motorists.'

The White Lion, Hope

Outside there is a date stone showing '1828' but it is almost certain that the building is much older. The old rectory is thought to have been on this site. Against the inn was a small building, a bier house, where the horse drawn hearse was housed. From the late 1850–80s Mary Langford was the innkeeper and a farmer of 30 acres, her son helping her on the farm. In 1903 travellers could stay the night, in the two bedrooms and there was stabling for two horses. A year later, landlord Alfred Hill was summoned before the licensing committee for selling underproof whisky. F. W. Soames and Co. of Wrexham supplied the beer and ales. In 1953, Price Griffiths was the landlord and there was a public bowling green behind the inn.

The White Lion, Hope.

The Crane Inn, Hope

In 1838 the Crane Inn was for sale as part of the Hope Hall estate. It is not known when it was closed. It was part of the building now known as Sarn House, which used to be a small farm. The magistrates held the Petty Sessions in an upstairs room before they moved to the Glynne Arms in Caergwrle. Later, the front room of Sarn House was turned into a grocery store by Mr Henshaw. This closed in 1967.

Roper's Arms Inn, Rhos Estyn

There was an inn at Rhos Estyn in 1849 but it could date from an earlier period. The inn was named after C. B. T. Roper who owned land in the vicinity. It was still an inn in 1852, but by 1875 sale details call it Rhos Estyn Farm or Old Roper's Arms as it had ceased trading by then.

The Stocks, Shordley

A public house and lands called the Stocks, in Shordley, were for sale in 1799.

The Temperance movement

During the 1800s concern was mounting about the effects of excessive drinking on the lives of men and their families. Some men and women forgot their responsibilities and spent their limited income on drink, leaving their families in financial distress and even destitution. It was accepted that drunkenness affected an adult's ability to work and could lead to immorality. A temperance movement, originating in England, began in the 1820s. The British and Foreign Temperance Society was formed in 1831 and over the next ten years extended to the rest of Britain. By 1847, young people were being encouraged to join the Band of Hope. All members, some as young as six years old, took a pledge of total abstinence from intoxicating liquors and attended lectures on the 'evils of drink.' Local competitive meetings were held and outings arranged and it proved to be a popular youth organisation in our area. From the 1850s onwards, a powerful Nonconformist temperance crusade took hold in Wales. As the Nonconformist religious groups became widespread, so did the philosophy of teetotalism. It was hoped that by refusing alcohol adults would become 'self-respecting responsible citizens' on the road to purification and salvation. A branch of the Church of England Temperance Society was established in Hope in 1879. The *Parish Magazine* of July of that year stated that, 'a special effort should be made to counteract our great national sin of drunkenness ... this society admits not only total abstainers but all who are prepared to pledge themselves to the practice of moderation in use of strong drinks.' By the following year, 91 men, 42 women and 98 children were members and meetings were held in the Bridge End schoolroom.

Despite all these measures, drunkenness in Hope and Caergwrle was a concern that some residents decided to address. In 1880 local men formed a committee to raise £300 to build a British Workman's Hall and Reading Room as an alternative venue to the public house. Here men could relax and not be tempted by intoxicating drink. There would also be opportunities for 'self improvement and educative recreation.' This public-spirited venture succeeded and a hall was built in Lower Street but, over the years, the lack of support meant that the hall eventually closed and the premises were sold. In 1905 there were draft details of the sale of the Workman's Hall on land known as Trewynfa. It is now a private house.

The Welsh Temperance movement instigated the passing of the Welsh Sunday Closing Act of 1881. When this new law was enforced in Caergwrle, on 27 August 1882, local miners walked to Hawarden to get a drink as the public houses there did not close until 10 September 1882. The Act caused financial hardship to the innkeepers as most men worked six days a week, so Sunday was the only day they had the money and time to drink.

The Bridge Temperance Hotel and Refreshment Rooms proved to be very popular with visitors from the early 1900s and many temperance groups came to enjoy the spa, the castle and Hope Mountain. In the 1930s, the Queen's Temperance Hotel, opposite the railway station, had apartments and served meals.

Friendly Societies

The public houses were the venues for meetings of the local Friendly Societies. With no state welfare benefits or National Health Service available, workers could protect themselves and their families by becoming members of, and paying subscriptions to, a friendly society. These societies encouraged self-help and were organised to provide financial security. They would offer welfare protection such as payments to cover sickness, accidents and old age, as well as death or burial insurance and savings clubs. Throughout the nineteenth century these societies grew in popularity and by 1900 it is estimated that half of the working population were members, enjoying social activities and companionship. In Caergwrle friendly societies were associated with individual public houses.

The Halfway Inn

The Order of the Oddfellows, formed as a breakaway group in Manchester in 1810 and was the richest and largest society by the mid nineteenth century.

The Glynne Arms

The Royal Antediluvian Order of Buffalos. The Buffs now describe their society as a fraternal and charitable order, raising funds for worthwhile causes, a 'band of men where friendship and everlasting companionship is real and rewarding. It is not a secret society but a society with secrets.'

The Glynne Arms

The Loyal Order of Shepherds in 1894 had 250 members.

The Derby Arms

The Ancient Order of Foresters which had 112 members and £334 capital in 1895. Colonel Trevor Roper was president. This society originated in Yorkshire.

PROPOSED

BRITISH WORKMAN'S HALL AND READING ROOM,

CAERGWRLE.

Our object in forwarding this circular is to enlist the sympathy and assistance of the Benevolent and Philanthropic, for the purpose of providing Caergwrle with a "BRITISH WORKMAN'S HALL AND READING ROOM," where working men can resort after their day's labour is over, free from the temptation of intoxicating drinks.

For a population of less than one thousand almost entirely composed of working people, we have Eight Public Houses, but we have no place or suitable Building where the temperate and abstainers can meet for recreation and for improving their minds. Under these circumstances, it is not surprising that drunkenness is so prevalent; sobriety and frugality rare, and the labours of our clergy and ministers but poorly responded to.

Some friends of Temperance have laboured here with some success, many of the former drunken characters have become sober and steady; but the want of a place where their leisure time can be spent without going into the Public House, is much felt and needed, and there is a danger of them falling back to their former habits.

A Committee of working men, who are abstainers, has been formed, determined to make an effort to erect a suitable place, to include a Reading Room, a Library, and also a room for entertainments.

They have subscribed among themselves about £30; but it requires about £300 to erect the desired building, and we beg to appeal most earnestly and confidently for assistance to our funds, from those whom God hath blessed with means and noble hearts.

The Rev. J. Williams, Rector, Hope, has kindly consented to act as Honorary Treasurer to whom all contributions may be sent.

Committee.

PRICE MICHAEL	SAMUEL GRIFFITHS
JOHN S. MORRIS	GEORGE EDWARDS
JOSEPH GRIFFITH	T. CUNNINGHAM
JONATHAN GRIFFITHS	JOHN WELCH

EDWIN HAYES,

Abermorddu, Caergwrle,

Secretary.

The Workman's Hall

The Rechabites were a temperance friendly society originally founded in 1835. The Caergwrle branch was founded in 1883, and their first meeting was held on 7 July. This branch was known as the 'tent'.

All the societies had annual 'feast' days when a band led a parade of members, celebrating later with a meal, games and dancing. All the family enjoyed the feasts. With the introduction of the Welfare State in 1948 the need for Friendly Societies diminished and over the years their roles have changed.

[Castell Alun Resources]

13. Interesting Houses

In both Hope and Caergwrle there are a number of beautiful houses with fascinating histories.

Bryn Iorcyn

Bryn Iorcyn, situated high on the eastern side of Hope Mountain, just below the summit, was the home of the Yonge family for four hundred years. The Yonge family were a perfect example of how the gentry class became socially and politically powerful.

It has been suggested that in the eleventh century the site of Bryn Iorcyn was part of the property of Sanddef Hardd, lord of Burton and Llay. Then, by the fourteenth century the ownership of land had transferred to Gruffydd ap Llewelyn ap Ynyr of Bodidris yn Iâl, Steward of Hope. It was inherited by his son Madog Foel, then by Tudor and later by Tudor's daughter, Gladys, who became heiress of Bryn Iorcyn. She married Jenkyn Yonge from Hanmer, Maelor Saesneg and they lived in the house. The Yonges were an important family in the Maelor area and claimed descent from Tudor Trefor.

The first documentary evidence of the Yonges at Hope is a land deed of 1427/8 which names Morys Yonge. One hundred years later, Ellis Yonge made an excellent marriage with Lowri, verch Lewis of Y Galchog, Northop. Her father transferred land

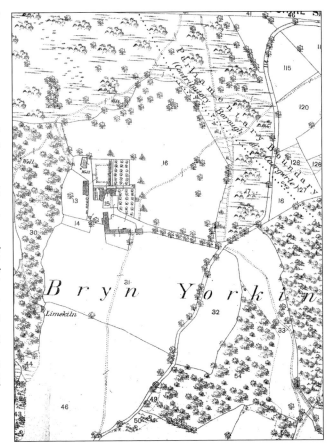

Map of Bryn Iorcyn, 1870.

Bryn Iorcyn.

to Ellis (1568/9) who was appointed escheator of the county of Flintshire in 1581, a position his son Lewys held in 1607. Richard Yonge, Lewys's son, married twice (in 1628 and 1652). Both wives were from affluent families and further land was added to the Yonge's estate. About 1628, the Bolde's of Plas yn Bwl, Caergwrle decided to move to Wrexham and Richard purchased their house and lands.

During the Civil War, Richard was a Royalist and was involved in the fighting in the area. After the surrender of Chester to the Parliamentarians, a pass dated 9 February 1646 permitted Richard Yonge, his servant and horses to travel to his home in 'Cairgurley'. He was very fortunate not to have his estate sequestrated and quickly resumed his position in society and was a Justice of the Peace. It is very likely that it was Richard who had Bryn Iorcyn remodelled to reflect his family's growing prosperity.

Ellis, Richard's son, became High Sheriff of the County of Flintshire in 1690 as did his son, William in 1716. Both men were also Justices of the Peace. William's two marriages were most advantageous, the first to Anne Lloyd of Fferm and the second to Barbara Lloyd of Llanarmon. The Yonge family, through good marriages, were now part of a complex social network and were accumulating land.

The jackpot winner was Ellis, William's son. His first marriage was to Dorothy Robinson of Gwersyllt, whose mother was Elizabeth Jefferies of Acton, Wrexham. In 1745 Ellis bought the Acton estate and Pant yr Ochain, Gresford, using a parliamentary procedure, for £6,500. He was appointed High Sheriff in 1750, and three years later married Penelope Stapleton of Bodrhyddyn, Rhuddlan. Through this marriage he obtained the large Bodrhyddyn estate and slave plantations in the West Indies. His two daughters, Barbara and Penelope, inherited his estate in 1785. Penelope married the Revd. William Shipley, later to become Dean Shipley of St Asaph. Barbara was to remain unmarried. On the death of Barbara in 1837 the lands of Bryn Iorcyn were taken into the Bodrhyddyn estate and the Bryn Iorcyn Manor was rented.

In the 1851 census Thomas Peters was the tenant farmer, his household included his wife, seven sons, two daughters, four servants and a labourer. On 16 June 1915 the Bryn Iorcyn estate was sold in 69 lots, but the manor house and 235 acres were sold to the tenant, Mr Thomas in 1919. To supplement the farm income, Mrs Thomas took in visitors from all over the world. The farm remained in the ownership of the Thomas family until 1963 when Mr Frank S. Whittingham bought the house, farm buildings and 144 acres. After the death of her parents Miss Rosemary Whittingham decided to sell Bryn Iorcyn and it was bought by Mr Davies who converted the barns and outbuildings into houses.

Bryn Iorcyn was originally a late medieval timber-framed hall house, the remnant of spere trusses indicates the possibility of an ornate archway between the large main hall and a cross passage. During the seventeenth century the house was rebuilt and encased in locally quarried Cefn-y-fedw sandstone. The extensions were built in the same stone. As there is no trace of a medieval structure surviving in either wing they may not be part of the original house. A floor was inserted above the main hall to make upstairs rooms. Improvements were made outside, the gate piers are very imposing and are ball finialed. In addition, stone walled gardens with an integral dovecote were constructed. In the Hearth Tax returns of 1670 there were ten hearths recorded, indicating a large house. Two shillings per hearth was paid.

In the grounds there was a group of farm buildings, some probably older than the house, but they had been much altered over time: the great barn (which has an excellent example of an early medieval cruck); the granary loft; the stables (with a hayloft above and a room for a farm servant); a cowshed; a dairy; a cart shed; pig sties; and three dog kennels built in stone wall. There were also servants' quarters which comprised a separate building with a large inglenook fireplace and bread oven and in another room possibly the laundry. Beneath this was a cellar with a well and a drain/tunnel. The exit of the

The kitchen at Bryn Iorcyn, c.1950.

tunnel 500 yards east downhill could still be discerned in 1910. There were three bedrooms for servants on the upper floor. In another part of this building was the malt house, in which there was a grain drying kiln.

In the gardens the dovecote would have provided meat and eggs for the house and a large pond, fed from a mountain stream, may well have been stocked with carp. In the vegetable garden there still is a wall shelf for the bee skeps. In the corner of the garden is a communal privy with seating for several users! Another well is to be found near the fishpond and in a field close by, a lime kiln is still visible. As already stated, the farm buildings have now been converted into dwelling houses.

Rhyddyn Hall

In the late 1740s Sir John Glynne decided that his house, Broadlane Hall, Hawarden, needed to be rebuilt and moved with his family to live in Rhyddyn Hall, Caergwrle. This house had been mentioned by Edward Lhwyd in 1699 and had come into the ownership of the Glynnes through marriage. It is very likely that the house had to be extended to accommodate the Glynne family. During their residence the Glynnes took an interest in local matters and attended Hope Church, the Bishop of St Asaph giving permission for the erection of a pew in the south aisle for their use. Their daughter, Frances, was baptised there in March 1751. Sir John exchanged land with Ellis Yonge of Bryn Iorcyn to extend the grounds around the Hall, giving greater privacy.

When the building of Broadlane Hall was completed, around 1757, the Glynne family returned to live in Hawarden. In 1769, Sir John's wife, Honora, died and he married his children's governess, Miss Augusta Beaumont, in 1772. Two years later, he leased a field in front of Rhyddyn Hall from the Earl of Derby for, '15/- and a suit of clothes from the mill.'

In 1777, Sir John died and his widow was given Rhyddyn Hall as a jointure house, but never took up residence there, preferring to live in Bath. She did, however, take a keen interest in business matters concerning the house and often wrote to Thomas Boydell, land agent for

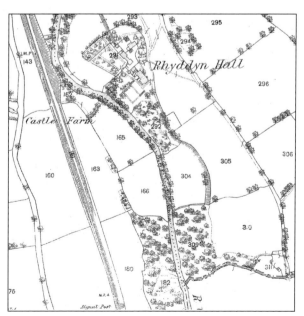

Map of part of the Rhyddyn Hall estate, 1870.

the Glynnes. In 1793 Frederick Phillip of Warwickshire paid £50 p.a. to rent the Hall, and by 1833 the rent had increased to £84 p.a.

In the 1840s, Sir Stephen Glynne was involved in a business venture and was obliged to sell land and other property to finance the scheme. On 22 September 1846 Rhyddyn Hall was auctioned and was sold again in 1852 and in 1875, when it was described as being 'suitable for a family of distinction.' Over the years the tenants of the house were influential men who readily took on the role of squire and benefactor within the community. Examples are listed below, dates indicate known periods of residence.

Rhyddyn Hall as an hotel — a Grade II listed building with a Doric porch.

1828 — C. B. Roper.
1839 — Richard Golightly (whom it is believed undertook some building and redecoration work in 1839).
1850 — R. C. Rawlins, Hope Paper Mill.
1861 — Captain J. C. Jones (retired). He had six servants living in the house.
1868 — Samuel Poole, coal and ironmaster at Ffrwd Iron Works and Colliery. He was a member of the Hope School Board in 1871.
1875 — Captain A. Adams who became an Overseer of the Poor.

Around 1900, the owner of Rhyddyn Hall was Llewelyn Roe Brown of Gwastad Hall, Cefnybedd. He decided to investigate the mineral content of two springs by the River Alyn below the Hall, which had been known for many years to have medicinal properties. Most tenants of the Hall, however, had refused public access to them, wishing to preserve their privacy. Roe Brown had the springs cleared

FLINTSHIRE AND CHESHIRE.
Amended Particulars
OF VALUABLE
FREEHOLD ESTATES
In the parish of Hope, in the county of Flint, and in the parish of Thornton-le-Moors, in the county of Chester, which will be again
SUBMITTED TO PUBLIC COMPETITION,
BY MESSRS.
CHURTON, ELPHICK, AND CO.
At the Grosvenor Hotel, in the City of Chester,
ON SATURDAY, THE 16th DAY OF OCTOBER, 1875,
THE RESIDENCE, BUILDINGS AND LANDS
KNOWN AS
"RHYDDYN HALL,"
The Plantations, &c., known as "Bryn-y-Gaer,"
And the three very fine FARMS, known as "Hope Hall," "Caeau," and "Shordley," with all the Mines and Minerals thereunder, close to several Railway Stations.
ALSO
THREE CAPITAL FREEHOLD FARMS,
In the Townships of Elton and Hapsford, in the parish of Thornton-le-Moors, extending in the whole to 434 Statute Acres, close to the Ince Railway Station.
MAPS MAY BE SEEN AT THE AUCTION MART, CHESTER.

[FRO D/BC/3307]

PARTICULARS.

Parish of Hope, County of Flint.

N.B.—The Lime Stone Rocks under all Land purchased from the late Earl of Derby are reserved.

TENANTS' NAMES.	Ordnance Numbers.	DESCRIPTION.	Ordnance Quantities. A. R. P.	TOTALS. A. R. P.
		LOT 1.		
		RHYDDYN HALL ESTATE.		
		IN ESTYN TOWNSHIP.		
Captain A. F. Adams	291	Rhyddyn Hall, Outbuildings, Yards, Gardens, and Pleasure Grounds	2 3 5	
	292	Plantation, &c.	0 2 30	
	293	The Lawn, &c.	7 3 17	
	279	Plantation, in ditto	0 2 13	
	295	Field	4 2 37	
	294	Plantation, in ditto	0 1 5	
	296	"	4 2 33	
	304	Meadow	1 2 6	
	305	Lawn	3 0 11	
	30C	Cae Pella	2 0 30	
	306	Cae Mawr	4 1 26	
	308	Wood in ditto	0 1 9	
	310	Costian-tan-y-ffordd	2 2 30	
	309	Wood and Dingle	1 3 38	
	311	House, Buildings, Garden, &c.	0 1 32	
	312	Occupation Road	0 0 24	
	314	Cae-wrth-bewyty	3 1 7	
	315	Wood, in ditto	0 2 14	
	282	Field	4 0 27	
	283	Field	3 1 24	
	297	Cae Pell	4 3 33	
	298	Meadow	2 1 13	
				56 3 34
In hand	241	Plantation	0 1 0	
	246	Plantation	0 1 29	
	280	Plantation	0 1 27	
	281	Slang Plantation	0 2 34	
				1 3 10
		IN CAERGWRLE TOWNSHIP.		
George Dutton	143	...	1 0 24	
	162	...	0 2 1	
	165 }	...		
	166 }	...	2 3 10	
	113	...	2 0 17	
				6 2 12
		246, Formerly Earl of Derby.		**66 1 16**

Such a property is seldom to be obtained. It occupies the Vale of the River Alyn, beyond which are the almost overhanging ruins of Caergwrle Castle. The House, Stabling, Gardens and Pleasure Grounds are suitable for a family of distinction. Approached by a carriage drive, only five minutes' walk from Bridge End Railway Station, and about half-a-mile from Hope Church.

[FRO D/BC/3307]

and the water analysed. The results were so encouraging that he decided to open the wells to the public. In 1907 he sold Rhyddyn Hall and the wells to a syndicate of local businessmen who converted the house into an eight-bedroomed residential hotel with other visitor attractions in the grounds.

In 1921, HPM Syndicate Ltd bought the spa for £3,550. Plans were prepared to extend the hotel to twenty-eight bedrooms, and later a more grandiose design for thirty-four bedrooms, but both came to nothing and in 1929 the hotel and spa were again for sale. The spa's popularity declined and Rhyddyn Hall reverted to being a private house, eventually, through marriage, coming into the possession of Mr F. Whittingham. In the 1940s it was let to R. W. Leaney. In 1963, Mr and Mrs Sherlock bought the house from a Mr Gunning and converted the coach house into a cottage.

In the late 1980s an application was made to turn the house back into a hotel, but, after further consideration, Mr and Mrs Sherlock decide not to proceed with the plan.

Hope Hall

In the early fifteenth century a *plas* or mansion called Brynni or Bryniau was forfeited by Llewelyn ap David ap Meredith for his involvement in the rebellion of Owain Glyndŵr and was acquired by Jenkyn Hope of Broughton Hall who continued living at Broughton and later, at Diglane, Hawarden. Through advantageous marriages the Hopes extended their estate and social standing so that by 1686 George Hope II was High Sheriff of Flintshire. From 1705, investment in unprofitable coal and lead mining ventures led to a steady decline in the family's fortunes. George Hope III borrowed £4,814 from Sir George Wynne of Leeswood, but was unable to repay the debt. When his son George Hope IV, inherited in 1740 he continued to invest heavily in coal mining but a slump in coal prices lead to great financial difficulties, forcing him to sell his properties and move to Bryniau at Hope. In the

Hope Hall.

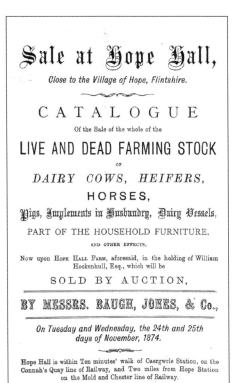

[FRO D/BC/3304]

1750s he built a handsome house of a classical design on an elevated site above the village. Bricks were made from the clay dug near by and stamped 'HOPE HALL'.

George Hope took an active role in local affairs and was a magistrate. Financial problems continued as his rental income was insufficient to support his life style, so he continued to mortgage his estate and his lands were managed by Sir Stephen Richard Glynne of Hawarden. When he died his finances were in a terrible state. As he had no son to inherit and his daughter had married the Revd. John Eyton of Old Leeswood Hall, Hope Hall was tenanted. Eventually Sir Richard Brooke of Norton Cheshire, who had earlier taken over the mortgage debts and the deeds of George Hope's estate, agreed a settlement payment of £5,000 to the family.

By 1838, when the tenant was Mr John Dutton, Hope Hall was up for sale at the Crane Tavern, (Sarn House) Hope. In 1843 George Chamberlain bought the Hall with other properties in the area, but by 1852 it was back on the market.

In September 1875 Hope Hall, two cottages and 139 acres of land were for sale in an obviously run down state, being described in the sale catalogue as 'capable of being made into a valuable property.' All the farming stock and equipment had been sold the previous year. By 1886, John Bowman had bought the Hall, and was living and farming there. He was also a noted rose grower. Hope Hall was a comfortable house with seven bedrooms and in the gardens was an orchard, a vinery, tomato houses and a tennis court. In addition to the usual farm buildings, there was a three-horse hackney stable.

After the death of J. B. Bowman, Flintshire County Council bought the Hall and 141 acres for £4,000. Then, under the provision of the Smallholding and Allotment Act 1908, the estate was divided into five smallholdings.

By 1970, the Hall was in poor condition, being attacked by dry rot and woodworm. Sadly Flintshire County Council decided that it was necessary to demolish the Hall and this was completed in 1974.

Plas yn Bwl

This was originally the seat of the Bolde family and a legal document of 1430, records a Richard Bolde buying land in Hope. The Boldes' held important administrative offices in Chester and were English settlers in the borough of Hope. Sir Richard Bolde or Bold, bought the land of seven of the Hope burgesses when they left the area, and by 1461 had an estate of note, west of the castle. Over the years the Boldes married into local Welsh families and became integrated socially into the area.

It is very possible that parts of the house date from the early fifteenth century, but over the years it has been greatly altered. However, what remains is a fine stone spiral staircase in a stair tower (possibly the solar end of the medieval house) and some moulded arched doorways. The house and lands were bought by Richard Yonge of Bryn Iorcyn around 1628 when the Bolde family moved to Wrexham.

Edward Lhwyd described the house in 1699 as: 'anciently a house of good note belonging to ye Bulls at present it is Mr Young's. There was formerly a chapel at Plas yn Bwl.' This would have been a private chapel for use by the family, to avoid the difficult walk to Hope Church. The Bryn Iorcyn estate was sold in 1915 and the house was bought first by William Whittingham and then by Mr Lewis. The photograph shows a former stable building which has been remodelled into four cottages.

Caergwrle Castle by S & N Buck, 1742. Plas yn Bwl to be seen upper right.

Plas yn Bwl. The outbuildings on the left have been converted into cottages.

Rhanberfedd

A lease of 1748 gives details of how a house at Rhanberfedd was to be built. It could be the smaller house attached to Rhanberfedd, the Grade II listed nineteenth century building.

18 February 1748

Between;

(i) Thomas Eyton of Leeswood co. of Flint Esq.

(ii) Richard Griffiths of Rhanberfedd co. of Flint. Carpenter.

The site of the house or building near the Lower Bridge in the parish of Hope, a parcel of land for a garden and a sitting, kneeling or standing place in the South Aisle of Hope Parish Church.

Term lives of (ii) and of Catherine his wife and John their son.

Rent: 12 shillings and two days reaping at harvest and two fat hens.

Consideration: building by (ii) of a substantial house on the site, to be of brick or stone with handsome glazed windows in every room, floors ceiled with lime and hair, the roof slated, hinged and locking doors to each room, oak floor boards to the chambers and convenient chimneys and hearths, a staircase and a cellar. Also (ii) to make a pew of well seasoned oak boards in the sitting place granted.

Estyn Grange

Sold July 1919 and was described as a 'country residence' with ten acres of land. There were five bedrooms, a nursery and two servant's bedrooms. Outside, there was a walled kitchen garden, an orchard, a tennis court, a coachhouse (with stabling for two horses), a shippon (to accommodate eight cows) and two piggeries.

Bryn Tirion

The first mention of this house is made in the will of John Jones in 1828. By the 1840s it had been bought and rented out, along with other local property, by George Chamberlain. The sale brochure of 1852 described the house and lands as being 'a handsome lot fronting the turnpike road with a highway at the back. Also a pew in Hope Church'. There were 24 acres with woods and an orchard and an extra six acres of rabbit land.

Throughout the years the tenants were well-to-do, often described as 'living on their own means' in the census returns. Most were benefactors of the community, allowing the grounds to be used for school and chapel outings. In 1885, all the pupils from Abermorddu school walked to 'Bryn Tirion Park to enjoy a variety of games.' In the 1920s a Russian immigrant, Baron Tobias Globe, was in residence. He was a timber dealer and property

owner in Liverpool and, to the locals, a colourful character. Older residents recall that he wore spats and drove a Rolls-Royce motor car. He was a generous man, paying for over 100 children to go to Rhyl for the day in June 1933, travelling in three charabancs. He also helped with fund raising during the Second World War.

In 1977, a community home for boys and youths in care was set up in the house. Bryn Tirion then became a nursing tome for twenty residents, but sadly it has now closed.

Bryn Tirion.

Map of Bryn Tirion.

Celyn

This house is situated on the lower slopes of Hope Mountain. In 1919 the house was for sale and described as being stone-built with five bedrooms. The grounds consisted of ornamental fruit and flower gardens with eight acres of pasture land. Water for domestic use came from the mountain. Also to be sold were an entrance lodge and gardener's cottage.

The previous occupants of the house reflected the steady industrialisation of the area. In 1871, John Hogg from Scotland, a colliery agent, was in residence and ten years later Adolphus Dear, the manager of the sand quarry. William Davies, a civil engineer, was living there in 1891, and became a stalwart of local society, serving as a Justice of the Peace and an Alderman of Flintshire.

14. Caergwrle Castle and Grounds

The children of the late nineteenth century provided their own entertainment on and around the streets. Some of their games are still played today whilst others are still remembered e.g. bowling iron hoops, spinning tops, walking on stilts, blowing bubbles with clay pipes, playing marbles, leap-frog, I Spy. Rounders and cricket were played and also 'bat and catty', kites were flown and 'bladders' (which were obtained from the slaughter house) were kicked about. Girls skipped and hopped on the pavement and played duckstones. Visiting circuses and carnivals were also very popular.

The adults had their own hobbies which included keeping allotments and pigeons. The River Alyn, at a point called the Causeway, provided a wonderful venue for swimming for those more adventurous youths. Fishing for trout and eels, in the Alyn and Cegidog, was fun but also provided food, and even the Coots were caught and eaten. Fishing permits were sold by local shopkeepers.

It's nice to sit and think and fish and fish and sit and think and think and fish and sit and wish that you could get a drink.
When you are fishing at
CAERGWRLE

The railway played a major role in bringing an ever increasing number of day trippers and weekend tourists to enjoy the clean air and beautiful countryside around Hope and Caergwrle. By 1896 a rail connection had been built linking Seacombe on the Wirral to Wrexham. Visitors from Liverpool crossed the River Mersey by ferry to Seacombe, then boarded the train to Caergwrle. Others came from the Manchester area as well as from local towns and villages.

The *Gossiping Guide to Wales* (1894) recommended that at Bridge End station visitors 'can leave the train, if so disposed, for a visit to the ruins of Caergwrle Castle which are seen on a mound to the left. Caer Estyn, an

Early twentieth century comic post card.

Visitors enjoying Caergwrle Castle.

ancient British camp is on the right. Still better, it would repay the pedestrian tourist to explore Hope Mountain.' By 1899 the cost of a weekend fare from Liverpool to Hope was 6s. First Class and 3s. Third Class.

Many visitors walked up Hope Mountain to enjoy the bracing air, excellent views and solitude. No doubt blackberries and whinberries were picked in the autumn. On a postcard sent 1911, Nellie wrote to her mother in Liverpool: 'sitting on a mountain a lovely view but very hilly. The last few days chronically wet, however we have a week left hope to goodness it will shape better.'

The castle and grounds were a very popular recreational amenity for residents and visitors alike. Dances, fairs, games, school and Sunday school treats were all held there. In fact it was a 'playground' for the village. In 1895 Henry Eccleston, landlord of the Derby

Arms rented the castle and grounds from the Earl of Derby erecting a notice by the gate: 'The Castle and Grounds are Private Property, permission to enter must be obtained from Henry Eccleston, Derby Arms. Persons doing damage will be prosecuted.' Villagers were dismayed as there had always been free access to the area. Mr William Roberts in his book, *Memories of Caergwrle* recalled that feelings ran high when local youths playing football in the grounds were deemed to be trespassing, and Mr Eccleston brought a prosecution against them, the hearing taking place in the Magistrates Room at the Glynne Arms. Such was the controversy that the local councillors decided to apply to Lord Derby to take over the lease.

On the 24 February 1896 Lord Derby offered the castle and grounds to the Parish Council on a lease for 999 years at a rental of £2 10s. p.a., on the understanding that any repairs and improvements would be undertaken by the Parish Council. A month later the Councillors voted to accept Lord Derby's offer and so the castle and grounds were officially leased on 25 August 1896.

The Parish Council formed a castle sub-committee to supervise the management of the site. In 1907 a rumour spread through the village that the council was going to charge an entrance fee to the site. This was denied, but funding was a concern. It was suggested that a subscription list be established and a collection box placed at the entrance.

The castle committee organised catering facilities on the castle site and set fees for stallholders, reduced by a third for residents. The owners of the swingboats paid £2 for the season, coconut stall or shie 7s. 6d. per day. Mr Marubbi of Wrexham offered to pay 30s. for the right to sell ice cream and Mr Allen's band was engaged to play for dancing. The caravans of the swingboat and stallholders caused a problem, and were eventually allowed on castle hill, but not by the entrance.

The committee appointed a caretaker of the castle who was paid £2 10s for the season. In 1913 a request was made to the Chief Constable for a plain clothes policeman to assist him. In June of that year it was decided that a 'noticeboard' be obtained, embodying a warning against 'using obscene language, climbing walls on the ruins, taking heather and breaking bottles etc.'

The Parish Council worked hard to beautify the castle grounds and provided seating made from 100 sleepers donated by the Great Central Railway Company.

Throughout the years the castle and grounds have been enjoyed by many people and the area has been the focus of village festivals. On 9 September 1962 the Earl of Derby gave the castle and grounds to the Parish Council.

Caergwrle Spa and Wells
The wells consisted of several springs on the Rhyddyn Hall estate, lying beside the River Alyn. Their popularity and unusual properties drew many people to Caergwrle seeking a

health cure. The first mention of the saline well was by Edward Lhwyd in his book *Archaeologia Cambrensis Parochialia Queries* 1690; 'Ffynnon Deg—a place below Kaer Gwrle on ye bank of Alyn which affords salt water.' In 1740, Dr Short of Sheffield published a book giving details of the most prominent springs:

> There are two wells, the further more salt and brackish than the nearer, it is 5 feet 9 inches deep. The last is most commonly used and carried away, it is 19^1/2 feet deep. About forty years ago (i.e.1700) they were cleared to the bottom...The water is as clear as crystal, none can be finer. It has been much used as of late as a purge and is sent for a great way into Wales... One Eliza Jones of Mold having a great scurf all over her body that she was even loathsome, drank for some time of the water, about three pints a day and is now cured.

Thomas Pennant in his *Tours of Wales* (1773), also expressed his amazement with the curative properties of the waters, reporting that:

> Patients drank a quart a two a day and some boiled the water till half was wasted, before they took it. The effect was purging, griping, sickness of stomach which went off in a few of days, and then produced a good appetite

After the death in 1777 of Sir John Glynne of Hawarden, owner of Rhyddyn Hall, the house was rented to different tenants with the result that public access to the wells was restricted as some occupiers insisted upon privacy. In 1846 the Glynnes sold Rhyddyn Hall and by 1900 the owner was Ll. Roe Brown of Gwastad Hall, Cefnybedd, who employed a number of men to clear the wells and had the water analysed. The results of the tests were published in 1902 and stated:

> From the saline spring an excellent aerated table water was obtained, found

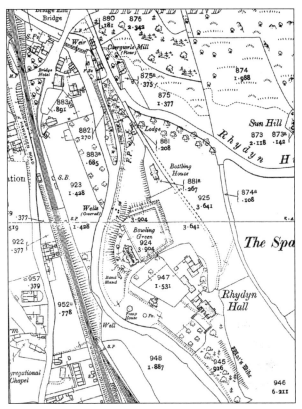

Map of Rhyddyn Hall and Spa, 1912.

Rear view of Rhyddyn Hall Hotel, showing the cast iron verandah.

equal if not superior to the much vaunted German water. The water from the sulphur well was also found to be most valuable for certain disorders.

The first pump house, 1905.

In the same year the *Chester Courant* claimed that: 'The discovery of the wells ... is an important step towards making the village of Caergwrle a popular holiday resort.'

As there were already many visitors attracted to the area Roe Brown realised the business potential of the wells and opened them up to the public. A correspondent for the *Chester Chronicle* described a visit in 1906:

> Go through ordinary field gates walk along the footpath by the River Alyn and reach the pump house, little more than a small wooden erection painted white and blue with a tiny veranda and furnished in front with a few seats. After sampling the water, drawn from a very prosaic looking iron pump, which is clear and pungent, glance around there should be a great future for the wells.

In 1907 Roe Brown sold Rhyddyn Hall and 80 acres of land, including the wells, to a syndicate represented by R. N. Woolett of Wrexham, who was the managing director of a brewery Messrs C. Bate & Son, Wrexham. This syndicate developed the wells as an outstanding tourist attraction.

The railway was to prove essential in the growth of the spa. The station at Caergwrle was originally named Bridge End, but was later changed to Caergwrle Castle and Wells. In 1910 the platforms were extended to accommodate the longer excursion trains — the railway offering 1s. a day excursion tickets on a Wednesday, Saturday and Sunday, and the visitors took full advantage of this cheap day out. On busy weekends, seven or eight trains a day would bring hundreds of people. Local papers gave estimated visitor numbers...

St Cuthbert's Tower with the castellated gateway (complete with portcullis) and pay booths either side of the entrance.

One day in June	1906 — 800
August Bank Holiday	1907 — 1000
May Bank Holiday	1914 — 1,500
20 June	1914 — 2,000–3,000

Outside the railway station visitors would have faced three or four Liverpudlian ladies with shawls over their heads, and at their feet large baskets bearing fruit, toffee, rock and sweets. They would shout, 'Caergwrle Rock One Penny a bar, two bars for 1½d' They would then pass the Bridge Inn, go over the bridge and turn right along the River Alyn. Ahead was a tall castellated stone wall with a dramatic portcullis gateway. On each side were stone pay booths. Having entered the spa grounds the visitors would see a four storeyed tower on the left, St Cuthbert's Tower, the house for the spa's manager. Further on, close to the saline spring, stood a very large bottling plant built of Ruabon brick. Here 14,000 bottles of saline aerated table water were produced daily. Small bottles were sold at 2s. 6d. per dozen, and large bottles 4s. per dozen. The registered trademark was 'Girlie'. The suffix of the place name Caergwrle was often pronounced as girlie/girly (particularly by outsiders), and

Caergwrle Natural Mineral Waters bottling plant.

this in turn, can be wistfully associated with a young healthy girl.

Ahead was an impressive pavilion and tearoom. The pavilion had french windows leading to a terrace. It was ideal for all sorts of entertainment, having a stage and two convenient dressing rooms. Pierrots often performed there and ' proved to be a great attraction.' Behind the pavilion was a bowling green. Down the slope a picturesque pump house was built over the sulphur well where visitors could sample the medicinal waters. It was said that some drank bottles of saline and sulphur water and then refilled them with water from the River Alyn, selling them as genuine spa water back home in Liverpool!

Other attractions kept the visitors amused. The Buckley Band often played on the bandstand and dancing and games took place especially on bank holidays. A water fountain and penny machines were in the grounds. Many people strolled along the pretty river bank and in the grounds which covered 26 acres.

Early in the 1900s, Rhyddyn Hall was converted into a small eight-bedded hotel, said to be, 'of high class character and lavishly furnished.' The spa was bought by a new syndicate in 1922 and there were ambitious plans to extend the hall into a 28- and 34-bedded hotel.

With so many outsiders visiting Caergwrle, many local residents took the opportunity to make money. Some housewives served teas and many households offered accommodation. Some of the youngsters from the village met the trains and escorted the visitors to the various houses where they could have refreshment.The Tate family ran a shop and also took in visitors. A joint of meat was served every day for dinner at noon and tea was served at 5pm prompt. In the shop they sold ice cream, postcards and pop. In all, there were seven assistants serving in the shop on a Sunday and another two outside. The Queen's Hotel and Café had a dancehall, accommodating 150 dancers, while the Temperance Tea Rooms, opposite the Bridge Inn, met the needs of the teetotaller.

In June 1910, the parish council applied for urban powers to deal with and regulate the

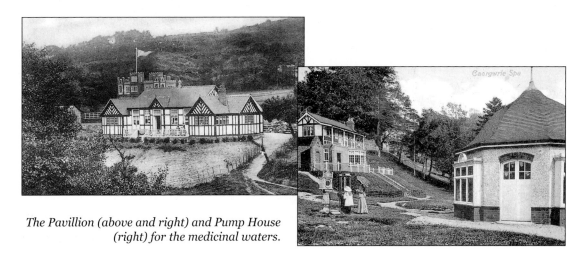

The Pavillion (above and right) and Pump House (right) for the medicinal waters.

vehicular traffic, including traps that were plying for hire and ice cream vendors. Cab stands needed to be provided for a small charge and hawkers supervised. The construction of a hackney cab stand was delayed as there was a dispute as to who would pay for the paving and drainage.

The Queens Temperance Hotel opposite the railway station.

With the arrival of so many trippers it was inevitable that tensions would arise in the community. In August 1891 the *Wrexham Advertiser* warned that, 'some of our young people will be getting into trouble if they are not more civil to the visitors in Caergwrle.' Many local residents were upset by the level of drunkenness, rowdiness and foul language, remembering that the major influx of people came on the Sabbath day. On 23 October 1905 a public meeting was chaired by the rector of Hope, the Rev. T. E. Jones, to discuss, 'The Detrimental effects of Sunday excursions.' One lady was criticised as she had once been a regular church attender but was now engaged in preparing teas for trippers. A man spoke of a party going down the street singing, 'A Lassie from Lancashire.' One irate resident spoke of the ' dumping of these undesirable aliens' Another said,

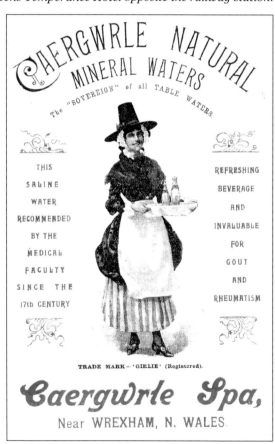

'begrudge not the poor people of the slums of Liverpool a mouthful of fresh air upon the only free day they had. A large proportion of trippers were of a respectable class.'

At one point a party of women entered the meeting, at great consternation to the men, however the men were assured that the women would not be allowed to vote! The meeting

The Bridge Hotel was very popular with visitors.

came to the conclusion that the Sunday excursions:

1. Kept away the best class of visitor.
2. Ruined the place as a holiday resort.
3. Were detrimental to the morals and religion of the neighbourhood.
4. Hindered the development of Caergwrle as a residential district.
5. Drove away some of the most respectable householders.

The arguments about the effects of a large number of visitors on Sundays raged on over the years. In 1912 Councillor Thorn declared that, '70% of ratepayers were in favour of the continuance of the Sunday excursions.' Another petition presented to the Caergwrle Licensing Justices in 1913 was supported by all churches and many local gentry, it stated that:

Chapels are compelled to close their doors and windows during services on Sundays to exclude noise, the yells, the singing of lewd songs and the profane and vile language so prevalent in the village.The behaviour of the trippers was becoming a disgrace to civilisation.

Unrest did break out and boys from around the area used to go to Caergwrle to watch the fights! Policing the area was difficult and when Police Sergeant Griffiths was on duty during the 1920s and 1930s, his main aim was to get all the visitors back on the train in good order! The Great Central Railway refused to reduce or stop Sunday excursions, but in 1915 discontinued the very cheap day tickets. This encouraged a large number of visitors to stay for a weekend or longer, some even decided to reside permanently in the area. Even in the

[Castell Alun Resources]

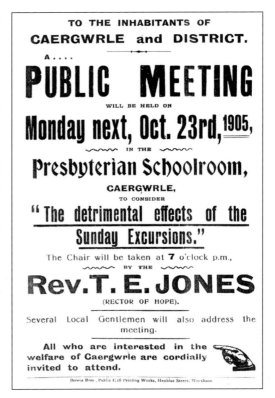

TO THE INHABITANTS OF
CAERGWRLE and DISTRICT.

A....

PUBLIC MEETING

WILL BE HELD ON

Monday next, Oct. 23rd, 1905,

IN THE

Presbyterian Schoolroom,

CAERGWRLE,

TO CONSIDER

" The detrimental effects of the Sunday Excursions."

The Chair will be taken at 7 o'clock p.m.,

BY THE

Rev. T. E. JONES

(RECTOR OF HOPE).

Several Local Gentlemen will also address the meeting.

All who are interested in the welfare of Caergwrle are cordially invited to attend.

Breese Bros., Public Hall Printing Works, Henblas Street, Wrexham

1920s tourists continued to travel to Caergwrle in large numbers, not only by train but also by bus, charabanc, bicycle, motorcar and motorcycle.

By the 1930s, the popularity of the spa was in decline. The reasons varied—many people were badly affected by the depression, especially those from the industrial areas and the cost of the railway ticket had gone up to 2*s*. 6*d*. from Liverpool. Fashions had also changed, and as people's health improved the need for a spa holiday resort diminished. Whatever the reason for the decline, Caergwrle Spa and Wells in its heyday was very popular and successful giving a great deal of pleasure to thousands of visitors. For many people, who worked under difficult conditions and lived in dirty, drab, overcrowded towns and cities, a trip to Caergwrle must have been a wonderful experience. This excerpt from a poem written in 1899 says it all (full version in Appendix):

A typical, slightly risqué *postcard of about 1905.*

> *From the toiling city hum*
> *Bands of happy tourists come,*
> *Climb Hope Mountain—this the sum*
> *Of thy bliss   Caergwrle*
>
> *Surely had thy kings of old*
> *Standing in thy castle bold*
> *Looking on meadow, river, fold*
> *All entranced   Caergwrle.*
>
> *Wales, bright gem of liberty*
> *Never conquered ever free,*
> *Many spots we love in thee*
> *Last, not least   Caergwrle*

The Bridge Temperance Tearooms.

15. Community Entertainment

As far back as 1651 there appear to have been visiting fairs to Caergwrle and throughout the nineteenth and twentieth centuries there have been various community carnivals, fetes, shows, fairs, enactments, which took place in different venues, Plas Teg, the Castle grounds, Rhyddyn Hall, the Glynne Arms, etc. One of the earliest recorded events was the Hope and Caergwrle Festival which had begun in 1837. The 1887 event was described as a celebration of the anniversary of the founding of the 'Anchor of Hope', No. 4138 of the Ancient Order of Foresters, (a friendly society). This took place at the castle, with members attired in the full regalia of the order. There was a march with the band of Flintshire Engineers playing. After the parade, a dinner was given at the Derby Arms, and ended with dancing at the castle.

Plas Teg was the venue for the Hope Bazaar on 13/14 August 1878, where the Royal Flint Band entertained the visitors. Admission was 1s. between 2pm and 5pm, and 6d. between 5pm and 8pm, children half price. Carriages were sent to Llong railway station to meet the 2.30pm train from Chester, and would leave Plas Teg at 6.29pm to meet the train back to Chester. Lawn tennis and other games were played. There were sales of cut and potted flowers as well as eggs and poultry.

Hope & District Horticultural Show began in about 1890 when the venue appears to have been Penyffordd School. This show was extremely popular and gave the community an opportunity to show their gardening skills. The list of flowers fruit and vegetables shown by villagers from all around was long, and the prizes were valued.

Goodwin Terrace, Hope.

Hope village with Sarn House on the left, Sarn Lane in the centre.

*Castle Hill,
Caergwrle with the
Derby Cinema on
the right.*

*Derby Road,
Caergwrle. The
cottages on the
right have been
demolished and
new houses built
there.*

The second Caergwrle Eisteddfod was held at the Drill Hall in 1890. Competitions included: spelling under thirteens; soprano solo; sketch; best 4lb loaf; baritone; knitting best pair of children's socks; piano solo. Directed by the rector, the Rev. John Rowlands, the proceeds went to Hope Church Restoration Fund.

In 1894 the Primrose League, which was part of the Conservative movement, organised a fête at Plas Teg with Mrs Trevor Roper as president. Events included cricket matches and dancing accompanied by the Buckley Band.

The Caergwrle Flower and Dog show was started in 1898, there were of course large numbers of visitors attending from Liverpool. The Ffrwd Prize Band played at the 1899 show. This show continued until the 1950s and 60s. However in 1899 the dogs were not mentioned again!

The Hope Cycle Carnival was, according to the *Western Advertiser*, held annually and on 4 November 1905 raised funds for Wrexham Infirmary. There was a procession and prizes for the following: best decorated car; best lady, gentleman, boy and girl collector; meritous historical character; Rum Tum Band; best decorated house.

Other fêtes in the 1930s were mainly held at Rhyddyn Hall. There were American tennis competitions in 1933, and afterwards, at 6pm, a jazz band competition, the Fielding brothers giving a boxing demonstration and the day was ended with a dance.

The Hope and Caergwrle Carnival of 1938, had obtained the services of 'Great Britain's Railway Queen' who came from Shildon. Carnival Day, 27 August, was held on the field of the Glynne Arms, admission was 6*d.* for adults and 2*d.* for schoolchildren. The Coed Talon Silver Band played. There was a fair on the field with numerous side shows and attractions. There were many field competitions such as: funniest couple in procession; jazz band contest; decorated trader's vehicle; ankle competition; slow cycle race; and identifying the mystery man. The crowning of the Queen was the highlight of the day.

Circuses and shows were a standard form of entertainment patronised by families until well into the Victorian era. There were a variety of acts and the travelling showman was a familiar figure who promoted 'freaks', variety turns or crude

The Historical Pagent, 1953.

A variety of entries and events from the Caergwrle Carnival. Starting from top left, clockwise: Castle Jazz Band; A decorated lorry; Carnival Rose Queen, Susan; Caergwrle Band, c.1912; Carnival Rose Queen, 1967; the National Savings decorated float; a decorated boat on the River Alyn; a group of competitors from the 1930s.

A parade through Caergwrle, possibly to celebrate the Coronation of King George V.

melodrama at the fair grounds. Most of these took place in the towns such as Wrexham and Chester, with children and their families visiting them.

Royal events were always occasions for local celebrations. The wedding of the Prince of Wales's in 1863 was celebrated in Hope with great rejoicing on 10 March. Rosettes and medals were given to the people and the church bells were rung in celebration. The coronations were all celebrated in different ways. In 1911 coronation of King George V and Queen Mary was celebrated by children and those over sixty years with an 'excellent repast at the Castle Dining Rooms. The Ffrwd Band then played for dancing and sports held in the castle grounds. Lassell and Sharman gave all the older residents a pint of beer in a coronation mug, which they kept.' The 1937 and 1953 coronations were also celebrated. A pageant was staged in the castle grounds in 1953, showing how the villages had developed since Roman Times.

The carnivals and fêtes of the twentieth century were very popular and well attended. On the 1 July 1967 in the grounds of Rhyddyn Hall the Boys' and Girls' Brigades organised a carnival and fête. As can be seen on the poster there was a great deal of entertainment and fun for all.

The Caergwrle Historical Festival was started in 1987, with the aim of re-creating history from the time of the Iron Age Celts to Edward I and beyond. This event was very popular and everyone joined in, dressing up in ancient costumes and bringing the celebrations into the streets.

A group of 'medieval' ladies at the Historical Festival

The Derby Cinema

Mr and Mrs Rollason of the Derby Arms Inn commissioned the building of a cinema in Castle Street. It was built by W. E. Eccleston & Son of wood, steel and asbestos, and opened in 1920. There were approximately 380 seats with a balcony, and a 22-foot wide proscenium (an arch over the stage). The projection room was metal clad as the early nitrate films were highly inflammable.

The Derby Cinema, Castle Street, Caergwrle.

In 1936, it was known as the 'Cosy Cinema'. There was one show each evening and two on Saturday. In one week in 1938 it showed *Charlie Chan on Broadway* on Monday and Tuesday, *Riding on Air* on Wednesday and Thursday, and *Said O'Reilly to MacNab* on Friday and Saturday.

During the Second World War the cinema was very popular and people often had to stand in long queues if they had not booked a seat. The manager had to have a standby film in case the delivery of a new film was delayed or the audience had to be retained in the cinema due to an air raid. The films were shown earlier in the evenings as blackout regulations made travel difficult.

In the 1940s Mr J. Jervis of Buckley bought the cinema and later introduced cinemascope. In the 1950s the charge was 5*d*. for the front stalls, 7*d*. for the middle, 10*d*. for the back and 1*s*. 3*d*. for the balcony. The sound of heavy rain on the roof made it difficult to hear the soundtrack! For many years the projectionist was Alfie Williams of Caergwrle, who also worked as an electrician at Llay Main Colliery.

The cinema was a popular local amenity and patrons would travel from all the surrounding villages. Mr Jervis continued to run the business until the early 1960s when Mr Gilbert Hughes took charge for a short period but sadly, it closed in 1962. It was sold in the early 1970s and the site redeveloped.

The cinema was also the venue for plays and concerts.

Amateur dramatics

Caergwrle Amateur Dramatic Society; The village players were very active during the 1940s and 1950s, but had a short break before recommencing their activities in the 1960s. They

The cast of Happiest Days of Your Life.

presented plays such as: *Blithe Spirit* by Noel Coward; *The Cure for Love*, Walter Greenwood; *The Reluctant Debutante*, William Douglas Home. The *Wrexham Leader* in November 1952, reported on *The Happiest Days of Your Life* by John Dighton:

On three nights this week the Caergwrle Village Players strayed into the carefree realms of pure and unalloyed farce for the first time, and one can only regret after seeing their performance in the Happiest Days of your Life, that they did not make the move long ago. The Institute resounded with laughter, the play was a triumph of team work. (Alistair Sim and Margaret Rutherford played in the film version). Hazel Underwood played the part of a boy—cut her hair—' a noble spirit of sacrifice.'

The Church Institute

In 1906 Hope National School closed and the children transferred to new premises in Hope, the redundant school building becoming the church institute, available for communal use. During the winter of 1919 the institute was open every evening as a recreation room where billiards, draughts and dominoes were played. Debates and talks on 'profitable subjects' were also held there. The Dean of Manchester encouraged the church to make use of the modern passion for dancing as it had a 'refining influence'.

In the *Parish Magazine* of October 1924 the vicar suggested that the billiard room should be utilized for 'something more of deeper character and have papers read — say once a month — on some topic of the day.' During the winter months of 1932 children were encouraged to come every Tuesday evening to 'a warm room,' where toys, books and games were provided. It proved to be so popular that two sessions had to be organized. In the summer all the children, over 100, were taken to Rhyl for an outing paid for by Mr B. T. Globe of Bryn Tirion.

The following year the executors of the late W. Thorn gave land to allow an extension of the Institute to proceed. Stone was removed from behind the old building, allowing the middle section to be doubled in width. The modernised and enlarged Institute was opened on 15 May 1934 by Mr and Mrs A. Scott of Gwastad Hall, Cefnybedd. The building work cost £1,550 and was paid off by 1941.

Flintshire County Council Education Authority established a school canteen in the Institute in 1942, the children walking daily from Hope and Abermorddu Council Schools, this continued until 1951 when a kitchen was built at Hope School. Flintshire County Council paid compensation to the Institute for wear and tear of the fabric while it was used as a canteen.

During the Second World War, between 1941 and 1945, there were many dances held here for the Home Guard, the Royal Engineers, the ARP, the Police, War Weapons Week and a 'Salute the Soldiers' dance.

Over the years the building has been a very popular venue for whist drives, political meetings, concerts and plays. The Village Players, the Boys' Brigade Pantomime and other local groups, have performed there. However with the building of the Church Hall adjacent to Hope Church, the need for the Institute declined and it was sold and converted into cottages and a dental surgery.

16. Organisations

The Boys' Brigade (1st Caergwrle Company)

The Boys' Brigade has been around for more than 110 years and is part of the boyhood experience of many adults in the Hope and Caergwrle area. The founder, Sir William Alexander Smith, encouraged, 'The promotion of habits of obedience, reverence, discipline, self respect and all that tends towards a true Christian manliness.' He believed the Boys' Brigade would care for and challenge young people for life through a programme of informal education underpinned by the Christian faith. The new organisation's badge was an anchor, with the motto 'Sure and Steadfast'. This was taken from the authorised version of the Bible, from the Epistle to the Hebrews, chapter 6, verse 19: 'Which hope we have as an anchor of the soul, both sure and stedfast.'

The 1st Caergwrle Company of the Boys' Brigade was formed on 20 February 1929, when some 50 boys gathered in the school room of the High Street Methodist Church invited by Mr Cecil Jones to hear Gerald Pugh describing his plan to set up the Boys' Brigade. Within a few weeks the company was in full operation, although reduced in numbers as some of the boys at the initial meeting were only interested in football and cricket.

The established programme, which is largely unchanged today, included drill parade, Bible class, team games and camp. The first parade was the enrolment service on 7 April 1929.

Football was very popular and in the first year the company gave a good account of itself in the *Wrexham Leader's* Chums' League. The band has always been a prominent feature, leading the way in many fêtes and fairs and travelling all over the county. In the first year, fund raising was essential to buy instruments and some 'old boys' recalled selling chocolate bars and packets of soap. The band was trained by Mr Jim Lawler, and they soon played a wide

Boys' Brigade.

range of tunes. The Boys' Brigade concert was always popular. Mrs May Morris was a great friend of the company, training and accompanying the various musical items.

When the Second World War started, many officers were called up for active service and sadly, several of them never returned. Captain G. Pugh was doing war work, which meant long absences from the village, but nevertheless the company flourished being run by the NCOs. During this period the company rented an empty shop opposite the railway station for a clubroom.

The minutes of the NCOs' meetings, 16 May 1943–2 March 1947, were written by the secretary, John Williams. They make very interesting reading, giving us a delightful picture of the company during this period. Captain Pugh remained in charge with Staff Sergeant Ken Williams, Sgt. Piercy Chesters, Corporals Ray Martin, Eric Hughes and Keith Roberts, Lance Corporal Dennis Ledgard, Mervyn Bignall and Jack Garston and Privates Roy Smith and Elwyn Jenkins.

On 29 May there was a 'Wings for Victory' parade in Leeswood. For this they travelled by bus, and ' hoped the second bus would be able to get up the hill better than the first!'

It was not always praise for the company however, a member of the Castle Street Methodist Guild had heard language coming from the club, which to quote one comedian 'would have abashed Billingsgate!' After this complaint the boys were warned that any boy

Boys' Brigade, Naval Company.

using such language would be kicked out of the Brigade.

Despite the war they still had their camps. Rationing however affected the food supplies needed. For their camp to Porthmadoc they needed 1,179 points. It was decided that:

> 1. Failing to get points meant no food, and it is important that we get a fair number of points due to the fact that we have a number of foodstuffs reserved at the shop.
> 2. We only accept and use the very best foods (salmon grade 1 was approximately 350 points).
> 3. If there is not a vast improvement by next meeting on 6 June, the camp will either be curtailed or cancelled.

There were often problems at the camp, since the instruments had to be cared for in sometimes wet conditions, and the boys were very untidy. The secretary records that it was suggested that the sergeant should be detailed to look after things, but the captain said that 'this was ridiculous as the Sgts could not look after their own tent properly let alone a marquee!'

Caergwrle Boys' Brigade.

In February 1944 these yearly minutes recorded:

Billiards, Darts competitions held last year quite successful, no one interested in tennis. The tennis courts were now under cultivation for the 'Dig for Victory' campaign. Football successful won 12 lost 2 games, topping the Boys' Brigade league. Wrexham companies thanked 1st Caergwrle for making it possible to hold camp, and assistance in providing list of needs for camp.

Cost of last years camp £95.

Members of the Boys' Brigade and the Girls' Brigade work closely together.

In June 1944 there were some changes, possibly because of the war, and the boys had to be 15, 16 or 17 years of age to be warrant officers or colour sergeants.

Every Christmas the NCOs had a social:

NCOs' social', what magic words they seem to the ears of our romeos. First question, are we having one? Answer Yes! Second question, When? 23 December at Somerset House. The boys social to be held the following Saturday 30 December in the Castle Street Methodist Hall.

There were 50 boys on the roll at this time. The NCOs had to give in their young ladies name so that they could be sent an invitation. The Master of Ceremonies was to be Captain G. Pugh.

The company did a lot of charity work, giving concerts at Meadowslea (the local tuberculosis hospital) and making donations to the Nursing Association, the British Sailors' Society, and many others. They also provided a good example to others, such as the Ewloe Company, who, after seeing their display at Hawarden, decided to reform and make a fresh start. They also had firm links with the 2nd Wrexham company. In April 1945, it appears this company had been helping to organise a Boys' Brigade Company in the badly blitzed area of the East End of London and, although the company had not been formally enrolled, had decided to invite eight boys to the Borth y Gest camp. The 1st Caergwrle agreed that they should attend camp, and as they felt they had done so little to help the 'bombed out' they sent them a donation of £10.

Carnivals and fêtes were also organised by the Boys' Brigade. As the premises for the Brigades became inadequate, Dennis Ledgard, who was the captain for many years, raised

234

the question of a building fund (1 February 1946) and the formal opening of new premises took place in November 1946.

The Girls' Brigade

The Girls' Brigade celebrated one hundred years in 1993. This movement came about with the amalgamation of the Girls' Brigade (Ireland), the Girls' Guildry (Scotland) and the Girls' Life Brigade (England).

The Caergwrle Girls' Brigade came into being on 1 February 1946 and was affiliated to the Boys' Brigade. Their motto being 'Seek, Serve and Follow Christ.' Mrs Joyce Ledgard was the captain, and is now currently the president, with Mrs Pat Dudds as captain. They meet on a regular basis, and once a month attend the Methodist Church for Church Parade.

Children can join when they are four years old and are called the Little Explorers. Juniors are eight to eleven years old, seniors eleven to fourteen years old, becoming Brigadiers until the age of eighteen when they may become Leaders or Officers. They take part in many activities including sport and first aid. Their programme is in fact 'four square' spiritual, physical, educational and social.

Caergwrle is certainly a successful Brigade, and in 1996 they celebrated 50 years and next February will be their diamond jubilee. In 1985, six of the girls were awarded the Duke of Edinburgh award.

Every year since the 1960s, they have had a camp in Pwllheli, following the same rules as the Boys' Brigade.

During the last few years the Boy's and Girl's Brigades have sponsored a school in Gambia, a very poor school belonging to the Massembeh people, who belong to the

Caergwrle Girls' Brigade Jubilee, 1996.

Mandinka tribe. On their first visit 1,800 books and pens were taken out. At that time only 100 children attended the school, but now approximately 400 children attend. As a result of this sponsorship they have built new classrooms, and a new well for the area. This started as a small venture, but is still growing with plans to provide a health clinic in the school grounds so that the local people do not have to travel miles.

Girls' Brigade knitting class.

Both Brigades serve the community well and continue to thrive.

The 1st Hope Scouts and 1st Hope Cub Scouts

The Boy Scout Hope Church Troop was set up by Mr Boosie, a local school teacher, in 1916. One of its tasks was to help guide parishioners out of church on a Sunday night, and another to help at whist drives! The troop must have disbanded at some stage as it was revived in 1923 with the aim to 'train boys in self reliance.' The Hope Scouts were part of the guard of honour when HRH Prince Henry opened the War Memorial Hospital in Wrexham, 1926, and in the same year they went to the Welsh National Camp at Llandrindod Wells. Three years later the boys took part in the World Jamboree at Birkenhead, where scouts from over 40 countries attended.

On 29 October 1941, Ivan Moore, a Scout with the Hope and Caergwrle Church group, was posthumously awarded the Cornwell Scout decoration. He was described as a 'model Scout and during a long drawn out illness he bore his sufferings with great fortitude and cheerfulness.' He had died at Meadowslea Hospital Sanatorium aged 19. The decoration was presented to his widowed mother, Mrs W. Moore, by the First Lord of the Admiralty, upon his visit to Wrexham. The newspaper reported that 'Ivan Moore had lived up to the Scout Law — clean in thought, word and deed.'
The Cornwell award was known as the Scout Victoria Cross and was awarded for courage. Named after Jack Cornwell who was born in Essex in 1900 and became a Scout. During the First World War he was involved in the Battle of Jutland, when he remained at his post

Hope Boy Scouts.

236

Hope Scouts, Cubs and Beavers: Top left, clockwise: Scouts at camp; Beavers and Cubs Scouts at Rowallan Hut, 2006; Whit Camp, 1955; Cub and Beaver Scouts, 1990; Beaver Scouts, 1999.

on HMS *Chester*, despite being mortally wounded. He became a national hero. He was one of the youngest to receive the Victoria Cross.

After the Second World War, the Scout troop became more active and the leaders decided to move from the scout room by the church to the old spa pavilion on Rhyddyn Hall land where they could meet and also establish camping facilities.This served both the local Scouts and Guides well, until the building began to suffer structural problems. It was agreed that it should be demolished and a new Scout headquarters be built on land nearby. The Scouts raised £60,000 with grants and voluntary effort in three years. It was opened in 1988 by Sir William Gladstone, the former Chief Scout of the Commonwealth. The facilities included a main hall, camping and barbecue sites, committee room and kitchen. It was hoped that the centre would become a national and international camp site. It was visited by the Chief Scout in November 1989, a red letter day for Hope Scouts.

George (Skip) Evans and Derek Holroyd were long serving and very influential Scout leaders in the area. In 1983 Ian Sumpter became Scout leader and then Group leader after Mr Holroyd's death, when he was assisted by Kelvin Arden.

Irene Clegg and Janet Arden ran the Cub Scouts for sixteen years and Liz Sumpter set up the Beaver Scouts for the younger boys. She became Assistant then District Commissioner for Beaver Scouts. Over a period of time the Beaver, Cub and Scout leaders resigned and this led to the cessation of Scouting activities in the villages for a few years. However, in 2005, Ann and David Lovatt re-established the Beaver Cub Pack. In time it is hoped that a Cub Pack and Scout Troop will be formed.

Over the years, the 1st Hope Scouts and the 1st Hope Cubs have learnt new skills during indoor meetings, and have participated in outdoor pursuits. The Cubs have camped at Rowallan, Bryn Iorcyn and Bodelwyddan. The Scouts have enjoyed the challenges of camping in the Snowdonia National Park and have visited Germany, France and even Gambia. The Scout movement has trained boys to become ' responsible members of their local, national and international communities.'

1st Hope Girl Guides 1st Hope Brownies

The Girl Guide Association was set up by Robert Baden-Powell in 1910. The first mention of a Hope Troop was in June 1925 when there was a general inspection and enrolment by the County Commissioner. At this time annual county rallies were held at St Asaph and Flint and camps at Nannerch and Kinnerton. In 1932 a pageant in London to celebrate 21 years of guiding was cancelled due to 'economically depressed conditions', but it was celebrated locally in Hawarden Park.

The Guide meetings lapsed during the Second World War but were restarted in 1946. A committee of the local association of Hope Guides was reformed in 1951 to raise funds to buy equipment and to help with proficiency badges. Miss Vera Lewis was captain of the 1st Hope Guides for some time and then became a long-serving District Commissioner. Over the years Guide leaders, too many to mention individually, gave their time willingly and without their commitment the guiding movement would not continue.

The 1st Hope Brownie pack was well established when their numbers increased in 1965 due to the closure of the Presbyterian Church Brownie Pack. In 1971 Margaret Hillman took over the running of the 1st Hope Brownies with help from Assistant Guiders Mavis Hughes, from 1969, and Kathleen Roberts, from 1983. These ladies were the stalwarts of the Brownie movement in the area. Margaret Hillman serving as District Commissioner 1978–83,

*Hope Guides and Brownies. Top left, clockwise:
Brownies at Chirk Castle, 2004; 1st Hope Brownies,
1980s; 1st Hope Brownies at Llandyrnog, 1980s; 1st
Hope Guides, 1920s; 1st Hope Guides, 1950s; 1st Hope
Rainbow Guides, 2006.*

Divisional Commissioner 1995–2001 and is now County Administrator. In 2003, a pack of Rainbow Guides was set up for girls aged between five and seven years.

Venues for meetings were the Church Institute, where a guide hut was sited, and later Rowallan and more recently Ysgol Estyn. Guides and Brownies are busy with activity filled meetings, parades, visits, day hikes, swimming galas and the adventures of the annual camp. These have been held at Rowallan, Hawarden, Chirk and Erddig, as well as further afield in Llandyrnog, Llanfairtalhaiarn and Prestatyn.

Throughout the years the principles on which guiding has been based have not wavered. It gives girls of all ages opportunities to learn new skills and to become, 'resourceful, responsible and able to think for themselves' Above all Guiding is fun.

The Women's Institute

The Women's Institute (WI) is a non-sectarian and non-political organisation opened its first branch in Britain in 1914. The Hope and Caergwrle Women's Institute was formed in 1927. It offered women a chance to learn new skills and crafts, to keep informed through a programme of talks and demonstrations, and to take part in musical and dramatic activities. The members met at Hope Council School, then at the Church Institute, now meeting at the British Legion in Caergwrle.

During the Second World War the WI helped with the evacuation of children and families to the area. Women took up vegetable and fruit growing and learnt canning and preserving skills in the Cookery unit at Hope Council School. 'Make do and mend' classes were very popular to help overcome wartime clothing shortages.

As the population of Hope was growing, a decision was made to set up a separate WI and this ran for some years until falling membership meant its closure.

In 1988 a group of women got together and decided to re form the WI in Hope. An advertisement read, 'members are provided with a wide range of activities

Chester Musical Festival.

FIRST CLASS CERTIFICATE

Presented to

Hope & Caergwrle W. I. Choir

Class 41

Maud E Glanthone
President

Robert McLeod
Judge.

Hope & Caergwrle WI Choir certificate.

... most of all friendship and fun.' It is now a flourishing Institute, meeting at Heulwen Close, and it is the proud winner of the 2004 Clwyd/Flint WI dart tournament.

240

Caergwrle W.I., 2006.

Caergwrle W.I. at Ruthin Castle..

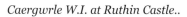

Caergwrle W.I.

Hope W.I.

Hope W.I. at a Victorian School.

Hope W.I., 2006.

Both Caergwrle and Hope WIs offer a great deal to women of all ages and continue to be an important voice in their community

TOC H

On 11 December 1915, the house at number 43, Gasthuisstraat at Poperinge in Belgium opened its doors for the first time, welcoming British soldiers to a new club. This large house was owned by a wealthy brewer who, because of bomb damage, had removed his family and offered the empty house for rent to the British Army. It was set up to provide basic comfort to young men going into war and returning. It was named after Lieutenant Gilbert Talbot who was killed at Hooge. Talbot House soon became known to soldiers as Toc H, Toc being the army signallers' code for 'T'.

Toc H is a movement concerned with Christian values and there are many branches throughout Britain, with Hope and Caergwrle being one. The meeting room was initially in Castle Street, above the barber's shop, but other venues were used later. The organisation provided many charitable things such as logs for Christmas for the older generation, the wood being provided by Mr Frank Whittingham of Bryn Iorcyn Manor.

Mr Ron Evans was the chairman when Hope and Caergwrle Toc H teamed up with Buckley and Mold Toc H, in order to build the new facilities at Meadowslea Hospital. At this time Meadowslea was a tuberculosis hospital and many inmates were patients for very long spells — months, even years. Toc H was the ideal vehicle to fulfil the needs of patients. There were a lack of suitable facilities to cater for the social and religious life of this community and Toc H initiated a project to build a recreation room and chapel. The hall was to be large enough for bed-fast patients to be wheeled in and a relay system from the hall and chapel to the wards ensured that everyone could enjoy the entertainment or religious services. The fund-raising appeal began on 21 June 1954. Site clearance was tackled by many volunteers from the surrounding villages and, with the help of a tractor called the 'Green Linnet' and a mechanical shovel, it was soon ready for the foundations. The chapel was dedicated on 25 June 1955 by the Bishop of St Asaph, just a year after the appeal began. This was a considerable

Members of the Hope and Caergwrle
Toc H, c.1950.

OAPs' Group Committee.

achievement and one which served the patients well until the closure of the hospital in December 2004.

Late twentieth century

There were many clubs and societies in Hope and Caergwrle during the latter part of the twentieth century. We have listed the ones known in 1986 in order to show the variety of interests held by the people of these two villages:

Hope and Caergwrle Ladies Club, met at Heulwen Close.

Hope and District Gardening Society, met at Castell Alun High School.

Caergwrle Women's Institute

British Red Cross, Hope group

Ladies Circle, Caergwrle Methodist Church

Hope, Caergwrle and District Amateur Wine Makers Society, met at Red Lion.

Caergwrle Angling Club

Caergwrle Senior Citizens Club

Caergwrle and District Aged
    Pensioners Society

Whist Club

Camera Club

17. Public Services

Community Councils

A series of Acts of Parliament in the sixteenth and seventeenth centuries encouraged the Vestry, which was the governing body of the parish, to take more responsibility for secular matters. Legislation allowed the parish to levy a rate for poor relief and the upkeep of the highways. The churchwardens and the sexton were appointed at the Vestry meetings. In addition overseers of the poor, the surveyors of the highways and constables, were also chosen with the approval of the local Justices of the Peace.

With the 1894 Local Government Act, the civil functions of the Vestry were transferred to an elected Parish Council. On 16 May 1894 it was decided to divide the parish of Hope into three wards:

Higher Ward: Uwch-y-mynydd Uchaf
              Uwch-y-mynydd Isaf
              Cymmau
To be represented by six councillors

Middle Ward: Estyn
             Rhanberfedd
             Caergwrle
To be represented by five councillors

Lower Ward: Hope Owen
             Shordley
To be represented by four councillors.

The following were later elected to serve as councillors:

Higher Ward:

Thomas G. Lewis	farmer	Bryn Iorcyn
Isaac Williams	farmer	Plas Maen
J. O. Smallwood	teacher	Bridge End
E. Jones	collier	Ffrith
Thomas Griffiths	innkeeper	Ffrwd
John Williams	collier	Uwch-y-mynydd

Middle Ward:

Ed. O. Probert	builder	Hope
D. G. Evans	physician	Cefn-y-bedd
W. R. Savage	cashier	Caergwrle
G. Griffiths	butcher	Caergwrle
D. Roberts	builder	Caergwrle

Lower Ward:

W. E .J. Swetenham	farmer	Shordley
Wm Speed	huckster	Sryt Isa
Wm. Roberts	wheelwright	Lower Mountain
J. Howarth	clerk	Penyffordd

In 1974, the parish councils in Wales were replaced by Community Councils. The first chairman of Hope Community Council was Councillor E.Holroyd of Caergwrle. He was very active and influential in local politics.

The present Hope Community Council is as follows:

Mrs M. Cokayne	Mr P. Evans
Mr G. B. Griffiths	Mr R. J. Harrison
Mr D. J. Healey	Mrs G. Healey
Mr B. Hughes	Mrs S. Jones
Mr E. A. Parsonage	Mr P. R. Pemberton
Mr C. Shone	Mr K. A. Shone
Mr K. M. Shone	Mrs M. D. Williams

Medical Care

In 1909 the possibility of providing a qualified nurse for Caergwrle and District was discussed. Meanwhile First Aid evening classes were held in the early years of the twentieth century.

In January 1917 there was a meeting to discuss the need for a Parish Nurse. The meeting was addressed by Miss Rowlands Assistant Superintendent, North Wales Nursing Association. The Following resolution was passed:

That this meeting is in full sympathy with the establishment of a branch of the Flintshire Nursing Association in the Parish and pledges itself to do everything possible to support the matter.

In April 1917 there was a meeting of the general committee — 350 members being enrolled. It was felt imperative that the services of a qualified nurse should be gained by September. This committee met on several occasions forming rules and inviting the public to subscribe.

In September 1917 the Hope District Nursing Association was formed and became affiliated to the Flintshire County Nursing Association, The Hon. Mrs H. N. Gladstone being the President.The Flintshire Association was in turn affiliated to the Queens Institute of District Nursing. Public Health was of great concern and in 1919 the Queen Victoria Jubilee Institute for Nurses provided a model scheme showing how the County Nursing Association could cooperate with the County Council in this work.

There were charges for the services of the nurse, from 4s. to 10s. per year, donations could also be given. The doctors also charged, for instance in 1928 for three visits, 15s. was charged. The doctors in Caergwrle in this period were Dr M. A. Thomas, Dr Dalling and Dr H. Sparke Welton of Abermorddu.

The fund raising committee and the car bought for the district nurses in 1937.

In 1931, the village nurse at this time was L. B. Williams, CMB. and the number of cases she attended were 27 midwifery, 11 maternity, and 10 general. Hope population was 3,300 at this time. The nurse was paid 11s. per midwifery case and 4s. 6d. for maternity cases.

The village nurse in 1933/34 was M. Lloyd, CMB, and in 1935–37, L. V. Williams who was independently trained.

As this was such a large district, with 3,000 visits (on average 60 visits per week) it was decided in June 1937 to launch an appeal to buy a car for the Hope and Caergwrle district nurses. There was a house to house collection with the slogan 'Save the Nurse'. It was hoped to raise at least £100.

In the early days, Hope included Caergwrle. However, in 1940, as the workload increased with the inclusion of Higher Kinnerton, a second nurse was employed, A. C. Hughes, SCM.

It is interesting to note that one chemist in Caergwrle was Thomas William Williams who was originally a haulage driver at Llay Hall colliery. His aunt, Betty Parry, was a very keen herbalist, which inspired him to become a chemist. He made a salve for boils, calling it Betty Parry salve. He also became a dentist!

18. Sport

Boxing

Caergwrle can be proud of the fact that they had the flyweight champion of Wales in their midst. There were six Fielding brothers listed as professional boxers in the early 1930s, Jack, Joe, George, Syd, Albert and Bob. As members of a family steeped in boxing tradition, it was little wonder that the brothers became so well known. Their father Billy, a talented boxer who was known throughout north Wales, acted as trainer and advisor to his sons.

The brothers travelled with fairs including Hughes' Fair, taking on opponents, giving exhibitions and also giving local demonstrations. Bob's career was quite short-lived, for after starting professional boxing at 16 years of age he retired six years later. However during this time he become the Flyweight Champion of Wales. His first professional fight was on 6 February 1932, in Merthyr, against Freddie Morgan, which he won points. His second fight was against Jackie Brown, in Blackpool, on 1 August 1932, which he won on a technical knock-out, but unfortunately his eye had been damaged. Bob's next two fights were against the experienced fighter, Tut Whalley in Hanley, Stoke-on-Trent. These took place very close together, with the first on 4 July 1933, which he lost on points, and the second on 18 July 1933, which he won on a technical knock out. This latter fight was said to be one of the finest bouts ever seen in the area.

Bob's last recorded fight was against Benny Lynch, 'the Kid from the Gorbals', in Liverpool. This was fought on 9 November 1933, and was drawn on points, at the Liverpool Stadium. Unfortunately, because of a recurring problem with his eye, Bob was forced to quit boxing after fighting over 200 bouts, but he retired as the undefeated Welsh Flyweight Champion. He went on to coach and give exhibitions.

Bob's brother Joe was a good lightweight boxer, fighting over a 100 bouts. George, another brother, fought Jim Crawford for the North Wales Featherweight Championship in Wrexham and knocked him out in the twelfth round.

Jack, Billy and Bob Fielding.

Syd and George Fielding.

Albert Fielding fought at the Liverpool Stadium 3 May 1949. His other brother Syd had over 72 fights. He also fought whilst in the army during the Second World War, where he became the 'All Services Boxing Champion'.

Syd pioneered the then newly formed Maelor Amateur Boxing Club at Cefn Mawr, Wrexham, devoting his time and passing on his considerable knowledge to the young boys. He befriended one famous boxer, Chris Eubank, a 'quiet shy 13- year old' who was staying at a children's home in Llangollen, and encouraged him to box. Chris went on to become the World Middleweight Champion. He and other boxers still visit Syd.

A quote from Bobby in a local newspaper; 'We are a boxing family but not a fighting family and are all rather quiet really.'

Another local boxer was Cyril Jackson from Hope. Cyril started boxing at the Mold Amateur Boxing Club when he was 14 years old. His trainer throughout his boxing career, both amateur and professional, was Gerry Greaves, himself a well-known boxer. As a young boy he won his first Welsh schoolboy championship and, by the age of 17, had fought his way into the Welsh Amateur Boxing squad and was rated as one of the top four welterweights in the country. Cyril made his professional debut when he was 23 years old, and as a light middleweight won many fights. When he was 27 years old he was about to

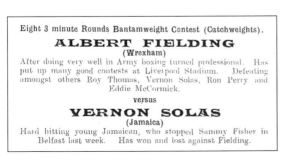

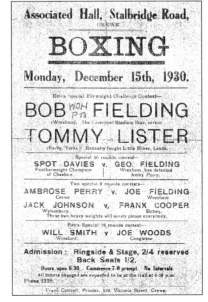

248

Cyril Jackson.

fight his first title fight when he was involved in a road accident, which left him with serious injuries. He was out of boxing for about a year and returned only until he was 31, when he decided to retire. He then took a number of fitness courses to prepare for 'life after boxing.' During his career Cyril had worked as a driver and also part time at the Sports Centre at Castell Alun. Gerry Greaves, his trainer, had been in charge of the Mold Amateur Boxing Club for many years and when he retired Cyril took over and enjoys training young boys the art of boxing. He is now also the supervisor of the Castell Alun Sports Centre, teaching 'boxercise' (no contact boxing), weight and circuit training.

Football

Caergwrle Wanderers

The first recorded mention of this team was when they played at Flint against Bangor Athletic Reserve in 1894/5, winning the Amateur Cup Final.

There were football pitches on various sites in the villages: alongside Hope School (where the houses are now built), Stryt Issa and Abermorddu. Those who played at Abermorddu in the early 1900s had to change at the Castle Inn.

Local players of note were: George A. Godding (born in Caergwrle, 1896) was a goalkeeper playing in the local team. He then went onto the Wrexham books and twice played for Wales in 1923. He was said to have a 'safe pair of hands and good judgement'. He was secretary to Caergwrle Football Club in the 1930s. He went on to run a garage in Caergwrle. His son Earl was a goalkeeper with Wrexham in the 1950s.

Wynne Crompton (born in Cefn-bedd, 1907) was a fullback who played for Oak Alyn Rovers and then Wrexham. He also played for Wales three times in 1931. A knee injury ended his football

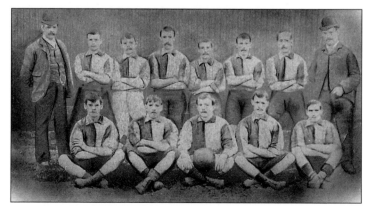
Caergwrle Wanderers F.C., 1892.

Castell Alun F.C., c.1960.

career. He worked as a miner in Llay and then went to Shotton Steelworks.

Roy Cunnah played for Wales as a schoolboy in the 1930s.

Castell Alun Colts Football Club, 1972–2006

The authors are indebted to Mr Warren Gittins for this account of the club. He has always enjoyed participating in football and played for Wales as a schoolboy, as did his son Andrew who later became semi-professional with Caernarfon Town.

This club was formed in July 1972 from a Caergwrle Boys' Brigade under 18 youth team, who were too old for the youth league. To obtain funds to get started and to buy a football strip we went around the local businessmen and shopkeepers who responded very well. We also held discos at Castell Alun and shared the profit with the school, and every year we would have a Colts Football Queen.

The football club has long serving officers who have given up their time willingly:

Committee Members

	1972	2006
President:	Geraint Williams, OBE	Geraint Williams, OBE
Chairman:	Harold Pearson	Dion Williams
Vice Chair:	Henry Kirkham	Warren Gittins
Secretary:	Warren Gittins	Brian Davies
Treasurer:	Mike Reilly	Dion Williams
Manager:	Warren Gittens	Gary Crewe
Coach: Tony Hughes		

From the start the players paid £2 subscription towards the running of the team. Over the years the club has been indebted to many local businesses which have been generous sponsors. In 2005/6 Mr Mike Norton of the Bridge End dental practice sponsored the kit.

The enthusiasm and hard work of all the coaches, managers and team players has led to great success:

Castell Alun Colts F.C., 2002.

1973/4 Division 4 — league and cup; Horace Wynne Cup.

1974/5 Division 3 — league and cup

1975/6 Division 2 — league

1980   Horace Wynne Cup.

1997/8 Division 1 — league and cup

1999/0 Premier league cup at Wrexham Racecourse.

2002/3 Premier league and finalist in Welsh National League, Wrexham Area Cup.

Henry Kirkham was with the football club from the beginning serving in many capacities as vice chairman, secretary, coach, manager and groundsman. He only retired from the club due to ill health but still came to watch the team play. He died in 2005 and a Henry Kirkham Memorial Trophy has been set up to be awarded annually for services to the football club.

Bowling

Bowls has been played in the villages for many years judging by the bowling greens in various places, i.e. the White Lion, Rhyddyn Hall Spa, and the Castle Inn. However we have not been able to find out about the earlier teams.

The Castell Alun Bowling Club was opened in February 1982 by Lord Barry Jones. Its aim was to provide crown green bowling for the community of Hope and surrounding area. It is a very active club, which is affiliated to the Wrexham Area Bowling Association, Deeside and Flintshire Bowling Association.

The founder members included:

W. Millington, E. Abram, P. Ager, B. Cooper, S. Walls, J. Ankers, V. Lewis, K. Rathbone, A. Bhatt and P. F. Vision.

Present members are:

President: W. Millington (retired)
Vice President: K. Dodd
Chairman: E. Abram
Vice Chairman: P. Muncey
Treasurer: M. Abram
Secretary: B. Watkins
Committee: P. Williamson, T. Jones, B. Jones, G. Jones, A. Muncey, M. Bagnall, F. Tonks and C. Watkins.

There are six teams:
Deeside Veterans League A. Team Division A Captain P.Williamson
Deeside Veterans League B.Team Division B Captain M.Haggie
Wrexham Veterans League Division 1 Captain G.Jones
Wrexham League Division 2 Captain E.Abram
Flintshire A.League Division 1 Captain M.Bagnall
Flintshire B.League Division 5 Captain F.Tonks.

The bowling green behind the Bridge End Hotel.

Castell Alun Bowling Team, 2005.

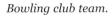

Bowling club team.

Hope and Caergwrle Cricket Club

The early history of the game of cricket in the two villages is rather hazy, but there were a few cricket pitches, including one where the garage now stands on the Mold Road. The club then moved to another on Porch Farm land, but this was not ideal as a bank running parallel to the wicket caught out unwary fielders! In addition to the serious matches 'Knockout' games were played on a 'matting' wicket, (to protect the proper pitch) and these were very popular. Teams were drawn from local organisations and public houses and often involved the younger generation who went on to play as adults. The third pitch was in Stryt Issa and is now under Castell Alun High School. It was the loss of this pitch that led to the closure of the club. There are many well-remembered players but there is only room to mention a few: Ronnie Pye, a wicket keeper who could knock a six into the cemetery; Percy Chesters; Ron

Cricket team, 1977.

Williamson; Archie Kirkham; Peter Lee; Fred Whittingham; and Dennis Bulmer, a bowler of note.

Castell Alun Cricket Club

In February 1976 Phillip Owen and Des Scragg decided to start a cricket team. A group of volunteers prepared an area of the Castell Alun High School's sports field as a pitch and played a few friendly games. In 1977, the team began to play in the Flintshire League and the following year won the Division II championship and was promoted to Division I where it remained for the next ten years. In 1990 the club joined the North Wales League as an affiliated member and became a full member in 1992. The team did very well rising from Division VI to Division I. New young players were encouraged to learn cricket skills by Phillip Owen, a school teacher, who took lunchtime and after school practice sessions. Many of these boys went on to join the first and second teams or played with other clubs.

The club has encountered some difficulties since the pitch has always needed a great deal of attention, but Phillip Lloyd has worked diligently to keep it in good condition. In the early days a redundant mobile classroom served as a pavilion, but now a converted farm building is in use.

Some of the founder members are still playing namely Colin Purton and Phil Owen, and Ian Stent has been a long-serving secretary. It is a very successful club and there are two Saturday league teams and one Sunday team which plays friendly games and a midweek team playing in the evening.

Pigeons

Many farm houses in Wales bear the name *Colomendy*, which is the Welsh for pigeon house/dovecot, there is one in Pigeon House Lane. Dovecots were detached buildings in which several hundred pigeons were encouraged to nest in order to provide fresh meat and eggs for the privileged. There is a dovecot at the manor house, Bryn Iorcyn. It is a square building in which there were 560 'L' shaped nests, 6" square by 14" deep. It had a wooden floor 6' 6" above the ground floor. It is believed to have been erected in the seventeenth century.

Caergwrle Cricket XI, winners of the Chester and District Midweek Cricket league, Division I, 2002. Presentation by Derek Randall, England and Notts player, to Mike Arden (Captain).

In 1871 during the Franco-Prussian War when Paris was surrounded by troops, hot air balloons were used to transport homing pigeons past enemy lines and messages were then able to be sent to Paris from as far away as London.

Messenger pigeons were used extensively in the First World War. In 1914 the French had 72 pigeon lofts which advanced with the troops. This was the only method of communication in many instances. Pigeons were decorated for bravery when delivering messages.

During the Second World War the UK had 250,000 messenger pigeons. Thirty two of which were awarded the Dicken Medal, which is the highest award for animals. There was an 'Air Ministry' Pigeon section, and the pigeon policy committee made decisions on how to use the pigeons. It was in 1948, after the War that the military decided that these pigeons had no further use.

Unfortunately pigeons could also be a nuisance particularly to the newly sewn crops. In February 1917 a newspaper reported on an organised pigeon and sparrow shoot, which provided food and also prevented the birds eating the crops.

Pigeon fancying became popular as a hobby with miners and working men. Although not used as messengers they now race and we still see flocks of pigeons flying around Caergwrle and Hope. Mr Ronnie

Dovecote at Bryn Iorcyn.

254

Mr Ron Bradshaw demonstrating at the W.I.

Presentation of cups to the pigeon fanciers.

Bradshaw has kindly provided the history of the Caergwrle Homing Society.

The club was formed in 1919 and is believed to be the oldest club in the village. It became a member of the North Wales Homing Association, before joining the Wrexham and District Federation. The Federation is still in force for the true enthusiasts. The club membership has always been good, having between 25 and 30 members. Some of the past presidents have been:

Mr Ronnie Pleavin (farmer)

Mr G. Godding (ex Wrexham goalkeeper)

Mr J. Wright (farmer)

Mr J. O. Hughes (postmaster, Caergwrle)

Mr Brunning (chemist)

The season extends from April to September, with racing every Saturday (an average of twenty one races), of between 70 and 500 miles, i.e. Hereford to Saints in France. The presentation evening is in November when up to 110 people attend. The present secretary is Mr Harry Loundes of Gwersyllt, and one of the longest serving secretaries was Mr Ellis Manford of Caergwrle. He was also a good pigeon fancier, often winning races.

These are just a few of the sports that have been played in the parish. There are however other sportsmen and women to remember, i.e. Julie Ralphs who was in the Girls' Brigade and became Table Tennis Champion of Wales and Adam Robertson who learned to play table tennis in the Boys' Brigade and went on to play for Wales in the Olympics.

Appendix

Caergwrle

Roaming o'er thy lanes and hills,
With delight my spirit fills,
As the fragrance sweet distills
From thy flowers, Caergwrle.

Robed in charming scenery fair,
Blessed with sunshine, bracing air;
'neath the earth, too, wealth dost share,
rich in ore, Caergwrle

Pictured hedgerows, flowering gay,
Song birds warble all the day,
Cheer the traveller on his way,
Passing through Caergwrle.

From the toiling city hum,
Bands of happy tourists come,
Climb Hope Mountain-this the sum,
Of thy bliss Caergwrle.

Sacred temples meet our gaze,
Worthy board schools stud thy ways;
All who seek thee sing thy praise
As they roam Caergwrle.

But there comes a day of rain;
Hid is mountain, hamlet, plain,
Till the sun restores again,
Beauty of Caergwrle.

Surely had thy Kings of old,
Standing in thy castle bold,
Looked on meadow, river, wold,
All entranced, Caergwrle

Wales, bright gem of liberty,
Never conquered, ever free,
Many spots we love in thee,
Last not least Caergwrle

Praise the Giver of all good,
From the mountain, streamlet, wood,
For His truth, which aye hath stood,
Like thy hills, Caergwrle.

Written by Annie Clegg (New Brighton), 1 July 1899

Caergwrle

There's a little spot in Flintshire on the border of north Wales
So profusely decked by nature, through the hand that never fails
So delightful and enchanting, circumspect if you will
'Tis the village of Caergwrle with its Castle on the hill.

The hills are clothed with verdure with their fern and foliage fair
The fragrance of their perfumes intermingles with the air
Little need for appetisers neither indigestion pill
In the village of Caergwrle with its Castle on the hill.

Should you ever need an outing to eliminate dull care
Visit where the songs of nature fill the balmy air
Pretty song birds will greet you with their twitter and their trill
In the village of Caergwrle with its Castle on the hill.

If you take delight in climbing, there's Hope Mountain close to hand
It takes 'ouff' to reach the summit but the scene's extremely grand
But be careful with your footing, and remember Jack and Jill
In the village of Caergwrle with its Castle on the hill.

Or if you're fond of fishing, surely get your tackle out
For the famous stream of the Alyn, just abounds with speckled trout
Chief delight of all the sportsmen is to hook them in the gill
In the village of Caergwrle with its Castle on the hill.

One other great attraction is the famous mineral spring
Experts and great physicians have pronounced it just the thing
To rejuvenate the system and abolish every ill
In the village of Caergwrle with its Castle on the hill.

Yes, the lean, the lank, the weakly quickly change to strong and stout
And also very strangely the dwarfs are lengthened out
St Winifred's not in it with those who drink their fill
Of the waters at Caergwrle with its Castle on the hill.

There are good accommodations to supply the inner man
Substantial food or dainties just whatever suits your plan
You will find that you are treated fairly when you come
To the village of Caergwrle with its Castle on the hill.

No surprise that crowds of trippers, during summer gather there
Such delightful scenes of landscape they cannot enjoy elsewhere
Nothing seen like it at Blackpool or Llandudno neither Rhyl
In the village of Caergwrle with its Castle on the hill.

by Griffith S. Davies of Braddock. Pennsylvania

Sources

Early History
Adam Gwilt, curator, Cardiff Museum.
Roman Roads in Britain, Vol. II, Ivan D. Margary, London, 1957.
Prehistoric and Roman Roads of Flintshire, Ellis Davies, Cardiff, 1949.
Dr David Mason.
Clwyd–Powys Archeological Trust, CPAT Report No. 527.
Cyril Fox, 'Wat's Dyke a Field Survey'
Margaret Worthington Thesis, 'Wat's Dyke'.
Royal Commission of Ancient Monuments in Wales and Monmouthshire—Inventory of County of Flint (II)
HMSO, 1912.
The Archeology of Clwyd, David Hill.
Flintshire, A History for Schools, Vol. I. C. R. Williams, Denbigh, 1961.
North Wales in the making, Michael Senior, Llanrwst, 1995.
Clwyd Magazine for North Wales, First Issue.
The Place Names of E. Flintshire, H. W. Owen, Cardiff, 1994.
Growth and Development of Settlement Population in Flintshire 1851—91. K. Davies, Msc.
New Dating for Wat's Dyke, *Wales History Today*, Keith Nurse, August 1999 (Look Smart web site).
Who's Dyke—Mind numbing links, web site, 9 Jan. 2003.
Wat's Dyke; A North Welsh Linear Boundary, Keith J. Matthews.
Stephen Aldhouse-Green, National Museum and Galleries of Wales, Art Ritual and Death, pre History, 1996.
Map of Wat's Dyke/Offa's Dyke, RCAHMW.
Cheshire under the Norman Earls, B. M. C. Husain, Vol. IV, Cheshire Community Council, 1973.

Early Modern Wales, 1200–1542
D. G. Evans (ed.) Flintshire Ministers Accounts 1328-1353, *Flintshire Historical Society Pub.* 2, 1929.
FHS, Vol. 8, Flint Pleas 1283—1285, edited by J. Goronwy Edwards, 1921.
Lordship of Hope, D. G. Evans, 1985, unpublished.
FHS, Vol.6, Ministers Accounts.
Flintshire, A History for Schools, C. R. Williams, Denbigh, 1961.
Medieval Archaeology, volume xxxviii, 1994, 'Excavations at Caergwrle Castle, Clwyd North Wales 1988-1990'.
John Manley, Chief Executive Sussex Archaeology Society.
The Black Prince, David Green, 2001.
The Hope Castle Account, A. J. Taylor, *FHS*, Vol. 33, 1992
FHS, Vol. 23, 1967-68, The County of Flint and the Rebellion of Owain Glyndwr in the Records of the Earldom
of Chester, J. E. Messham.
The Revolt of Owain Glyndwr, R. R. Davies, Oxford, 1997.
The Last Prince of Wales, David Stephenson, Buckingham, 1993.
Flintshire Quarter Sessions Rolls 1747-52, Derrick Pratt, Clwyd Record Office, 1983.
In Search of Owain Glyndwr, Chris Barber. Second Edition. 2004.

The Civil War, 1642–46
A Nation under Siege, The Civil War in Wales, 1642-48, Peter Gaunt (Cadw), 1991.
North Wales in the Civil War, Norman Tucker, 1958.
FRO D/DM/1411/41, Sequestered Land from the Earl Of Derby.
FRO Bodrhyddyn schedule no. 306, Travel Pass.
FRO Bodrhyddyn schedule no. 311, Pardon.

Religion
FRO D/G/3276/69, 1651 letter re Churches without Rectors
FRO P/31/1/20, Queen Anne's Bounty

FRO P/31/1/23, Hope Parish Overseers Account Books 1781-1804
FRO D/LE/1129, List of Subscribers for relief of the Poor 1800
Hope Parish Magazines 1872 onwards.
They lived in Flintshire, Huw Williams, Wrexham, 1960.
The Salvation Army, International Heritage Centre, London, Gordon Taylor Archivist.
The Stanley Manor of Hope 1484-1790, Clwyd Record Office (unpublished), D. G. Evans.
Forging of the Modern State 1783-1870, Eric J. Evans.
A History of Hope Parish Church, written and compiled by Mr David Evans, Hope.
www.historyonnet.com/Tudors Poor Law 1601.
A Pictorial History of the Revival, The Outbreak of the 1904 Welsh Awakening, Kevin Adams & Emyr Jones, Farnham, 2004.
Welsh Church Commission — County of Flint, The Statistics of the Non Conformist Churches for 1905.
Programme Capel Horeb y Mynydd, 1837-1987.
Old Newspaper cuttings Howell Hughes.
David Healey, editor, *Hope and Caergwrle Heritage Trail*,Wrexham, 2002.
William Roberts, 'Memories of Caergwrle'.
I. G. Jones, *Religious Census of 1851,* Vol 11, Cardiff, 1981.
FRO DD/G/2039, *Official handbook of a Grand Bazaar July 1908*, New Welsh Congregational Chapel.

Education

Hope National School
    FRO E/LB/31/1, Hope School Log Book, 1898-1906.
    FRO E/LB/31/2, Hope School Log Book, 1906-1921.
    FRO E/LB/31/3, Hope School Log Book, 1921-1963.
    FRO E/X/1/4, 300 + 308 Lease and Release 1838.
    FRO P/31/1/20, Churchwardens accounts 1859-1891.
    FRO E/X/1/ 7-9, Education Act 1900 Accounts Flintshire schools.
    FRO FC/3/25, Minutes of school accommodation 1904-10
    FRO E/MB /31/1, School managers minutes 1930-69.
    FRO FC/E/8/49+50, Hope C.P. Correspondence 1925-62.
    Topographical Dictionary of Wales, Vol.1, Lewis, 1838.
    Report of Commission of Inquiry into the State of Education in Wales, 1847.
    Hope Parish Magazines, 1878-89 1954.
    Act to make provision for meals for children attending Public Elementary School in England & Wales, 21 Dec. 1906.
    Newspaper Cuttings Cliff Shone.
    Newspaper cuttings Howell Hughes.
Abermorddu Board School
    FRO E/LB/31/5,6 & 7, Log Books 1883-1972.
    FRO E/SB/2/1/,3 & 6, Contract for erection of school.
    FRO E/ SB/2/8, Ledger of Hope School Board 1871-82.
    FRO E/AR/31/1-6, Abermorddu School Attendance records.
    FRO FC/E/8/1, Correspondance 1927-1958.
    FRO E/MB/31/2, Managers' minutes 1935-76.
    FRO E/A/2/42, Plan of school.
    Newspaper Cuttings H. D. Davies.
    The Wrexham Advertiser, August 1883.
Castell Alun School.
    FRO FC/A/2/98, Ground plans of proposed Secondary Modern 1956.
    FRO E/SS/4/1, Castell Alun Sec. School Governors Minutes 1958-1966.
    FRO D/DM/994/6, Papers relating to Castell Alun 1967-1985.
    FRO FC/A/2/29, Plans of alterations at Comprehensive School 1973 + 1974.
    FRO D/LE/1752, Programme for opening remodelled Castell Alun High School, 1975.
    FRO FC/E/8/49 +50, Castell Alun Correspondance.
    Programme to mark celebration of extension and refurbishment of Castell Alun .
    High School 1996 Newspaper Cuttings, Cliff Shone.
    '*Pont*' school magazine 1st edition.

The Historical Development of Community Schools within Clwyd, Alwyn Morgan, unpublished M.A. thesis.

Transport

FRO BD/No. 310, Petition to repair bridge 1654.
DRO DD/HB/1194 , Bryn Iorcyn Sale 1915 toll bar cottage.
FRO QS/MB/1, Quarter Session minutes book.
FRO QS/DT/15, Kingsferry to Abermorddu road, 1834.
FRO QS/DT/2, Wrexham to Pentre Bridge road, 1818.
FRO D/E/753, Assignment of Tolls 1758 Wrexham to Mold.
FRO D/BC/3121, Mortgage of tolls 1765 Wrexham to Mold.
FRO D/E/756, Appeals for subscriptions.
FRO D/GW/492, Correspondance re tolls Kingsferry to Abermorddu, 1834.
FRO D/BC/3137, Letting of tolls Wrexham to Mold, 1845.
FRO D/BC/3131, Accounts of Wrexham Turnpike Trust, 1810-11.
FRO FC/C/4/2/38, Road widening Hope, 1922-27.
FRO QS/SR/623, Diversion and stopping up of Bedlam Lane Hope, 1924.
CRO Flintshire Quarter Session Rolls 1747-52, D. Pratt 1983.
Hope Parish Church Vestry Minutes.
FHS, Vol. 17 Flintshire Packhorse Bridges, George Lloyd.
FHS, Vol. 21 The Roads and Turnpike Trusts of Flintshire Roads.
Newspaper Cuttings Howell Hughes.
Hidden Highways of North Wales R.J.A.Dutton Pub. G.Emery Chester.
Article of early roads, Wrexham Leader 10 January 2003 D.Pratt.
Articles on Packhorse Bridge Caergwrle Chester Chronicle 10 November 2000,also Wrexham Leader 8 November 2000.
Ordnance Survey map, 1st Edition, 1871.
Information from Clwyd Powys Archeological Trust Records.
Caergwrle, The Gem of Lovely North Wales Official Guide, Caergwrle Development Association.
Wrexham, Mold & Connah's Quay Railway, James I. C. Boyd, 1957.
*Great Central on the Welsh Borde*r (part one.) J. M. Tolson.
FRO D/WM/210.
Mr Reg Carter Stephensons Society.

Agriculture

FRO DD/HB/1194, Corn Mill Cefn y Bedd.
FRO D/WM/70, Corn Mill demolished Cefn y Bedd, 1848.
FRO D/GL/6568, 1848 Corn Mill.
FRO D/G/2692, Water and Mills, 1347.
FRO D/G/2707, 3 Water and Corn Mills, 1662.
FRO D/LE/146, Lease George Hope, 1662.
FRO D/LE/147, Lease George Hope, 1682/3.
Mr Alun Parsonage.
Mr D. G. Evans.
Extracts from Flintshire Ministers Accounts, 1349.
FRO D/GL/6568, Cefn y Bedd Water Corn Mill.
Notes G. Lloyd.
Denbighshire Historical Society *Transactions* No. 29, D. Pratt.
Census Returns/ Trade Directories.
FRO DD/G/2936, Sale of the Bridge End Mill Caergwrle, 1921.
The House of Stanley, Peter Draper, Ormskirk, 1864.
FRO D/DM/1411/36, Letter re trial, 8.4.1794.
FRO D/LA/11/12, Hope Enclosure Act Hope Manor, 1791.
FRO, 31.3.1794. (John Hitchinson to Rev Hope Eyton, the Mount Wrexham).
FRO D/LE/687, Pardon.
FRO D/LE/679, Inclosure.
FRO D/LE/682, Inclosure Trial.

FRO D/LE/683, Military/Inclosure.
Hope Marriage Register, 1780-1804.
CRO P/31/1/23.
Leeswood Hall Estate Papers.
Chester Chronicle, July 29TH 1791.
FRO D/LE/686 Letter re trial, 31.3.1794.
CRO Eaton Hall estate Papers 58.
FRO D/WM/50 Lime.
Flintshire Quarter Sessions Rolls 1747-1752, Derrick Pratt, Clwyd Record Office,, 1983.
FRO D/LE/591 Labourers wages 1787.
FRO D/DM/850/3 Hope Parish Poor Rate book 1883-1884.
The Forging the Modern State 1783-1870, Eric J Evans, 2nd Edition, London, 1996.
FRO Earl of Derby box 8 G 1345.
FRO 19/323 box 8 /1-4 Sir Stephen Glynne's estate.
Industrial conflict 1870—1914 Clive Emsley, Open University.
FRO D/WM/ 283 Hafod Farm.
FRO QS/DE/10 Hope Enclosure Act plan & award 1797-98.
FRO QS/DE/7 Map ref. Enclosure Penyffordd records 1890.
History of the Old Parish of Hawarden, T. W. Pritchard, Wrexham, 2002.
David Healey, Bryn Iorcyn.
FRO D/LE/591 Labourers Wages 1787.
FRO D/LE/1686 Agricultural growth NLW Great Sessions (Flint) Wales, 4/1012/10.
FRO DD/469/54 M Farmers' Calender, 1804.
Bryn Iorcyn, a working Farm 17th Century to 20th Century.
FRO D/WM/186 Programmes of Caergwrle Show and Gymkhana.
www.ukagriculture.com/farming-today 15/11/04.

Industry
FRO D/GR/353 Sale of property of J.Kyrke, 1849.
FRO NT/ 180 N.Wales Iron Industries R. Mead.
FRO E/LB/31/1-3 Hope School Logbooks, 1898-1963.
FRO E/LB/31/5-7 Abermorddu Log Books, 1883-1972.
FRO D/C/110—25 Sale detains of Llay Hall Colliery, Iron Works and Clayworks.
FRO D/WH/283 Whittingham family scrapbook.
FRO D/G/3311-2 Coal Accounts, 1630-31.
FRO BC/2424 Agreement to supply Cefn y Bedd Colliery with electric power.
FRO D/BC/2382 Llay Colliery Accident and Compensation.
Castell Alun archives details of lease re Silver and Lead mining.
R.Burt The Mines of Flintshire and Denbighshire, Metalliferous and associated Minerals, 1845-1913.
FRO Census Returns, 1841—1901 (every 10 years).
FHS NO. 33, The Hope Castle Accounts of 1282, A. J. Taylor.
Industrial Railways in North Wales—The Birmingham Locomotive Club Industrial Locomotive Information Section. 1968.
Lordship of Hope, D. G .Evans, 1985, unpublished.
North wales Coal Industry, A. H. Dodd, *Archeologia Cambrensis*, 1929.
The Industrial Revolution in North Wales, A. H. Dodd, Cardiff, 1951.
The Development of the Flintshire Coal Industry up to 1740, K. L. Gruffyd, M.A. Thesis, 1981.
The North Wales Coalfield a collection of pictures, Ithell Kelly, Wrexham, 1990.
The Collieries of Denbighshire, G. C. Lerry, Wrexham, 1968.
Industry in Clwyd, C. J. Williams, Clwyd Record Office, 1986.
The Ellesmere and Llangollen Canal, Edward Wilson, 1975.
Brymbo and its Neighbourhood, Graham Rogers, 1991.
Century of Coal, K. Gildart, lecture, 28-2-04.
Wrexham Advertiser, 1893.
Scrapbook of newspaper cuttings, H. D. Davies.
Scrapbook of newspaper cuttings, Howell Hughes.
Article on Hope Colliery, Llew Fidler.

FRO NT/1432 Mills of Caergwrle.

FRO D/WM/78 Sale details of saw mill, 1929.

FRO D/GL/68, Hope Paper Mill, 1965.

FRO NT/481, Paper Making in North Wales.

FRO NT/ 1587, History of Paper making in Flintshire S.Wicklen.

FRO D/WM/ 70, Sale of Bryn Iorcyn Estate, 1915.

FRO D/BC/2366, Agreement for use of railway.

FHS vol. 34 1996, Vim, The Flintshire Connection, Bryn Ellis.

Papermills and Paper Makers in Wales 1700–1900, Genuki.

Bennetts Business Directory, 1913-14.

Copes Directory, 1932.

Newspaper article on closure of Gwalia Forge undated.

Newspaper article, obituary R. W. Lea, 1947.

DRO DD/HB/1191 Lease to Griffiths Bros. Forge by Packhorse Bridge, 1890.

FRO D/GL/ Notes on Brewery.

Prince of Ales, Brian Glover, 1993.

Hope and Caergwrle Past and Present, S. G. Jarman, 1908.

Wrexham, Mold and Connah's Quay Railway, J. I. C. Boyd, 1991.

Newspaper cutting on C. R. Averill paint manufacturer, undated.

FRO D/BD/298.

FRO D/WM/ 4, Sand Account.

DRO DD/HB/1197, Sale of land A. V. Kyrke, 1920.

Correspondance and newspaper cutting T. E. and H. Roberts.

Life in Victorian Brickyards of Flintshire and Denbighshire, Andrew Connolly, Llanrwst, 2003.

FRO D/DM/1057, Property sale.

FRO D/BC/ 3307, Property sale, Oct. 1875.

FRO D/BC/3304, Property sale, Sept. 1875.

Utilities

D/DM/661/6 Sanitary work.

Cutting from *Western Advertiser*.

Mr Fidler.

Caergwrle Official Guide, 1925.

Mr A. Parsonage .

D/DM/400/1-6 GPO Medic .

Law and Punishment

Flintshire Historical Society *Journal*, volume 35, 1999. The Early Years of Flintshire Constabulary 1856-88, A. Geoffrey Veysey.

FRO FC/A/3/1, Plans 1902 police station.

FRO FC/A/3/2, Plans 3 police houses etc, 1968.

FRO D/BJ/38, Murder of 1734 journal.

M. H. Lee (ed) *Diaries and Letters of Philip Henry MA*, 1882.

Folklore as an HistoricalScience, G. L. Gomme, 1908.

The Brave Men and Women of Hope and Caergwrle

Memoir of Flintshire Yeomanry Cavalry commanded by Major the Earl Grosvenor, Chester, 1838.

The Archives Photographs series, *Bwcle-Buckley*, Paul Mason, FRO.

FRO D/WM/ 121, Gospel of St John.

FRO D/WM/123, F.S.Whittingham 1918 joined up.

FRO D/WM/124, F.S.Whittingham 'Journey through France'.

FRO D/WM/125, Tank course.

FRO D/JB/96, (Feeding and shelter, food from the Red Cross, + Stirrup pump).

Hope Parish Magazines.

Leader, 24.7.1942, HMS *Niger*.

FRO D/DM/294/22, Home Office Register of Aliens.

Chester Chronicle, Mr Howell Hughes.

A Dictionary of Military Uniform, W. Y. Carman, London.
Luftwaffe over Clwyd, Ivor Wynne Jones, The Air War over Flintshire, Gee and Son.
FRO D/JB/148, Wartime leaflets.
FRO FC/C/6/245, Searchlight at Hope Hall.
FRO, *Clwyd at War 1939—45.*
FRO D/WM/130, Blackout times.
FRO D/DM/1277/1, Women's Land Army, Flintshire, WWII.
Information from The Regimental Museum of the Royal Welch Fusiliers via Lt-Col. P. A. Crocker.
FRO FC/E/8/78.
Mrs K.Gabriel, Hope Hall Farm.
Evening Leader, January 1997.
Village Nurse and Doctors.
    FRO D/DM/130/3, Bye laws, costs and charges.
    FRO D/DM/130/1-13, Annual reports of Flintshire County Nursing Association.
    FRO FC/C/6/585, Public Health rules.
    FRO D/DM/709/1, First meeting NWNA.
    D/WM/291, Chemist.

Social Life
NT/1000.
Reminiscences of Mrs D M Eccleston, 1911/13 .
FRO D/P/341,, Sale of Rhyddyn Hall, 1846.
FRO D/DM/1057, Sale of Rhyddyn Hall, 1852.
FRO D/BC/3307, "   "   1875.
DRO DD/W/826,   "   " 1880.
FRO D/DM/599/8, Sale of Rhyddyn Park Spa, 1921.
FRO D/DM/464/11 Plans of extension of Rhyddyn Hall.
DRO DD/G/2937, Sale details of Spa, 1929.
O/S Map 25" to 1 mile, 1912.
FRO D/DM/269, North Wales, Liverpool Wirral timetable, 1899.
FRO PC/31/1, Hope Parish Council Minute book, 1910—22.
H. D. D., *History of Caergwrle Castle and Neighbourhood*, 1902.
Tours of Wales, T. Pennant, 1773.
Hope and Caergwrle Past and Present, 1908.
Gossiping Guide to Wales, 1894.
Archaeologia Cambrensis, Parochialic Queries, 1690, Edward Lhwyd.
Rambles Around Caergwrle, 1936, T. Lloyd Jones.
Newspaper cutting from local unnamed papers, Howell Hughes.
Reminiscences by Mrs Mary Vaughan of Caergwrle, 2000.
Shops 1936.
Bennett's Business Directory, 1936.

Interesting Houses
FRO, D. G. Evans, History of Hope, unpublished.
HMSO, 1975, *Houses of the Welsh Countryside*, P. Smith.
The Buildings of Wales, Clwyd, E. Hubbard, London, 1986.
Royal Commission Survey of Ancient and Historical Monuments in Wales, 1966.
An Inventory of the Ancient Monuments in Wales II County of Flint, 1912.
The High Sheriffs of the County of Flint 1300—1963, E. Breeset and Jones Mortimer.
Buildings of Special Architectural or historic interest, Hope, CADW, 1998.
Archaeologia Cambrensis, Parochiahia Queries 1699, E. Lhwyd.
Coleman's Calendar of Deeds and Documents, Vol. III.
History of the Old Parish of Hawarden, T. W. Pritchard, Wrexham, 2002.
Slater's Trade Directory, 1850.
Census returns 1861, 1871, 1881, 1891, 1901.
Collection of newspaper cuttings, Cliff Shone.
Hope Parish Magazines.

Abermorddu School Log Books.
Bryn Iorcyn.
    (Note B.D. = Bodryddyn Documents).
    FRO BD 568, Deed of land of Hope 1427/8.
    FRO BD 270, Marriage agreement 1568/9.
    FRO BD 281, Appointment of Escheater of County of Flint 1581.
    FRO BD 293,   "   "   1607.
    FRO BD 302, Inventory of goods belonging to Lewys Yonge 1626.
    FRO BD 305, Marriage Richard Yonge 1628.
    FRO BD 306, Pass for Richard Yonge to return home 1646.
    FRO BD 320, Ellis Yonge High Sheriff 1690.
Rhyddyn Hall.
    FRO P/31/2/1, Hope Parish Record.
    FRO Hope Parish Baptisms, 1751.
    FRO Coleman's Calendar, no. 1349.
    FRO, National Library of Wales MSS No. 4110/4111.
    FRO D/P/341, Sale of Property, 1846.
    FRO D/DM/1057, Sale agreement, Sept. 1852.
    FRO D/BC/3307, Sale of Property, 1875.
    DRO DD/11/826, Sale of Property, 1880.
    FRO D/DM/599/8 + 11, Sale of Property, 1921.
    FRO D/DM/464/11, Plans for extension, 1922.
    DRO DD/G/2937, Sale of Property,, 1929.
    CRO DBC 102 Box 1/14, Supplement abstract of title of Sir S. R. Glynne, 1846.
    FRO D/DM/599/3, Analysis of water, 1902.
Hope Hall.
    FRO D/P/341, Sale of estate, 1846.
    FRO D/DM/1057, "   " 1852.
    FRO D/BC/3304, Sale of farm stock, 1874.
    FRO D/BC/3304, Sale of Property, 1875.
    FRO FC/LA/2/104, Sale of property, 1912.
    Postal Directory of Flintshire and Denbighshire, 1886.
Plas yn Bwl.
    FRO D/G/2702, Document re Richard Bolde, 1430.
    DRO DD/HB/1194, Property for sale, 1915.
Bryn Tirion.
    DRO DD/HB/1161, John Jones' Will, 1828.
    FRO D/DM/1057/3, Property sale, 1852.
Rhanberfedd.
    FRO D/LE/161, Lease of land to build house, 1748.
Celyn.
    FRO FC/LA/2/115, Sale of property, 1919.
Estyn Grange.
    DRO DD/HB/1195, Sale of property, 1919.
Inns of Hope and Caergwrle.
    Sutton's Trade Directory, 1889-90.
    Bennett's Business Directory, 1913-14.
    Slater's Directory, 1883-1895.
    Cope's Directory, 1932.
    Census Returns, 1861, 71, 81, 91, 1901.
    Hope Parish Magazines, 1879 1880.
    Hope and Caergwrle Heritage Trail, D.Healey, Wrexham, 2002.
    Caergwrle Official Guide, 1925.
    F. M. L. Thompson, *The Rise of the Respecable Society,* 1989.
    Peter Grey, *A Brief History of Friendly Societies* (Internet).
    Brian Glover, *Prince of Ales,* 1993.
    John Trematick.

FRO D/LE/665, Sale Advert, 1800 Bridge End.
FRO D/DM/1057/3, Sale of property, 1852.
FRO D/DM/495/23, Deed of land in Sarn Lane.
FRO D/WM/291, Newspaper cutting.
FRO D/BC/3304, Sale of details, Sept. 1875.
FRO D/WM/68, Sale of property Crown Inn.
FRO D/KK/1218, Draft sale Workingman's club.
FRO P/31/5/1, Parish vestry Book 1862-1896.
H. D. Davies's scrapbook of newspaper cuttings.
Wrexham Advertiser, 4 August 1891.

Community Entertainment
Derby Cinema.
Brian Hornsey, *Cinemas of North Wales*, 1996.
Kine Year Book, 1936, 1951, 1962.
Bennett's Business Directory, 1936.
Roger Shone, Chester.

Organisations
Hope Scouts and Cubs.
Hope Parish Magazines.
Cliff Shone, newspaper cuttings collection.
Flintshire County Council Community Directory.
Lynda Gray, Awards Administrator, Scout Association.
Leader, 12.12.1941, re Ivan Moore.
Hope Guides and Brownies.
Hope Parish Magazines.
Minute books of Committee of the Local Association.
The Guide Leaders' Handbook.
Women's Institute.
FRO D/DM/239/1, Caergwrle Women's Institute Jubilee Book, 1965.

Sport
Boxing.
Mr Syd Fielding.
Mr Albert Fielding.
Mrs Lil Fielding.
Boxing News, 25 July 1986.
Liverpool Echo, 13 April 1974.
Mr Cyril Jackson.
The Chronicle, 30 5 1980.
Boxing News;British rating, 4 Dec. 1987.
Football.
G. Davies & I. Garland, 'Who's Who of Welsh International Soccer Players, Wrexham, 1991.
Mr Warren Gittins.
Bowling.
Mr Paul Muncey.
Cricket.
Mr Phillip Owen.
Mr Harold Mount.

Public Services
Flintshire County Council